Fighting Sports, Gender, and the Commodification of Violence

Fighting Sports, Gender, and the Commodification of Violence

Heavy Bag Heroines

Victoria E. Collins

LEXINGTON BOOKS

Lanham • Boulder • New York • London

Published by Lexington Books
An imprint of The Rowman & Littlefield Publishing Group, Inc.
4501 Forbes Boulevard, Suite 200, Lanham, Maryland 20706
www.rowman.com

6 Tinworth Street, London SE11 5AL, United Kingdom

British Library Cataloguing in Publication Information Available

Library of Congress Cataloging-in-Publication Data Available

ISBN 978-1-7936-0063-9 (cloth : alk. paper)
ISBN 978-1-7936-0064-6 (electronic)

♾ ™ The paper used in this publication meets the minimum requirements of American National Standard for Information Sciences—Permanence of Paper for Printed Library Materials, ANSI/NISO Z39.48-1992.

Contents

Acknowledgments

There are so many people that were involved with, and helped me in, completing this project. I would like to start by giving thanks to my husband Michael Collins whose unwavering support in my pursuit of not only this research project but boxing more broadly, has been invaluable. When I came home and declared I wanted to jump in the boxing ring, he did not question why, but rather wanted to know what I needed from him to make it happen. I would also like to thank my parents and brothers for their support, entertaining my long-winded excitement about fitness accomplishments, running with me, and taking/finding me gyms when I visited so I did not fall behind in my fitness regime. I would especially like to thank my mum, who managed to find a boxing gym in an old warehouse for my visit to England. Boxing in an unheated building in the middle of winter was an experience only made more surreal by her telling-off one of the largest male boxers in her best teacher voice (she used to be a teacher), when he was cheeky to her when she came to pick me up! This kind of support goes above and beyond.

In addition to the support of family, I have to mention the wonderful academic friends who have helped me think through the framing of this project, offered feedback that was instrumental to its progress, and again humored me as I hammered on about it. These people include, but are not limited to, Travis Linnemann, Amanda Farrell, Favian Martin, Taimi Castle, Bill McClanahan, my EKU colleagues, and all the other wonderful friends I have talked to about this project. Thanks also to Scott Kulaga for the permissions to reprint his photographs and to Vicky Allaway for letting me use her likeness for the cover.

I would also like to extend thanks to my boxing/gym family who have shaped and encouraged me throughout this journey. Without them there would be no book. There are too many people to list individually, from sparring partners, to gym pals, to trainers, instructors, and coaches who really have been wonderful. I would, however, like to offer individual thanks to my friend Travis Conner from whom I have learned so much both about boxing and fitness more generally. He has not only been instrumental to this project by offering thoughts and feedback, but without him I would not have realized most of my fitness goals. I would also like to thank Kat Sasser for both her friendship in the gym and feedback on the manuscript. Her thoughts and stories helped reassure me I was on the right track. To all the men and women who were eager to chat with me about their thoughts and experiences on women, violence, and fighting sports, I will be forever grateful.

Chapter 1

Finding Boxing in a Strip-Mall

AN INTRODUCTION TO FIGHTING SPORTS, GENDER, AND THE COMMODIFICATION OF VIOLENCE

This project began in a nondescript strip-mall in small-town America. Much like any other strip-mall situated in a small southern city, it too is generic, decorated with the expected neon signage, mid-week advertisements, and characterized by its dated sprawl of a not-quite-urban public space. It is here, nestled between a hair salon and a Vietnamese Pho restaurant that you will find a storefront for a boxing club. Bright colors of red and black adorn the shop window and draw the eye upward to two large boxing gloves and the business name inviting the passerby to look through the glass windows to the activity inside. While pedestrian traffic is limited, the large supermarket franchise and restaurant clientele from across the street provide a steady stream of patrons whose curiosity peaked, cross the threshold into the space of the boxing gym. This space, this "boxing club," is the primary site and access point to a world of boxing. It is a relatively unremarkable storefront that encourages people to wander in and sign-up to "hit it hard."

My discovery of boxing did not start with me stumbling upon this boxing club, rather I purposely sought it out in an effort to take back control over my weight and health. For most of my adult life, I have been the "fat friend" or the girl who was "pretty in the face." I do not use these terms to elicit sympathy or to pass judgment on myself or anyone else. Rather, these are things that people, strangers and friends alike, have said to me. While I detest such terms and vehemently reject the utilization of labels that reduce people to a number on the scale, I am not immune to the socially constructed beauty ideals that pervade our everyday lives. Nor am I impervious to the hurt and harm that such characterizations cause, some of which I have internalized—so much so

1

that to this day, being in arguably the best shape of my life, I still struggle with body positivity issues and maintaining a healthy relationship with food. That said, my struggle with weight and body image is long-standing and deep-rooted, with some of my issues stemming from childhood. Also, although this work is not in any way a weight-loss testimony related to the benefits of boxing, it is an important motivational catalyst that led to my initial engagement with the sport.

Growing up in rural England, I was involved with sports and athletics as much as the next child. I went swimming weekly with my family, ran in a local village "fun run" and bicycled to the local store to buy candy with my friends. I was not particularly body conscious growing up, although I do have distinct childhood memories that influenced my perception of self, including my body image. One such memory was my dad teasingly calling me "tub" when I was around five or six years old, and another was my mum's refusal to let me pursue ballet as I was "too big for ballet"—so not slender like the other girls who pursued the pastime. I also recall being put on a diet at about 6 years of age† as I had gained considerable weight before a growth spurt. This entailed me eating less than my younger brothers and not being allowed to have dessert. I think this is the first prominent memory I have of feeling shame, confusion, and inadequacy because of my body. All this is not to launch criticism at my mum and dad's parenting, as I was a very loved and supported child, rather it is to highlight how formative socialization can have long-lasting impacts on our relationships with our bodies and sense of worth. For example, consider the following research note that emphasizes the distorted image of my body that is still embedded in my psyche.

I had arrived at the gym for training, but unlike our usual week-day sessions, my trainer had suggested we work out on a Saturday, so the gym was busier than I expected. When entering the space, I immediately noticed that there were two other women near the bags, an unusual occurrence as very few women frequented this fight gym. After warming up, I was asked if I wanted to spar with one of the other women and I jumped at the opportunity. As we both entered the ring, her coach and my own were having quite a loud conversation about our match-up. They pointed out that there was a significant age difference (she was 22), experience difference (she had been boxing approximately one year longer than I had), and weight difference, as one of us "had a good 15 pounds on the other." Eyeing my opponent up, I automatically assumed that I was the one who had the weight advantage, as in my mind's eye I was much broader and thicker than her, yet her coach yelled for her "to go easy on me." Funnily, she did not need to hold back, as it quickly became apparent that I could not only hold my own but was dominating the rounds. Afterward, in reviewing the session with my coach, the fairness of the match-up came up and he said to me, "Yeah

Victoria, I was worried for a second seeing how much bigger she is than you." I remember being quite visibly shocked at his comment, and when we talked about why, he said "you're not that big girl anymore Victoria." (Fieldnote, November 4, 2017)

The above fieldnote illustrates how difficult it can be to see yourself as others see you and how self-perceptions persist despite outward change. For me, a core component of my identity and body confidence (or lack thereof) was formed in part by being the first and only female child of three being raised by a mother who struggled herself with an eating disorder and a father who sometimes had an insensitive sense of humor.

Despite some of the above-noted childhood experiences, my parents always encouraged me to be active, supported me financially and otherwise in my pursuit of team sports at school, and as I grew into my teenage years, I did not struggle with my weight. In middle school, I played the requisite netball, ran cross-country, and occasionally danced around the Maypole. I attended a local high school that boasted a total student body of approximately 700 students, which included years 7–11 (grades 7–11). There, I played on the field hockey team participating in tournaments with other schools and clubs both in the United Kingdom and Holland. I also ran track and field, as well as cross-country but not particularly successfully. These pastimes were very typical of my white middle-class roots as well as growing up in the countryside. When I left high school and went on to Sixth Form College and University, I was not really involved in any sports, and I did not exercise regularly either.

After immigrating to the United States, I revisited field hockey in a local league and took up tennis for a while, but I also entered graduate school and health and fitness fell by the wayside. I had already begun to gradually put on weight before I started graduate school, but due to a number of factors including stress, inactivity, and diet, I gained more during this time period reaching 234 pounds at my heaviest. With the weight gain came some related health issues such as high cholesterol and thyroid disease. I was also not particularly comfortable in my own body, often self-conscious, and generally did not like how I looked and felt. Periodically, and with the support of my husband, I tried big box gyms but being particularly aware of my size, found myself intimidated by the machines and other gym-goers, which eventually would lead me to quit. I did, however, maintain a pool membership and regularly swam laps throughout my time at graduate school, and although this helped considerably with stress, my weight did not change significantly. It was not until approximately five years ago while attending a family reunion when my sister-in-law told me about a boxing class she had taken at a boxercise gym, that I decided something dramatic was needed in order to make some significant lifestyle changes. Approximately two weeks later, having decided I would like to improve my overall health and fitness; at 34 years of age, I found myself on the telephone with the cardio-boxing gym that later became the initial research site and catalyst for this book.

The boxing gym as a site of sociological inquiry is not a new phenomenon. From Loïc Wacquant's (2004) *Body & Soul: Notebooks of an Apprentice Boxer*, to Lucia Trimbur's (2013) *Coming Out Swinging: The Changing World of Boxing in Gleason's Gym,* to Benita Heiskanen's (2012) *The Urban Geography of Boxing: Race, Class, and Gender in the Ring,* to Deborah Jump's (2020) *The Criminology of Boxing, Violence and Desistance,* there is no shortage of research that studies the social significance of the space and human interactions that exist in boxing gyms. What is interestingly missing from many of these works, however, is an in-depth analysis of boxing from the point of view of women as their access to the sport, industry, and gym spaces has become more accepted (see Jennings 2015 and Channon and Matthews 2015 for some exceptions). This is especially important considering the increased popularity of novice and/recreational boxing that provides many women, myself included, their first introduction to the sport.

It was my personal engagement with the sport that provided the catalyst for this project and while it started with me taking a cardio-boxing class at the aforementioned cardio-boxing gym, it has developed into a pretty serious hobby where I have a coach, adhere to a strict training regimen and commit considerable resources and time to the sport. Like scholars before me (Jennings 2015; Nash 2017; Wacquant 2004), being immersed in the sport, gyms, and the training regimens, I began to notice behaviors and social interactions that not only shaped my own experiences but also impacted how women understand themselves and others in these spaces. This was especially so, given my age, race, gender, and class—a white middle-class woman over 30 pursuing fighting sports. For example, I have been called a number of things when hitting the heavy bag, including "terrifying" (Fieldnote, March 6, 2016), "frightening" (Fieldnote, April 17, 2016), and "someone you would not like to meet in a dark alley" (Fieldnote, September 15, 2015). This is not to say that men are not referred to in such a manner, and more broadly they are socialized to aspire to be physically imposing. After all, hegemonic masculinity prescribes that men are aggressive, dominant, and take up as much physical space as possible. Men are, of course, terrifying, frightening, and carry with them the threat of potential violence (Connell 1987; Hearn 1998). However, what is interesting here, is that such statements are more often made to and about women in boxing gym spaces to compliment or convey skill proficiency.

At times women, including myself, blindly internalize these narratives relishing the idea that they are intimidating and foreboding. For example, while attending one of the cardio gyms of focus in this study, during and following my workout session, a gym employee frequently approached me as I was walking to and from the changing rooms. He would often initiate a conversation (one that was undoubtedly always awkward), with a comment such as "you do some serious damage with those hands!" (Fieldnote, June 12, 2018) or "I can't wait to see you kill some bitches in sparring!" (Fieldnote, June 18, 2018). This fed into my own perception of myself as someone who was revered and respected by others as being good at boxing, but also led to conflicting emotions about this characterization. I began to question the feelings such comments would elicit, especially as they often blurred my skill proficiency in the sport of boxing with my broader perception of self and identity. I would often ask myself whether people viewed me as violent, aggressive, and intimidating beyond the space of the gym, or whether being characterized as someone who could "kill some bitches" was really a good thing? At its core, I think these questions confronted my own preconceived and embedded comfort with the gender binary, and how my behavior and engagement with the sport felt contradictory to who I am, or who I am *supposed* to be, as a woman and a person. The permission the sport gave me to engage with physical acts of aggression, at times, led to introspection and a larger unpacking of the heteronormative gender binary that still dominates US society. It is these contradictions that the book tackles, coupled with broader explorations about the treatment of gender in these spaces.

At first glance, boxing and the spaces that accompany the sport suggest an equaling or a traversing of the gender binary, whereby physicality and skill proficiency break down and eradicate differences based on femininities and masculinities. For example, other comments uttered by trainers and coaches center on the traditional gender roles attributed to men. These phrases were often intended to make me work harder and included phrases such as "defend your family" (Fieldnote, May 4, 2017) and "what you gonna do, he got your purse!" (Fieldnote, May 17, 2017). These ideas, rooted in the defense of both person and family, broadly represent more traditional responsibilities associated with men and seemingly, their application to women suggests an upending of the gender binary; however, and as examined in later chapters, this softening of difference between the feminine and the masculine is more complex.

As indicated in the following chapters, gender did not truly traverse heteronormative categories but became central to navigating space both inside and outside the ring. As illustrated by the following fieldnote, my place in these gym spaces was often questioned. "An older white man yells out "you trying to be a boxer?" a smirk on his face. I laugh, shrug, and respond "something like that" (Fieldnote, July 8, 2017). This prompted me to explore the role of gender in the social interactions, spaces, and gyms that surround fighting sports through the lens of amateur and novice women boxers as they increasingly engage the sport. However, outside of the gym space, my engagement with boxing was viewed as more of a violation of traditional gender norms and scripts. In telling friends and family about my hobby I am often met with shock and confusion, with some seeking to clarify what I mean by boxing "You really hit people?" (Fieldnote, November 19, 2019). While alternatively, some people express concern that I may get injured. Others in my life (all men) have suggested that it is "good for women to be able to defend themselves" (Fieldnote, August 8, 2016) while not fully acknowledging the problematic nature of such a statement—that is, the threat of male-perpetrated violence against women is not only a given, but both real and significant. One of the most telling reactions to me communicating my engagement with the sport was an almost comical reaction from a fellow academic.

I describe this interaction as *almost* comical as it really epitomizes the now popular phrase "mansplaining," whereby someone, usually a man, explains something to someone else, usually a woman, the latter having superior understanding or expertise in the topic. This unsolicited 'explanation' is often both condescending and patronizing, as well as being unsolicited. Frustratingly, the person involved here loudly claims a feminist identity without any self-awareness or sense of irony. On hearing about my engagement with the sport, from a seated position, he proceeded to "show me", in great detail, how to "throw a punch" (Fieldnote, March 3, 2016). This included a long explanation about thumb placement, wrist rotation, and knuckle placement. This continued despite me telling him I had been pursuing boxing for some time where throwing a punch is obviously a requisite core skill. This exchange represents many of the central issues addressed in this book. Namely, that larger understandings of femininity confine and normalize women to nonphysical behaviors and when women violate these societal dictates they are met with significant barriers, namely, the historically entrenched heteronormative and contradictory sex roles—ones that are represented by assumptions made in this interaction: that I, a woman, need a man to show me how to throw a punch correctly because I could not possibly be competent in such a physical and dangerous pastime.

It is these missing experiences of the amateur or novice women boxer that are especially important to understanding the sport. This is especially so, considering other scholars have claimed that boxing is exclusively for men and is a celebration of masculinity (Oates 1987; Sugden 1996; Woodward 2007), describing it as an animalistic based sport likened to cockfighting and bearbaiting (Sugden 1996). As a consequence, the boxing gym has become the site of focus for scholars that seek to unpack and understand regimes of masculinity, both physical and sociological, that have then become the socially accepted and taken-for-granted "common sense" on the topic. Framed as a purely masculine activity situated in a manly world, men who engage the sport are argued to embody machismo (Oates 1987) whose "passions revolved around blood, gore and a wager" (Sugden 1996, 15). Perhaps most often noted is Loïc Wacquant's (2004, 14) work on boxing where he describes the men of the boxing gym as a "commune in the plebian cult of virility that is the Manly Art." Not only does this framing narrowly draw on dualistic discourses grounded in anatomical sex (Butler 1993), but it also implies a biological predisposition that is rooted in heteronormative assumptions about gender. When Wacquant (1995a, 88) argues that "boxing is in your blood" what does that mean discursively, symbolically, and materially for the women of the boxing gym?

Ironically, and despite such sweeping and overly simplistic conceptualizations, there is a growing literature on women's experiences with boxing and fighting sports more generally that challenges this view. However, some of the literature that has emerged does not move beyond identities that frame women as doing masculinities (Gems 2014; Mennesson 2000; Oates 1987; Sugden 1996) or as spectacle (Randall 2004). When women are centered, the focus is documenting and acknowledging women's historical engagement as pugilists (Jennings 2015), women athletes and their experiences as professional fighters or competitors (Greenwell et al 2017; Lafferty and McKay 2004; Woodward 2014), and/or lone explorations of women who breach these male spaces (Nash 2017; Channon and Matthews 2015). Additionally, when amateur women fighters are discussed the historical framing of women in combat sports as "novelty" still endures (Boddy 2014; Woodward 2007). This neglects a large and growing sector of women who are introduced to combat sports through its growing popularity as a form of fitness.

Further, the role of commodification and consumerism as they impact women's access to the sport needs to be explored. It is in spaces that can be differentiated from the stereotypical boxing gym, such as the three cardio-boxing gyms featured in this research, where many women first engage the sport. Like the other storefronts in the strip-mall mentioned in the introductory paragraph, cardio-boxing gyms offer an experience for the consumer; the boxer's workout is packaged and sold to the corporate customer as an authentic boxing experience. While many women consume this packaged form of the sport *as boxing,* others, having enjoyed the experience, seek-out more serious participation in fighting sports. In *Fighting Sports, Gender and the Commodification of Violence: Heavy Bag Heroines* the question of women's experiences with boxing and fighting sports more broadly is addressed, examining the dualistic and historically entrenched heteronormative and contradictory sex roles (i.e., masculine versus feminine) and expanding on it to include considerations of aggression, self-defense, commodification and consumption, empowerment, and health and fitness. This also means it is necessary to go beyond the spaces that accommodate those women wanting to be professional athletes, to cardio-boxing gym spaces (i.e., fitness boxing), where the sport has been increasingly packaged, commodified, and sold to predominantly middle class, white female consumers as a means to not only improve their health and fitness (i.e., boxercise, punchfit, thump, bootbox, and kickboxing exercise classes) but also as a pragmatic way to defend themselves against a would-be attacker.

The increased popularity of the sport with women consumers is not only evident in the variety of exercise classes that have appropriated the boxer's workout, but it is also reflected in popular culture where references to women in the sport pervade our popular imagination. From the Hollywood Blockbuster film *Million Dollar Baby* (Eastwood, Ruddy, Rosenburg, Haggis and Eastwood 2004), to Ed Sheeran's recent music video *Shape of You* (Sheeran et al 2016), to the *Victoria Secret* underwear advertisements that feature models wearing silk boxing robes draped with boxing gloves (Dawson Hoff 2015), women engaging the sport increasingly propagate our popular consciousness and have, like women's access to sports more generally, become embedded in the larger global structure of sports capitalism. Coupled with the increased notoriety of female athletes in the fighting sports such as Ronda Rousey, Holly Holmes, Laila Ali, and Claressa Shields to mention but a few, women's combat sports seem to have experienced a revival and as a consequence are not considered as unusual as they once were.

Furthermore, there has been little academic consideration to the tropes and scripts that are reflective of broader heteronormative gender relations as it relates to women's health, self-defense, consumerism, and violence (consensual and nonconsensual) as they emerge in these spaces. *Fighting Sports, Gender and the Commodification of Violence: Heavy Bag Heroines* seeks to unpack dominant assumptions about gender and the sport through the eyes of the participant's understandings of gender norms, social assumptions about physicality and sexuality, and challenges to masculine and feminine performativity. Stated plainly, the goal of this book is to (1) provide a holistic and in-depth study on the subculture surrounding novice/amateur women in boxing; (2) better understand the body as a gendered project as it relates to health, self-defense, commodification and violence; and (3) launch a wider exploration of gender as women novice boxers navigate traditionally male spaces, defy prescribed notions of femininity and masculinity, and literally fight to be taken seriously. To do this, it is necessary to recognize the importance of gym spaces as research sites.

THE BOXING GYM AS A SITE OF INQUIRY

Essential to understanding and analyzing the role of the boxing gym as a site for sociological inquiry is to acknowledge its importance as a cultural, political, and economic landscape for social relations. This landscape includes the space as well as the spatio-temporal processes of the body as it engages the physicality of the sport and sites necessary for that engagement. It is through these processes that power relations are navigated and negotiated (Heiskanen 2012), as the body is simultaneously a product and producer of social relations. As argued by Griggers (1992):

> If we premise that the body is not outside textuality, that the body itself is a field of significations, a site for the production of cultural meanings and ideological ramifications, then we admit that we play the game this way or that, we can choose to pass or not within the scene and the next, but we can't choose to stop playing with signs, with our own *material* cultural production as a cultural (i.e., visibly signifying body).

Therefore, it is only through space that social dynamics and relations are given power and meaning (Lefebvre 1991). Space and place, including institutions, bring order to social relations, and they also fluctuate and change when challenged (Freidland and Alford 1991). This is especially important as it relates to gender regimes. This is because gender is not simply an individual attribute, but "an emergent property of social situations" (West and Fenstermaker 1995, 9). The social dynamics of the boxing gym, a historically male preserve, provides an apt site for sociological inquiry. This is especially the case, when considered through the lens of sport as an institution.

Sport, despite the considerable gains of women, has and remains a male-dominated institution especially as men not only organize and participate at a greater rate than women due to disparate resource allocation, but also because heteronormative masculinity is closely linked to attributes celebrated in sports such as physical power, success, and sanctioned aggression (McKay 1997; Messner and Sabo 1990; Theberge 1993, 1994; Trujillo 2000). Women's admittance into sport has generally been at the periphery and relegated to those activities that have been classified as feminine (i.e., figure skating and gymnastics). These sports are often deemed acceptable as they support socially accepted assumptions about femininity, such as the assumptions that women are smaller, weaker, and slower than men. Boxing is an important site for sociological inquiry, especially as the sport has long been equated with machismo (Wacquant 2004) and masculinity (Woodward 2007) but is undergoing change as it appears to be more accepting of women boxers. This is especially important when considering three of the research sites for this study openly advertised as boxing gyms, but primarily offered exercise classes (i.e., boxercise and kickercise).

Research Sites: Accessing the Gym

My first visit to the cardio-boxing gym was anxiety-inducing. Plagued by self-doubt and concerns over my poor health and body image led me to second-guess my decision to try the sport. After fifteen minutes of sitting in my car outside of the gym, I mustered the courage to enter the building where I was greeted by a very friendly petite woman who seemed genuinely happy that I had shown up. She quickly wrapped my hands in brightly colored material and brought me over to one of the many heavy bags (100 pounds) hanging from the scaffolding that almost covered the whole room (see figure 1.1. showing a typical cardio-boxing gym space).

She selected the bag I would be using based on its proximity to the center of the room where the trainer would be instructing the class, but she was also conscious of my nervousness and the bag I was designated was far back enough that it allowed me to feel relatively anonymous among the other gym goers. After explaining and demonstrating the fundamentals required for the class that included the proper boxing stance and four punches—jab, cross, hook, and uppercut—she left me to take the class.

The class itself consisted of a warm-up period lasting fifteen minutes, eight rounds of boxing on the heavy bag (each round three minutes each with a minute interval), and then a period for core exercises that also lasted fifteen minutes. My overweight and unhealthy body went into shock. I had to sit down twice over the course of the class, but I still tried. Afterward, with encouragement

Figure 1.1   Cardio-Boxing Gym Space. *Source*: Photo by author.

from the trainer, I signed up for membership and purchased boxing gloves and wraps. It is later that evening, when struggling to walk up the stairs to my bedroom because of stiff muscles and aches and pains, that I questioned this decision. However, I persevered and started going to classes regularly. Having lost approximately 85 pounds in weight and eliminated the aforementioned health issues, the pictures below illustrate the profound changes boxing has had on my life—and the extent to which I personally have found myself involved with the sport. The transformation has been dramatic as demonstrated in the self-indulgent yet illustrating image of me both before I started the project and today (see figure 1.2).

This book, therefore, in addition to giving voice to those involved in the sport, is a body project; my own. Perhaps not in the traditional sense where the focus is to attain heteronormative ideals of beauty and thinness as promoted by a capitalist hegemonic society (Bordo 1993; Sullivan 2004), but it would be misleading to divorce it completely from larger structural forces of influence and my own social identity, bodily conformity, and the habitual

Figure 1.2   Before and After Boxing. *Source*: Photo by author.

behavior of working out to achieve and maintain a fitness goal. However, while the body projects apparent in the gym spaces I traversed at times did "appear to be more reflective of male designs and fantasies than an expression of individuality" (Shilling 1993, 8), many women viewed their engagement with the sport as being counter to the dominant cultural expectations associated with gender norms and tropes within a heteronormative patriarchal society. As argued by Meredith Nash (2017), women in fighting/combat sports report experiencing increased agency and power as they become physically more powerful. The body project in the sport of boxing, therefore, could be framed as a form of resistance, or a physical feminism (Wedgwood 2004) that counters normative assumptions about boxing being male (Oates 1987).

The cardio-boxing gym that provided the initial site for this research is part of a franchise, one that has approximately 175 locations across North America and Mexico. Trainers offered group classes in boxing, kickboxing, and mixed martial arts, as well as personal training. Initial contacts were made in this gym and the study then spread to other sites that included six other gym spaces, two of which were non-contact cardio-boxing gyms and four gyms where sparring/contact boxing was permitted. Two of these gyms did not identify primarily as a boxing gym, but rather as gym spaces where boxing was one of many activities you could pursue. Two of these spaces fell under the more traditional understanding of a fighting gym, as not only was there sparring but one of the gyms regularly hosted bouts/matches. Contrary to the cardio-boxing gyms, these fighting gyms aesthetically typified what is thought of when conjuring the stereotypical image of a boxing gym or what is more often depicted in films such as the *Rocky* franchise that includes the more recently released films *Creed* (Winkler et al. 2015) and *Creed II* (Winkler et al. 2018). Over the course of the study period (2015–2019), my membership at these different gyms coincided with my coach's employment, so although I did not hold seven memberships at any one time, I very often held two memberships at once and spent considerable time in each of the spaces. Other sites included in this study were several outdoor spaces used for training/sparring at trainer's homes (flat concrete spaces about the size of a boxing ring and an enclosed grass area away from prying neighbors), several competition spaces, and some venues used for social events.

GAINING ACCESS: STORYING
MYSELF—A FEMINIST APPROACH

As is the nature of any ethnographic work, this book "seeks to capture, interpret and explain how a group, organization or community lives, experience and make sense of their lives and their world" (Robson 2000, 89). This requires a sociological *verstehen* allowing for meaning to be garnered from situational contexts, as well as interactions between the researcher and participants. As argued by Jeff Ferrell and Mark Hamm (1998, 14), ethnography "frees field researchers to embrace the situated meanings generated by their subjects and themselves; to value the insights and understandings gained from shared emotions; to explore the lived politics of pleasure and pain, fear and excitement." This requires an emersion into the researched environment to garner phenomenological insights from the perspective of that group (Krane and Baird 2005). In the case of boxing and fighting sports, as with other subcultures that require physical interactions, the researcher is required to go beyond the mind and "think with the body" (Scheper-Hughes 1994). This allows for autobiographical accounts that are inherently personal and political but are also reflexive as the research is participatory, empathetic, and subjective.

In many ways, I stumbled into the world of amateur boxing and pugilism by accident by signing up for a boxercise class that was a somewhat desperate attempt to regain some control over my own health. When I signed up for that initial class, I could not have anticipated how boxing would become an instrumental part of my life and my own social identity. Through my own experiences, and due to the physicality inherent to the sport itself, I not only found myself frequently questioning my own engagement and identity within the spaces I navigated, but also my assumptions about the people and places surrounding me. This retrospective reflexivity allowed for a greater exploration of the dialectic between my role as a researcher and the research process employed. As many researchers have argued, ethnography lends itself to feminist approaches where gender is seen as "a basic organizing principle that shapes the conditions of their lives" (Lather 1991). Tanya Bunsell (2013) notes this has resulted in an increased number of feminist ethnographers focusing not only on the quality of the research but also on the quality of the relationship between researcher and participant. It is this tradition that I seek to embrace here, where time, dedication, and personal embracing of the training regimes associated with amateur boxing led to the fostering of quality relationships with the research participants and a reflexive consciousness as I situated myself within the study. For example, the following field note is significant to my personal journey with boxing, emphasizes the quality of the relationship established between myself and my trainer, and my commitment to the role of participant/observer. It also represents a culmination of three years of working toward my own goals that were initially rooted in health and wellbeing but later transformed into a more complex amalgamation of identity, worth, competitiveness, fitness, and empowerment.

> As I stand on the squeaky raised platform of the boxing ring, in the unfamiliar space of a new gym, I am simultaneously filled with excitement and trepidation.

I have been invited here with my trainer to spar with a professional MMA fighter who has offered to give us both feedback me on my skills and him on his training. I am beyond nervous, the tension evident in my body as the fighter says, "relax, why you so tense?" I take deep breaths in effort to calm my anxiety and roll my shoulders from side to side in an attempt to relax my body. I try to take it all in, me at 37, a little woman from England, in a MMA gym in a small town in the middle of rural America. This situation strikes me as surreal and represents one that I could not have ever predicted, but it is one that means a great deal to me. I have to do well, I have to perform okay . . . I bring up my guard, we bump gloves and it begins . . . I hear in my periphery my trainer yell "don't be afraid to hit him Victoria!" (Fieldnote, June 1, 2017)

This field note not only emphasizes the participatory nature of this research but underscores two important reasons for unveiling the self in ethnographic research (autoethnography) (Chang 2008). First, that the very nature of research cannot be divorced from the personal or political (Becker 1967) and therefore infers a degree of subjectivity in the shared understandings and experiences between the researcher and the research participants (Ferrell and Hamm 2016). While this could be viewed as a potential limitation, I have endeavored to represent people and places accurately. My focus has been on both reporting events as they occurred, as well as reflecting on and analyzing these experiences as much as possible (Briggs 2013). Second, that striving for complete transparency is not without its vulnerabilities. My experience, while an essential ingredient to feminist approaches (Gelsthorpe 1990) may not be typical as it is informed by my personal history (i.e., race, gender, age, ethnicity, class, and other defining characteristics). Therefore, a complete and holistic account of women in boxing cannot truly be achieved solely through my biographic account not only because of the complexity of the subject matter but also due to the fragmented nature of ethnographic work (Bunsell 2013; Douglas 2009).

In addition, "writing in" the researcher's experiences as a method has been criticized for being narcissistic and self-indulgent as well as leading to ethical dilemmas related to anonymity, trust, and disclosure (Sparkes 2000). However, this method calls for the researcher to explore personal, emotional, and relational involvements allowing for the lived-sporting experiences to be relayed within the situational context of physical culture, as well as the emotional and special geographies in which they occur (Nash 2017; Sparkes 2000). Therefore, to guard against these potential vulnerabilities as they relate to the research subject, the focus here is the narratives and shared experiences of the women that occupy these spaces. As indicated by social-ist Howard S. Becker (1963, 183), it is necessary to "look at all the people involved in any episode of alleged deviance . . . all the parties to a situation, and their relationships." While Becker's focus is different than my own (i.e., deviance), his larger argument is that the researcher as a participant is instrumental to the scrutiny of the subject at hand.

PARTICIPANTS

In an effort to fully understand the role of gender and women's engagement and experience in the sport of boxing and fighting sports more generally, the participants in this study were both men and women. Their engagement with the sport varied along a spectrum of skill level from those who just hit the heavy bag at the non-contact cardio-boxing gyms, to those who were actively pursuing careers in fighting sports. The majority of participants were women (twenty-four) and eight were men. Several of the participants were gym-goers, some were trainers, and others were professional athletes. The participants ranged in ages from nineteen to fifty-five with the majority of participants being in their twenties. Many of the women participants were students, both undergraduate and graduate, as well as fitness instructors. Other women worked inside the home, while others had professional occupations that ranged from engineers to social workers, to surgical residents. There was less variation with the male participants who were either pursuing fighting sports as a career or worked in the fitness industry as coaches and trainers.

Important to the study of boxing is the issue of race and ethnicity, especially given its history of being a predominantly male, urban, minority, lower-class sport (Heiskanen 2012). However, largely due to the geographic location of this study (a small city situated in a state with a predominantly white population), all but two of the participants were white. However, one of the contact gyms featured was a black-owned business; therefore, a number of my own experiences with drills, partner work, and sparring involved black and Latinx men and women. Participants and interviewees either attended, trained at, or instructed others at one or more of the seven gyms sites included in this project. Therefore, there were some participants who only had experience with boxercise (i.e., non-contact boxing), while others trained seriously to compete. Furthermore, I attended several fights including white-collar, amateur, and professional events, where I was able to talk to the boxers and MMA fighters before and after their experiences. In addition, my own engagement as a regular gym-goer at both cardio-boxing gyms and fight gyms, attending classes and actively pursuing my own training, allowed me to immerse myself in the local fight community and document my own experiences through extensive field notes, and also capture situations and conversations as they occurred in public spaces.

Fighting Sports, Gender, and the Commodification of Violence: Heavy Bag Heroines attempts to broadly capture a glimpse into the cultural terrain of women's boxing and fighting sports more generally, especially as it manifests in everyday gyms for novice boxers. This project provides a vehicle for examining broader understandings of gender, violence, self-defense, commodification, and health and fitness. Commodification is a central theme to this book (see chapters 3 and 4 for further analysis) as it relates to the appropriation and commodification of the boxing workout and its sale to what emerges here as a predominantly white female consumer—a demographic that I myself occupy. While there are several ethnographic books that examine the world of boxing from varying disciplinary perspectives (see Heiskanen 2012; Trimbur 2013; Wacquant 2004; Weinberg 2016), several articles and book chapters that enter the boxing space for the purpose of sociological inquiry (Halbert 1997; Hargreaves 1997; Mennesson 2000; Sugden 1996; Wacquant 1992, 1995a,b, 1998a,b, 2001), as well as research that tackles the topic of masculinities and MMA (Vaccaro and Swauger 2016), there is yet to be a comprehensive in-depth ethnographic study of novice women's engagement (at a variety of skill levels) with the sport that places the experiences of women at the center of the analysis. Rather, the studies that do exist, primarily due to men's historical and current domination in fighting sports, tend to focus on men's experiences and the resistance/ acceptance women encounter when entering the traditionally male spaces of the boxing gym and ring (see Nash 2017 for an exception). The little research that does address women's experiences focuses solely on their discriminatory experiences in the sport (Halbert 1997; Oates 1987), narrows the focus to competitive boxing (Lafferty and McKay 2004), tracks the evolutionary history of women's involvement in boxing (Hargreaves 1997; Jennings 2015), provides a cursory glimpse into the female experience as part of a larger project (Heiskanen 2012; Trimbur 2013), and/or examines how celebratory characteristics of hypermasculinity bleed over into other aspects of fighters lives with detrimental consequences for women, that is, intimate partner violence (Vaccaro and Swauger 2016). While these studies have been instrumental to developing a growing knowledge of the topic, they often omit the complexity with which gender informs not only the sport of boxing but also the decision women make, and at what level they choose, to engage the sport.

Furthermore, there is a need to further unpack the relationship of women's boxing to health and fitness, especially the repackaging and commodification of a traditionally male, urban, minority, lower-class sport that has been coopted by recent popular culture as a means to sell goods (i.e., the 2015 Victoria Secret advertising campaign), and exercise regimes in gyms across the United States as it is sold to predominantly middle class, white consumers in the form of health and fitness classes, that is, boxercise. Therefore, with this in mind and drawing on literature from the sociology of sport, American studies, women, and gender studies as well as criminology, the purpose of this book is to provide a more holistic and in-depth ethnographic account of women in boxing and fighting sports at all skill levels.

Contrary to more orthodox approaches whereby a particular theoretical perspective is advanced to aide in the analysis of the research phenomenon of focus, the approach here is integrated. In chapter 2, I provide a brief overview of the history of women in boxing before addressing the emergence of white-collar boxing/novice boxer both as a conceptual term as it relates to attracting women to the sport. This is followed by an overview of some important concepts such as gender, hegemonic masculinity, and emphasized femininity as they are understood and applied here. This chapter closes with an examination of the benefits to women who engage boxing and how their participation relates to gender structures, roles, and norms including women's expressions of aggression and anger.

Chapter 3 takes the focus beyond the interactional level to examine general perceptions of women in boxing and combat sports. Drawing on media accounts, social media feeds, and commentary, as well as a more generalized understanding of women in the sport, this chapter examines how women pugilists are socially and culturally understood. This is unpacked at the amateur level where societal constructions of the sport, especially as it relates to sexualization, beauty, and the commodification of these constructions through the health and fitness industry manifest in boxing gym spaces. Novice women boxers not only navigate deeply embedded understandings of women in combat sports, but they too can contribute to, both willingly and unwillingly, the reification of the same patriarchal scripts that marginalize women.

Chapter 4 continues with an exploration of cardio-boxing gym spaces and women's introduction to boxing. Drawing on elements of feminist perspectives that examine gender performativity (Butler 1990; Connell 1995; Connell and Messerschmidt 2005; Crocket 2012; Halberstam 1998; Messner 1992), the importance of these space as sites where social dynamics, identities, performativity and relations are given power and meaning as they are explored. The body in this context brings power from the abstract to the material (Fiske 1992) as the body itself becomes the site for personal expression and empowerment, the navigation of interactions and relationships, and as a target for consumer marketing. This chapter reveals considerable differences between those gyms that offered cardio-boxing as compared to those that focused on adversarial/contact-boxing. These differences are situated within the larger societal structures of gender and sport and are related to the spatial boundaries that either invite women into these spaces or purposely exclude them.

Chapters 5 and 6 tackle the topic of adversarial/contact boxing. The emergence of an "all women's fight club" as a nontraditional foray into adversarial/no-contact boxing, is the focus of chapter 5. Framed by the organizers as feminist in its origins, the motivations and happenings surrounding this groups' Fight Nights, are unpacked and analyzed as it relates to emphasized femininity (Connell 1987), alternative femininities (Schippers 2007), precorporation (Fisher 2009), and gender maneuvering (Schippers 2002). Although clearly distinguishable from more orthodox and less commercialized understandings of boxing and combat sports, this chapter offers up women's fight club as an alternative space for the physical expression of empowerment, anger, and frustration at the constraints provided by heteronormative gender structures. Chapter 6 focuses on the bodily regimens, inter-gendered sparring, and coaching relationships that are characteristic of traditional fight gyms. This includes discussions of challenges women face, as well as how they navigate relationships necessary to remain safe in these male-dominated spaces. This chapter also examines how gender is used and exploited as a teaching tool by coaches and the excess emotional work women boxers do to be taken seriously. Coaches emerge as important gatekeepers because of their considerable power in deciding who has access to traditional fighting gym spaces.

Given the ever-present threat of men's violence against women, chapter 7 tackles the broader conversation of violence as it relates to boxing, self-defense, and fighting sports more broadly. This includes addressing the catalyst for women to initiate engagement with the sport, where victimization provides the motivation for a temporal reclaiming of body and space in efforts to resist and recover social power. This leads to an in-depth examination of violence as an appropriate vehicle for self-defense—a form of physical feminism (McCaughey 1997), something that has received considerable criticism from feminist scholars. In addition to analyzing the pragmatism of fighting sports as a defensive tool, the self-defense script is unpacked as a point of sale for cardio-boxing gyms. This is explored not only as it relates to possible themes of consumerism and false senses of security but also conversely as it relates to empowering women, reclaiming the body, power, and space.

Chapter 8 focuses on the fight as a spectacle where the culmination of body work is reduced to the minutes of a competition. With the emergence of athletes such as Claressa Shields, who has been said to have sparked a revival in women's boxing (Spezia 2017), the fight as spectacle is no longer exclusively the domain of men. This chapter explores what this means for the female fighter as she not only navigates the boxing ring but also the physical, social, and bodily demands necessary to prepare for a fight. Furthermore, the carnival of the white-collar boxing event is analyzed as it relates to novice/amateur boxers and the spectacle of entertainment. In acknowledging that women on these fight cards have become more normalized, this chapter asks the question, "What does this mean for women who are trying to pursue a career in boxing, versus those who are entering the ring for fun?"

Chapter 9 concludes the book by providing some thoughts on the future of women's boxing and fighting sports more generally. These thoughts are specific to the themes that have emerged throughout the book. Possible topics for further examination include projections about gender equality, health and fitness, and consumption, as well as the role boxing and fighting sports have when it comes to women embracing the potential of their own physicality. I leave the reader with a few suggestions for future research that includes the continued centering of women pugilists to better understand the social and cultural world in which we live.

Chapter 2

From Amazonians to Cardio Classes

Women, Consumerism, and Combat Sports

INTRODUCTION

Boxing has historically been marketed as a male-dominated sport with its genealogy configured around masculinity. While there are notable exceptions, with increased frequency, those that take part in, consume, and the language surrounding the sport remain male-dominated. As argued by Joyce Carol Oates (1987, 72), "Boxing is for men and is about men, and is men." Yet, while this may be empirically true, both classically and currently, it omits the reality of women's involvement with the sport. The record of women engaged in fighting sports remains largely undocumented as they are often discounted or excluded from the history books (Jennings 2015). However, there are descriptions that can be traced back to Roman poetry (Ovid 1990; Propertius 1994), albeit often conflated with broader understandings of women warriors, or military fighters. For example, Propertius (1994, 91) describes two Amazonian women as "One soon to be prize boxer, the other horseman." From Sparta, to the Amazonians, to fighters in WWII, women have fought for thousands of years (Jennings 2015).

Although important to acknowledge, historical accounts of women fighters are often conflated with soldiering, which is decidedly different from the engagement of women in fighting sports—the focus here. In this chapter, I briefly trace the history of women in boxing, before examining the emergence of white-collar boxing/novice boxer and the proliferation of the cardio-boxing gym as it impacts women. This is followed by an overview of some important concepts such as white-collar boxing and emphasized femininity as they are understood and applied here. This examination acknowledges the classed, gendered, and raced history of the sport before examining the benefits of women engaging the sport, how this relates to gender structures, roles, and norms including women's expressions of aggression and anger.

WOMEN FIGHTERS: A BRIEF HISTORY

While the emergence of women in fighting sports in the Global North is generally traced back to eighteenth-century England (Boddy 2014), there are sporadic records of women engaging in fighting events hosted at fairs, carnivals, and more professional/elite events throughout history. The documentation of their appearance in the sport, however, is not because of a spiked interest in women's participation, rather it can be attributed to the emergence of less restrictive print media that began to increasingly proliferate. Women almost certainly engaged in fighting sports prior to the eighteenth century; however, it is not until this time period that records of such happenings began to emerge. In addition, it is important to recognize that because of their exclusion from the sport, when women have competed historically, it has been at unsanctioned events that have lesser chances of receiving public and political acknowledgment. The exclusion of women from sanctioned boxing events has largely been justified because of the contentious nature of the sport more broadly (i.e., its framing as violence) that contradicts dominant qualities and characteristics of femininity. Compounding this further was the institutionalization of inaccurate medical information that excluded women from engaging in sport more broadly. For example, consider that historically women have been barred from running for fear their uteruses might fall out of their vaginas, in addition to claims that women who move around excessively might become sexually aroused (Jennings 2015). Yet, the involvement of women in fighting sports has persisted and over time has become gradually more socially accepted (Greenwell et al. 2017).

In the early eighteenth century, bare-knuckle fighting gained popularity among the working classes and fighting with gloves became a sought-after recreational pastime for the upper class (Boddy 2014). Although this sparring remained the pastime of men, there are journalistic accounts that detail women fighting for money. Popular women fighters of the era included Mrs. Sutton and Elizabeth Stokes. They were not boxers in the traditional sense, rather they fought with short quarter staffs and their fists, but they were often celebrated for their efforts. However, it must be noted that the focus of the press coverage tended to be less on their athletic prowess and more on their appearances, with media reports detailing the description of their "bosoms bare, and the clothes nearly torn from their bodies" (Hickey 1913, 82–3). The sexualizing of the feminine form represents a common stereotype of the female fighter (Boddy 2014; Jennings 2015), and throughout history, women boxers have been repeatedly portrayed to the larger public in ways that titillate and amuse male spectators.

From the 1800s to the 1950s, there was not a lot of change in the world of women's boxing, and although matchups and events occurred, they were sidelined to fairground attractions and vaudevi_le (Toulmin 1999). In the United States in the 1950s, a small profession.al boxing circuit emerged headlined by Barbara Buttrick, who emigrated to the United States and fought in several exhibition and competition bouts. She established several firsts for women in boxing including the first televised match, first feature in boxing magazine *The Ring* in 1957, and receiving one of the first boxing licenses issued to women along with Phyllis Knight (Dunn 2009; Hargreaves 1996; Toulmin 1999). While running the risk of gleaning over decades of time and the contributions made by many other women pugilists, the following section will highlight some of the more impactful accomplishments of women who have shaped the sport.

Further momentum in the sport gathered in the 1980s and 1990s, when resources, accessibility, and appeal to women increased. Here, women, attracted to the workout the sport provided, invested in classes that are often described as boxercise, as well as self-defense classes (Dunn 2009; Trimbur 2013). There have been many accounts from amateur boxers that have helped carve out a space in women's boxing. The 1980s saw the admittance of women to archetypal boxing gyms signifying a shift in sentiment toward female boxers. For example, in 1983 women were admitted to Gleason's gym in Brooklyn, New York, and according to Hass (2000) by the year 2000, 15 percent of their memberships were women (116 members).

Despite being permitted to train in "authentic" boxing gyms, it was not until the late 1980s when countries began to lift bans on women boxing competitively. In 1988, Sweden was the first to lift the ban. In the United States, it was up to individual states as to whether individual women could obtain a boxing license and there were no federal regulations, rules, or national competitions where titles could be won (Jennings 2015). This changed in the 1990s following several cases litigating women's right to compete in amateur bouts. The national sanctioning body for amateur boxing, the United States Amateur Boxing, Inc., refused to recognize women as athletes and consequently their right to fight, something they justified by advancing medical and safety concerns. This was challenged in the courts over the course of several years. For example, following eight years of litigation, Gail Grandchamp won her case against USA Boxing and the New England Amateur Athletic Union and was granted the right to compete as an amateur. Similarly, Dallas Malloy sued USA Boxing on the grounds of gender discrimination and won her case. These cases established precedent for the inclusion of women in amateur boxing as well as provided the catalyst for further challenges in court that led to an increase in the number of registered women amateur boxers (Dunn 2009). In 1993 USA Boxing created a women's program with accompanying rules and regulations (Trimbur 2013). This paved the way for thirty women to fight in the Golden Gloves tournament in 1995 (Jennings 2015).

Following the Golden Gloves tournament in 1995 women's boxing gained momentum. The first Women's National Championship was held in 1997, and the first Women's World Championship was held in 2001. The momentum and acceptance of women's amateur boxing culminated in the decision of the International Olympic Committee to include women's boxing in the London games in 2012. Although the focus of this book is predominantly women's amateur boxing, it is important to acknowledge the developmental trajectory of women's professional boxing, especially considering that the wider public acceptance of women in fighting sports can be associated with particular professional pugilists such as Leila Ali and Ronda Rousey.

Professional women's boxing paralleled that of amateur boxing, only insofar as it emerged in the United States during a similar time period. In 1995, Christy "The Coal Miner's Daughter" Martin, an American boxer from West Virginia, and Deidre Gogarty from Ireland, were featured on the undercard of the Mike Tyson and Frank Bruno title fight in Las Vegas. Martin received considerable attention because of the fight and appeared on the cover of *Sports Illustrated* magazine (Boddy 2014). However, despite becoming the new face of women's boxing, Martin created controversy. Instead of being an advocate for the advancement of women's boxing—a voice from the inside—she engaged in considerable criticism of other women boxers creating considerable tension in the then-emerging professional boxing circuit. Compounding her impact on professional women's boxing was the polarizing press coverage of both her career and her person (Jennings 2015). For example, the *San Diego Union-Tribune* in an article titled "Is She Admirable or Abominable?" undermined her skills as a fighter arguing that her success was not about her boxing ability, deeming the act of women fighting as "sickening." Rather, they attributed her success to her appearance. In addition, Don King commented, "Christy Martin is attractive. She can fight, and she is a novelty" (King as cited in Jennings 2015). Despite media coverage framing women boxers as novelty, Martin's professional debut and her subsequent career that boasted 49 victories, inspired many women to engage the sport (Boddy 2014). This does not mean, however, that she was the only female fighter that was deserving of public attention. Others such as Bonnie Canino and Lucia Rijker, whose boxing followed careers in other martial arts, were equally worthy of notice. However, media coverage of these women, especially Rijker, demeaned their appearances so much so that when she approached Christy Martin for a match-up, Martin's camp responded by asking Rijker for a DNA test to prove her biological sex (Dunn 2000).

Popularity of women's boxing gained momentum in the late 1990s into the early 2000s with the introduction of Laila Ali, the daughter of professional boxer and now infamous heavyweight champion Muhammad Ali. Due to her father's notoriety, Laila's career received considerable public attention (Jennings 2015). The popularity of boxing for women and its legitimacy was further boosted by the emergence of Mixed Martial Arts (MMA) and a growing number of women fighters garnering public attention. While there are numerous fighters from all over the world that participated in early MMA matchups, including the first women's competition held in Japan in the early 1990s, it was not until 1993 that the Ultimate Fighting Championship (UFC) held its first event. Then, in 1995, Toyoko was host to the first all-female fight card boosting seven different matchups. Like boxing, women's fights became more frequent and competitions were arranged across the globe. There are numerous women fighters that are deserving of mention during this time period, including but not limited to Svetlana Goundarenko (Russia), Shinobu Kandori (Japan), Marloes Coenan (Netherlands), Yuuki Kondo (Japan), Laura DAuguste (United States), Tevi Sai (France), Meguimi Yabushita (Japan), and Jennifer Howe (United States). It was not until the early 2000s, however, that women's MMA gained greater public acceptance.

The early 2000s saw women fighters featured in competitions such as Hook-n-Shoot, King of the Cage, Bellator Fighting Championship, Strike Force, and Bodog Fight, to mention but a few. Many women began their careers in these competitions before being signed to the UFC. Some notable names include Debi "Whiplash" Purcell, Rosi Sexton, Lana Stefanac, Gina "Conviction" Carrano, Julie Kedzie, and Cris "Cyborg" Justino. Gina Carrano, often dubbed the first "face of WMMA" (Jennings 2015), and Julie Kedzie made history by being the first women to have their fight televised on *Showtime*. Arguably, however, it was not until the entrance of Ronda Rousey that women's MMA reached a level of publicity that acted to further normalize and legitimize the sport. This is not to say that all the women that came before her are not equally as important, yet it was Rousey's physical appearance that launched her, and by proxy women's MMA, into the spotlight. Capitalizing on Carrano's retirement, when Rousey entered into talks to fight Miesha Tate, she argued that she was more marketable than the alternative—Sarah Kaufman. She argued that she and Tate would be good for the sport as they were both more attractive than the other fighters that had been working themselves up through the ranks. Shortly after, Rousey was the first woman signed to the UFC and she has since become a household name.

Based on the albeit brief history here, women in combat sports more broadly have made considerable gains. Yet, despite their lingering status of anomaly, the gains that have been made have had the effect of making resources otherwise closed to women more accessible. Many training facilities, boxing gyms, and gyms more broadly have opened their doors to women (Trimbur 2013), not only including them but also structuring workouts and group classes based on a boxers' workout regimen. As women have increasingly been able to engage the sport, the spaces, and places that they traverse—historically masculine spaces—I now turn my attention to the emergence of the white-collar/novice boxer.

CLASS AND GENDER POLITICS: BOXING AS EXERCISE AND THE WHITE-COLLAR BOXER

Of focus here is the development of boxing as a form of exercise that has been targeted to a broader consumer, specifically the everyday woman. As Lucia Trimbur (2013) argues in a chapter examining white-collar boxing, there is a long history of people engaging the sport for the sole purpose of recreation. There are historical accounts that indicate that upper-class men in the 1700s taught themselves fighting skills and technique in effort to guard themselves against potential assaults. This was situated in class-appropriate constructs of gender allowing upper-class men to present a refined form of masculinity while still being able to protect both themselves and those who were dependent on them. Other histories examine college men who boxed at universities such as Harvard and Yale (Bederman 1995; Gorn 1986). Yet, Shari Dworkin and Faye Wachs (2009) note that by the end of the 1900s there was an increased interest in the sport as recreation and as the fitness industry exploded more middle-class and white-collar workers joined gyms to workout with competitive fighters and boxing trainers.

Class: The white-collar boxer

As argued by sociologist Pierre Bourdieu (2010, 212), the values of boxing, such as "strength, endurance, violence 'sacrifice,' docility and submission to collective discipline," are "contrary to bourgeois role distance." The argument being that people of different classes have different cultural tastes (Bourdieu 2010). However, post-industrial relations have changed insofar as there has been an economic shift to consumer capitalism where class distinctions have diminished (Blackshaw 2016). Identity under this structure has to be constantly, individually, and reflexively cultivated through consumption behaviors. Cultural tastes and the willingness to transcend prior hierarchal boundaries have increased; however, the willingness to consume across class does not eradicate class or differences in class consumption practices. Termed cultural omnivorousness (Peterson 1992), the dissolution of class boundaries in class consumption practices is a useful way to conceptualize white-collar or recreational boxing as conveying a novice status opposed to a particular occupational type/class positioning.

Other examinations of recreational boxing have focused on white-collar boxing, where the term white-collar does not operate as a class indicator but rather connotes the level of skill demonstrated by the boxer, that is, a novice status (Wright 2019). Edward Wright (2019) argues that the term itself is misleading, as it situates the boxers within a specific socio-historical context, the time period in which the term originated, that is, in Gleason's Gym in Manhattan New York in the 1980s. Sociological analyses have argued that boxing is a working-class sport (Wacquant 1995a; Woodward 2007). It is through this conceptualization that white-collar boxing can be better understood to include women, a demographic characterized as being distinct from white-collar and therefore analyzed separately (Trimbur 2013).

The term "white-collar" boxer to mean "novice" boxer is demonstrated through the varied occupational backgrounds of the participants in this study. Occupations included, but were not limited to, homemakers, graduate students, retail workers, engineers, social workers, and trainers. Of the twenty-four -(21) were categorized as "novice" boxers, meaning they did not engage the sport as a career or a professional athlete. The level of skill here varied significantly ranging from those who exclusively took cardio-boxing classes, to those that trained for and participated in amateur competitions. Interestingly, the majority of participants who identified as trainers/instructors also would be classified as recreational boxers as with the exception of nine participants, they had little actual in-the-ring experience. A larger number engaged the sport during their childhood and adolescence, competing as amateurs. However, as one instructor who identified as a professional MMA fighter at the time of the interview said, "jumping in the ring when you are ten-years old doesn't mean you are a qualified boxer when you're thirty" (Antonio, Personal Communication, July 9, 2018). The majority of participants in this study, therefore, fit Edward Wrights' (2019) definition of white-collar boxer as they cover a spectrum of engagement with the sport that is truly novice, and furthermore capture a demographic that has received little scholarly attention; women white-collar boxers or novice boxers.

Sex and Gender

A popular approach for examining boxing is to utilize masculinities as an analytical frame (Gorn 1986; Heiskanen 2012; Oates 1987; Messner 1992; Satterlund 2012). Violence is not incompatible with hegemonic masculinity and as a consequence becomes an available tool for men in its achievement. As argued by Jeff Hearn (1998, 35–6), "violence is dominance, is the result of dominance, and creates the conditions for the reproduction of dominance.

Violence is a means of *enforcing* power and control, but it is also power and control itself." Connell (1995, 51) argues that "the most visible bearers of hegemonic masculinity" such as celebrities are not always the most powerful, rather they are symbols or emblematic of its project. Celebrities as visible bearers include sports stars, and as Kath Woodward (2007) argues this is important as it relates to Connell's argument surrounding complicity.

Connell (1995) notes that most men are not sports stars and therefore are not emblematic of hegemonic masculinity, rather it is their complicity with its project that is worthy of consideration. However, they are complicit in the masculinity it promotes and affirms. This may happen through their consumption of the sport through their attendance at events, purchasing it via pay-per-view or simply watching it from the comfort of their own homes. Connell's (1995, 79) argument is that despite limited engagement, complicity leads to most men benefiting from the "patriarchal dividend, the advantage men in general gain from the overall subordination of women." Although not all hegemonic masculinity is visible, Woodward (2007) notes that boxing provides a space where masculinity, especially physicality, violence, and risk are very visible. Also, historically this has intersected with class as the boxing gym is a geographical space where masculinity, usually black, lower class, can be acquired by white middle-class men (Satterlund 2012; Trimbur 2011). But this leaves a gap in understanding when the focus is women who engage the sport as novices.

In spaces that have historically valued masculinity, viewing gender as performative (Butler 1999) lends itself to a more in-depth exploration of how gender is understood in these spaces. Furthermore, this approach establishes that gender identities are not only situational but accomplished interactionally (Messner 1992). Constructions of gender as an ongoing activity (Schwalbe 1996; West and Zimmerman 1987) offer understandings of the gym spaces of focus here, where masculinity has traditionally been celebrated, but to achieve it, that is to "do" gender effectively, requires the drawing on resources (whether internal or external) and behavioral skills that signify to others the successful expression of gender identity (Messner 1992). As argued by Schwalbe (2005) having or achieving masculinity is dependent on other people's interpretation of their gender expressions. These behaviors rely on established gender identities that are specific to those spaces. Behaviors and characteristics associated with hegemonic masculinity vary across time and space, but generally it can be achieved through the performance of, or perceived performance of, "risky" or pseudo-dangerous activities. This is of course situational, as engaging in risks that are viewed as unnecessary or nonsensical do not hold the same value as those that have been given purpose—those validated by societal gender norms. For example, displays of aggression by men in situations deemed appropriate by society, such as protecting a loved one from harm, taking on a position of power or leadership, or demonstrating physical dominance such as exchanging blows in the boxing gym, would qualify as performing masculinity. Therefore, in the space of the traditional boxing gym there exist gender signifiers or scripts where "masculinity is thus a quality attributed to people (males or females) based on interpretation of their expressive behavior" (Satterlund 2012, 530). In the gyms included here, the marketing of the boxing experience was very much dependent on understandings of gender and how it interacted with other demographics. This understanding began with the gym space itself, specifically how and to whom it was marketed.

MARKETING THE SPACE: CRAFTING THE IMAGE, SPORTS APPAREL, AND THE NEW MIDDLE-CLASS CONSUMER

There were obvious ascetic differences between the gyms included in this study with the three cardio boxercise gyms purposely appropriating common or perhaps stereotypical understandings of a boxing gym into their décor. For example, one of the gyms situated in a strip-mall near a busy shopping area that included a coffee shop and deli, identified itself as "the king of the boxing gyms." The gym itself had walls, equipment and flooring decorated in dark colors such as black and gray, as well as displayed graffiti-style white and orange writing across the walls. Furthermore, black and white photographs of famous boxers such as Muhammed Ali loomed above the equipment stations. The equipment (i.e., bags, ring, weights, bands, machines, etc.) were all new. This gym in particular appeared to be trying to capitalize on the history of boxing as being a sport associated with the urban, an activity that exists on the periphery of society with the practitioners of the sport stereotyped as operating outside of conventional society (Heiskanen 2012). This was especially so as many of the "heavy bag" classes were held in a darkened room, with loud music and strobe and spotlighting adding an element of excitement, despite the impracticality of hitting a target with little light.

As was the case for all three cardio-boxing gyms, the gym space could be seen from the street as the whole front of the building was glass, so those passing by could see inside. All three spaces had boxing rings, two falling within the standard sizing of 16 to 20 feet along the sides with a further two feet outside the ropes,[1] the other was much smaller. The rings were purposely situated near the front of the gym spaces where they were easily visible from the street (see Figure 2.1 for an example).

Also, at the front of each of these spaces as you entered the door, there were areas where merchandise was sold including gloves, hand-wraps, and

Figure 2.1   Street View of Boxing Ring in Cardio-Gym Spaces. *Source*: Photograph by Scott Kulaga.

apparel decorated with each of the gym's logo. All three of these spaces had a front desk that was manned by an instructor/gym worker who greeted prospective consumers with upbeat messaging and a reassuring smile. My own experience may have been quite different if I had not been greeted by such a friendly female staff member who not only allayed all my fears but encouraged me with kindness to try a class. The aesthetic and marketing of the sport as being friendly to middle-aged, white middle-class women was therefore effective.

These gyms were designed with the goal of maintaining the authenticity of a boxing gym, a historically masculine and classed space, but also to be appealing to a wide consumer base. This claim is supported by a comment made about the refurbishment of one of the commercial gyms that occurred during the course of this project. As indicated by a female trainer Agatha,

Um, now it's more. So, we took . . . We wanted to keep it masculine because we didn't want a man to walk in and be like this is the fru fru like . . . Lululemon, this is a boutique gym . . . this is, we still want to maintain a certain amount of masculinity but have it softer more modern. That's why we have the gray um, instead of the stark white and red . . . um, but if you walk into a new club that has the total new floor design it's very very feminine . . . um, because they have a very, at least the ones I've seen may have a storefront basically so it's a . . . It's like you're shopping, they push a lot more retail than we do, we keep our retail pretty small and focus more on the bag stand and the weight equipment. Um, and so we're like right in the middle. So as a concept [this gym] has moved much more feminine, and kind of because they found um, that their biggest demographic was 35-year-old women. (Agatha, Personal Communication, January 4, 2017)

This gym was marketed as "the best of both worlds, with the fitness and realistic boxing" (Margery, Personal Communication, December 5, 2017). Another trainer described it in the following way:

Now [this boxercise gym] definitely has more of a fitness aspect to it. You know it's definitely more about um you know, losing weight increasing your endurance, ah cardio workout. Um, and again, you get what you put into it so there are different ways to actually box to, you know either lose weight, to, you know gain some new muscle mass and all that stuff but primarily it is about the fitness. (Arthur, Personal Communication, December 27, 2016)

This gym was the only one that was explicitly no-contact and openly advertised as such. As stated by Maria, "we want to be the best at noncontact boxing" (Maria, Personal Communication, April 2, 2017). The other two commercial gyms were also primarily no-contact; however, one had a series of extra classes that were purchased as a package, advertised to advance the skills of the consumer to the point of being ready to "step into the ring." The goal of this program was for the participants to engage in a friendly controlled bout with opponents from another gym. The other gym boasted sparring and a step-by-step program was needed to be eligible to participate. This included taking a certain number of classes and passing a boxing-related skill and endurance test (i.e., running a mile under a certain time requirement, jumping rope for a certain amount of time, and showing proficiency on the pads, among other things). The sparring, however, never materialized during my time as a member there and rumors circulated that this was due to a lack of staff with the expertise necessary to supervise such sessions.

In many conversations in different gym spaces, more serious fighters, both boxing and MMA, suggested that these programs "set people up to fail" (Fieldnote, April 17, 2019), were more about "making money" (Fieldnote, November 2, 2018), and "preyed on people who did not know better" (Fieldnote, November 2, 2018). As indicated by a professional fighter interviewed for this project:

Because it's kinda like, it's kinda like Apple telling you, you got unlimited internet when really you only got 5 gigs and if you go over that 5 gigs they cut you down to like a lower level. You still got internet but it's not 4G like you think. But it's just there, I mean. They not gonna tell you hey I can't make you a better fighter because they gonna lose, they know people really want to learn too and that's why I don't lie to people. When they ask me, I tell em hey if you're looking to get in boxing shape, yeah, but if you're learning how to actually fight, no. I can't lie to people though coz, I wouldn't want someone to lie to me. You know, make me think I'm about to learn something I'm not. (Antonio, Personal Communication, July 9, 2017)

Interestingly, a handful of people who completed one of these programs expressed disappointment at the results of the program and then sought out training at one of the contact gyms. In fact, when I was at the contact gym, I was called on several times to get into the ring for some light instructional sparring to demonstrate to these gym goers that they were not in fact ready to "step into the ring." This often led to a switch in membership for those more serious about boxing.

Other gym-goers, however, were more praiseful of these programs proudly announcing they were part of the program in casual conversations in the gym and posting to social media about their upcoming "fight" (the end of program bout). Also, when others complained, one gym-goer who had enjoyed the program later said to me, "well what did they expect from this kind of gym" (Fieldnote, August 19, 2019). These programs offered a boxing experience more intensive than the cardio bag classes and marketed as being more authentic to "real" boxing. Interestingly, these programs were very controlled, only allowing for limited contact (not many contact drills) and focused a lot on fitness, that is, the roadwork necessary to be a boxer. Even though the target consumer here is not the competitive boxer, but rather people seeking to workout, the distinction seemed to frequently get blurred both in the marketing messages and by the gym-goers themselves.

Sparring and Contact Gyms

In contrast, the sparring/contact gyms were not situated in heavy shopping areas, nor did they have shopfront style glass windows or even color schemes for their décor. Three of the buildings were situated in manufacturing areas and surrounded by industrial buildings. They were converted warehouses with no air-conditioning, roll-up doors, and industrial fans. Two of them did not have new/modern equipment; rather, their machines, weights, and bags were well-used and often patched together with duct tape because of wear and tear. In one of the spaces, old couches and wicker furniture provided places where people could sit and watch. This gym also did not have a women's changing facility, instead you were expected to change in a small single cubicle public restroom that was often occupied. These gyms did not have large shop windows where the goings-on of the gym space could be seen from the street. Rather, it would be difficult to ascertain what the space was used for from the outside. Two of these spaces did not have air-conditioning and instead relied on large rolling doors, like you have in mechanic or auto-repair shops, that were lifted for ventilation in the summer. On more than one occasion at the height of summer, my coach physically placed me in front of an industrial fan at one of the gyms as I had become overheated and light-headed before he disappeared to find me crackers and Gatorade to assist in my recovery. During this time, other gym-goers checked on my welfare, teased, and even patted me on the head while asking "Aw, you okay champ?" (Fieldnote, September 2, 2018). I took this as being all-in-good-fun, but I am doubtful I would have received the same treatment had I not been a woman.

These gyms, one in particular, held full-contact classes that involved intensive full-contact partner drills (one person practicing their offense and the other their defense in scripted movements), which allowed people of all skill levels to practice both defensive and offensive moves. However, some of the classes at this gym, depending on the instructor, pushed participants to the extreme, taking a survivalist approach, with one instructor yelling at the class participants that he would "make someone throw-up in class, by the time they were through" (Fieldnote, December 1, 2017). These classes were heavily attended, as were most of the classes, by male gym-goers. Although I was not there for every class that was taught, I only ever saw one woman attend one of these classes in a twelve-month period. There were, however, women-only classes that occurred once a week and the gym itself did not openly exclude women. Rather, if asked, women were welcome to attend any of the classes. Therefore, the ideology of the gym itself was one that promoted itself as egalitarian, but it did not shy away from hyper-masculine ideals more stereotypically associated with fighting sports such as physical toughness and endurance. When there were opportunities to do so, it was not uncommon for gym members to display or perform prescribed forms of masculinity. This gym also had a handful of fighters who were pursuing professional fight careers and adhered to intensive training regimens. Unlike the cardio-boxing gyms, the staff did not greet you as you entered. Rather, when I attended, I often had to wait for someone to open the gym or for my coach to arrive and let me in, even if other people were there working out. The other gym also allowed full-contact boxing, but boxing was one of many foci for this gym; therefore, it was not technically a boxing gym but housed a lot of boxing equipment and permitted sparring. There were no friendly greetings when you entered, instead you were left to your own devices in navigating the space and the equipment. One of the gyms had merchandise for sale, but there was rarely anyone there from which you could make your purchase. Marketing inclusivity through the targeting of women gym-goers was not important in these spaces as there appeared to be less emphasis on the acquisition of memberships and targeting consumers was not a priority.

CRAFTING THE IMAGE: THE NEW
MIDDLE-CLASS CONSUMER

There was a clear distinction between the two types of gym spaces, one heavily commercial promoting a more friendly or women-friendly aesthetic and environment than the other. As indicated by a trainer at one of the non-contact gyms who provided the following reasoning for why people were drawn to this specific gym space. She said,

> The unity aspects, feeling like you're on a team, feeling like you have like a home to come home to . . . I'm there just to hang out sometimes because I'm like these people are awesome, and all the members feel like they're my homies. (Evelyn, Personal Communication, July 17, 2017)

This sentiment was reaffirmed by many participants describing one of the cardio-boxing gyms as welcoming, a community, and having a family environment. The overt goal was to foster an inclusive space, targeting gym-goers who may otherwise avoid boxing as a recreational activity—that of the middle-class, white woman who has considerable consumer power.

There were varying reasons that initially attracted women to the cardio-boxing gym, including it being "a good workout" (Marie, Personal Communication, June 18, 2017), "therapeutic...both physically and psychologically" (Hannah, Personal Communication, June 20, 2017), having interest in fighting sports more generally (Miriam, Personal Communication, March 4, 2017), and "wanting to be independent and tough" (Savannah, Personal Communication, April 4, 2017). Noting the wide variety of fitness classes available, many of the participants expressed that their interest in fitness boxing as opposed to jazzercise, barre, aerobics, or say spin was influenced by their conceptualization of boxing as a novelty. Participants chose cardio-boxing because they "wanted to try something different" (Evangeline, Personal Communication, July 17, 2017). Historically, understood as a male-dominated sport, boxing was not particularly accessible to the female consumer in the fitness market. It used to be that to pursue boxing you either went to a boxing gym (i.e., referred to as fight gyms here) described as "grimy, intimidating boys club[s] where fighters would go" (Glazer as cited in Klich 2018) or you did Tae Bo. There was no middle ground (Williams as cited in Heiser 2019). Cardio-boxing, however, takes the novelty of the perceived dangerousness of boxing and provides an accessible space to learn and employ tangible skills without the intimidation of navigating a fight gym. In a way, it demystifies the sport by encouraging the procurement of its basic skills (i.e., punching technique).

Boxing- or fighting-based exercise classes have garnered considerable popularity in the last ten years, predominantly because of an increase in women consumers. Unlike other forms of exercise classes like jazzercise, this is related to the idea that you are acquiring a skill that is transferrable beyond the fitness gym. The gym spaces capitalize on this selling point by emphasizing the skill-based components of the exercise. This converges with popular understanding of boxing that frame it as dangerous and build on the male-dominated legacy of the sport. It is, therefore, unsurprising that women gym-goers understand cardio-boxing as something "different" and are eager to sign-up for classes. For example, Forbes reporter Tanya Klich (2019) notes that over 65 percent of Shadowbox gym members are women. As indicated by Steph Dyksta of Iron Lion Training Inc (2019), "Boxing is an incredible sport that can offer surprising benefits—depending of course on what you're prepared to put into it! As an enthusiast, competitor, and now coach, I've frequently seen the transformative power of boxing, particularly with women." As someone who was considerably overweight when I started my relationship with boxing, I would agree that the sport and the training regime had a transformative impact on both my physical body and my mental health.

As mentioned in chapter 1, my first engagement with the sport was at an internationally known franchise gym that offered cardio-boxing classes. My initial draw to cardio-boxing was founded in concern for my health, both mental and physical, but particularly having reached my heaviest weight ever, 234 pounds at aged thirty-four. This experience was not unique to me, as many of the women included in this study who participated exclusively in cardio-boxing reported being attracted to the gym for the intensity of the workout. Faye said "I always know it's going to be a good workout. I know I'm never going to go in there and half ass it, and it's a good mixture of . . . I like how [it] is a good mixture of cardio and like squats (Faye, Personal Communication, December 15, 2016). Faye is not wrong, the workouts were vigorous and intense leaving you feeling thoroughly exhausted and sweaty. It was not uncommon for instructors to boast about the number of calories that could be burned in a class, some claiming 800 to 1,000 calories per hour. Beyond weight loss, women reported seeing muscle development, increased endurance, and general feelings of improved physical well-being. Yet, although physical benefits were noted, they were often secondary to psychological and emotional changes they saw as being instrumental to them retaining their gym memberships.

Of note, was the emergent theme that many of the women communicated that cardio-boxing was superior to other types of workouts (i.e., crossfit, jazzercise, HIIT, or spin), as the benefits extended beyond the physical to include psychological wellness. As indicated by Hannah, "I think cardio-boxing is all around, I just think it's better. I used to take classes at [another gym] and I would do it and I would feel good with it, but not the same combination of mental and physical" (Personal Communication, June 20, 2017).

The women boxers felt like the cardio-gym boosted their self-confidence, perceptions of self, and acted to empower them in other aspects of their lives. For example, as expressed by Elizabeth:

> But I think that women taking boxing, you know, the other women in the class, I think that's so good for them. It helps your self-esteem, gives you some confidence, that, you know, to learn how to throw a punch, even, what are the chances of them getting into a fight anyway, but . . . To throw a punch, is a good thing to be able to protect yourself, or be physically self-aware, you know. (Elizabeth, Personal Communication, April 21, 2017)

Savannah also stated, "I like just the confidence it gives me the feeling of yeah like I may be a girl, but I can kick your butt" (Savannah, Personal Communication, April 4, 2017). Interestingly, many of the participants who exclusively engaged in cardio-boxing attributed their increased confidence to having the ability to execute the punches, and to do so with good technique. Confidence was associated with more typical masculine traits, such as being able to "throw a punch," "kick butt," and "protect themsel[ves]." Women, therefore, were learning to and embracing behaviors that more broadly speaking would be classified as unfeminine. They were subverting larger societal, taken-for-granted, gender norms.

Gender norms are most often misrecognized as innately natural and a factual way of life. Yet, women are socialized through the repeated rehearsal of characteristics deemed appropriately feminine from a very early age, such as weakness, being small (occupying as little space as possible), and passivity. Throwing a punch clearly contradicts these characteristics and signifies a deconstructing or unlearning of their socialized gender performativity. But women are not merely performing, as "masks become personas become people, socially, especially when they are enforced . . . It is not just an illusion or a fantasy or a mistake. It becomes *embodied* because it is enforced" (MacKinnon 1987, 119). Embodiment of heteronormative gender norms and roles are institutionalized more broadly, especially in sport, yet the cardio-boxing gym allows for dominant discourses about embodiment to be disrupted where previously socially prescribed behaviors, those learned through bodily enactment, can be unlearned. Boxing in this context, and the resulting confidence and empowerment, subverts the heteronormative scripts assigned to men and women as women can, and do, internalize a different image of their bodies and bodily capabilities having taken classes. Women reported feeling empowered making observations such as, "I just, I kind of feel like strong you know . . . I've always kind of been like a weakling my whole life and I just feel like I can, you know, I can do the same thing that everyone one else can too" (Terry, Personal Communication, January 5, 2017).

Sociologist Martha McCaughey (1997) addresses this subverting of femininity in her in-depth analysis of self-defense where she draws on several examples to illustrate femininity as socially and culturally learned. In discussing women's initial experiences with self-defense, she argues that one of the largest barriers is women's own socialization to feminine norms. As it relates to self-defense, McCaughey (1997) argues that women are tentative when first confronted with a weapon, fear getting hurt, or causing harm. They often apologize after kicking or hitting a pad in a drill or practicing a specific move. A similar pattern emerges with boxing. In my own experience when first ever given the opportunity to take part in adversarial boxing, I was asked by my trainer to hit him in the face. He did not try and defend himself from my punch. I was initially uncomfortable with the idea and proceeded to laugh. I also repeatedly asked if he was sure before landing the punch, and then immediately apologized and continued to say sorry for several minutes afterward. It felt strange, as if I had inherently done something taboo or wrong, something that is unpacked in more detail in chapter 6. Other participants involved with the sport beyond cardio-boxing reported similar experiences. For example, in talking to Angelina she said, "it was the first person I ever hit and I was like I don't want to hit you like at all... it's really weird" (Angelina, Personal Communication, February 16, 2017). It becomes obvious that McCaughey's (1997) observation that fighting is culturally and socially learned is true of boxing as well as self-defense. Dominant feminine scripts that are attributed to biological or natural differences between the sexes make women uncomfortable, insecure, and not good at fighting (initially). Being successfully feminine in the United States requires engaging in habits and behaviors that are incompatible with fighting sports more broadly. For example, the above quote from Elizabeth where she argues it benefits women to have greater physical awareness, something they garner from engaging boxing, is contrary to the socialization of women in the United States where early childhood dictates that women's bodies are not their own.

The difference between the socialization of men and women has long been recognized and critiqued in the fields of sociology, criminology, and beyond (Bem 1993; Deming 1977; Harding 2004; Renzetti 2013), and scholars have advanced different theoretical analyses, including sex-role socialization, drawing on these differences to explain varying behaviors. Common phrases like "boys will be boys" to dismiss mischievous of bad behavior not "girls will be girls," or "you've got balls" not "you've got ovaries" to compliment someone on a daring deed, signify a different social trajectory for men versus women. This is replicated throughout society and heavily institutionalized. Some examples include the differences in children's toys (Fox and Potocki 2016; Messner 2000), the framing of some careers such as nursing or social work as being more suited to women than men, and school-imposed dress codes that deem parts of girls bodies too sexually tempting to men and boys (Wang 2017). An instrumental and repeated component of this socialization process is for girls to reject aggression.

As argued by Jeffner Allen (1986, 39), "The ideology of heterosexual virtue forms the cornerstone of the designation of women as nonviolent. The ideology of heterosexual virtue charges women to be 'moral', virtuously nonviolent in the face of the 'political', violent male-defined world." To be feminine is to shy away from aggression and to embrace passivity and weakness. Boxing, independent of the level of engagement both undermines and violates this. As summarized by Elizabeth Swasey (1993, 18):

> From birth, most women are brainwashed into thinking the only proper response to physical aggression is submission. On the playground, we're told "girls don't hit"—even if we're striking back in self-defense to flee a much larger and stronger school bully. Later, we're told women should "submit to criminal attack for fear of injury"—as if the crime itself were not injury.

Boxing provides a space for women to unlearn these culturally embedded habits of femininity and the bodily, physical, and spatial assumptions that accompany them. In a patriarchal society where women are rewarded for exhibiting characteristics that promote their subordination to men, it is not surprising then that many of the participants here reported a resulting increase in confidence and feelings of empowerment when encouraged to undermine such behaviors. Hitting a heavy bag provides one such vehicle for such expression, an example of what Wacquant (2004) would term direct embodiment, as there is a reimagining of the relationship of women's bodies, aggression, and violence. The boxing gym provides an opportunity for the relearning of new social scripts. Another such script that emerged is that the boxing gym was a constructive space for the expression of anger.

In a similar manner to Cathy Van Ingen's (2011) study on boxing as a means to empower women, including trans-women who have experienced violence, anger emerged as dominant theme for why women were attracted to, and continued to come to, bag classes. As expressed by Terry, "I don't . . . I feel kind of silly to say it, but like I've always, sometimes I just get angry at things . . . and I really just like, I don't know I just had an idea through my head I'm always like gosh I want to punch something" (Terry, Personal Communication, January 5, 2017). Another woman cardio boxer stated, "I think women stay because it's such a good workout and good way to release that stress . . . energy and anger" (Faye, Personal Communication, December 15, 2017). Some women acknowledged the source of the anger (i.e., divorce, children, work situations), but the majority of women signified that it was "maybe just sort of like ugh generalized anger it helps to express" (Angelina,

Personal Communication, February 16, 2017). When asked to further explain what they meant by such assertions, Faye's response was typical as she emphasized the importance of the space to legitimize the expression of both her anger and aggression. She said:

> It's just a good way to be able to feel the anger and feel that passion but let it out like I said in a good controlled setting, where it's like accepted . . . without you know like being out there, like being . . . in the gym without looking aggressive. So, I think it's like a good way to kind of, I mean to me it's the most aggressive way you can release your stress, but without pushing it, you know, to being like some crazy, like people think you're crazy if you go to boxing . . . I think women start by going because they want to lose weight, but I think they stay because of the releases . . . I think it just a good release of it . . . because I think you know women aren't supposed to be seen as aggressive . . . or you know anything like that, so I feel like it's a good way for them to be able to be aggressive and to be able to let it out in a controlled setting. . . . (Faye, Personal Communication, December 15, 2016)

Boxing provided a constructive and sanctioned way for women to express their anger and aggression, legitimizing the physical embodiment of this emotion.

Of importance was the idea that anger was not a permitted feminine quality, but was one that women have been socialized to repress. Research on anger expression has indicated that there is little difference across gender as to the amount of anger men and women expressed and suppressed (Faber and Burns 1996; Kring 2000; Thomas and Williams 1991). However, there is a reported difference in the way women express their anger as compared to men, with the latter reporting acting out physically (Deffenbacher et al. 1996), and women being more likely to cry when angry (Crawford et al. 1992; Thomas 1993). This difference has been related to gender roles, with men who identify more strongly with characteristics of hegemonic masculinity having a higher propensity to express their anger physically than women who reported identifying with characteristics associated with emphasized femininity (Kring 2000).

Furthermore, men and women are judged differently with men's anger expression being generally considered more acceptable than that of women. When women do express their anger they have an increased likelihood of being sanctioned (i.e., being labeled as hostile or being called names such as "bitch"). This difference has been related to gender roles in the larger heteronormative patriarchal society (Friday 1977; Lerner 1977) where women's value is associated with passivity, weakness, and general submissiveness, and any characteristics that violate these traits (i.e., the expression of physical anger) are sanctioned as being inappropriate, unladylike, or unbecoming.

Therefore, the aforementioned catalysts for anger mentioned by the participants here, coupled with the structural oppression of navigating the embedded nature of sexist-based oppression characteristics of a patriarchal society,
found a physical release at the boxing gym. Not only was the expression of
the anger permitted, it was celebrated and normalized in this space, eliminat-
ing any social judgment and legitimating aggressive physicality. As argued
by Audre Lorde (1984, 127), "every woman has a well-stocked arsenal of
anger potentially useful against those oppressions, personal and institutional,
which brought that anger into being." Here, the boxing gym permitted the
embodiment of this anger. It must be noted that through the creation of a
space that permits women's expression of anger, there exists an irony. By
providing a legitimate space for the expression of women's anger, one that is
closed from public surveillance, the cardio-boxing gym conforms with larger
societal gender scripts. Through this lens, women's aggression and anger is
"okay" when confined to these spaces, kept separate, and distinct from their
everyday lives. To be an angry woman is sanctioned in these spaces, but
when moving beyond the space of the gym, women have to revert back to the
socially prescribed heteronormative gender roles that requires the suppres-
sion of anger and aggression.

NOTE

1. The standard varies with the professional organization, and as there are a
number of organizations, there is not one set size.

Chapter 3

Commodifying and the Woman Boxer

Popular Culture, Media, and the Sexualized Fighter

INTRODUCTION

The commodification and subsequent consumption of the sport of boxing as it manifested in the cardio-boxing gyms for novice boxers was introduced in brief in the last chapter. Other scholars, such as Lucia Trimbur (2011, 201), have also drawn attention to the issue as it relates to race and class dynamics arguing that "Clients are drawn to a perceived peripheral relationship of men of colour to the social or economic mainstream, or by the thrill of being in proximity to the dangerous, the wild, and the most cliched tropes of primitivism." Yet, as women increasingly enter the sport of boxing and combat sports more broadly, with Ronda Rousey and Laila Ali becoming household names, this explanation should be further examined as it relates to the experiences of women. Drawing on media accounts, social media feeds, and commentary, as well as more generalized understanding of women in the sport, this chapter examines how women pugilists are socially and culturally understood as it relates to engrained and bifurcated categories of heteronormative gender. While I acknowledge the growing literature on non-binary, queer, and LGBTQ+ people in sport (Anderson and Travers 2017; Carroll 2014; Griffin 2014; Love, 2014), the focus here is the long-enduring heteronormative categorizations largely due to the dominance of the gender binary as a theme that emerged in the spaces studied in this research.

The focus for this chapter is a broader unpacking of how women engaging the sport of boxing at the amateur levels understand societal constructions of the sport, especially as it relates to sexualization, beauty, and commodification of these constructions through the health and fitness industry as they manifest both in gym spaces and at the interactional level of analysis. Novice women boxers not only navigate deeply embedded understandings of women in combat sports, but they too can, both willingly and unwillingly, reify the same patriarchal structures that marginalize women. I will begin with an overview of the treatment of popular cultural and media portrayals of women in fighting sports.

POPULAR CULTURE AND THE SEXUALIZED BOXER

It has been widely acknowledged that when women athletes enter certain spaces they are subject to differential treatment than their male counterparts (Adams and Tuggle 2004; Cooky et al. 2013, 2015; Jennings 2015; Messner et al. 2003; Turner 2014). Nowhere is this more evident than in media presentation/coverage of sports (Cooky et al., 2015). Media presentations of sports have reflected societal understandings that sports are centered on men (Adams and Tuggle 2004; Billings and Young 2015; Caple et al. 2011; Cooky et al. 2010; Kane et al. 2013; Rightler-McDaniels 2014; Sheffer and Shultz 2007; Turner 2014; Webber and Carni 2013; Whiteside and Hardin 2012), so much so that whenever an event does not center men, "women's" is used as a qualifier, that is, "women's soccer." This means that, with the exception of the Olympics (Billings and Young 2015; Hardin et al. 2002) and the occasional collegiate event (Kane and Buyssee 2005; McKay and Dalliere 2009), media provides very little quality coverage of women athletes and their sports (Bruce 2013; Cooky et al. 2013). When sportswomen are covered in the media they are depicted in disparaging ways such as being infantilized or framed within overtly heterosexual lenses that sometimes question their femininity (Bernstein 2002; Cooky and Lavoi 2012; Duncan and Hasbrook 1988; Heywood and Dworkin 2003; Messner 2002). Although patterns of men's cultural centrality persist in sports, there have been some advancements over the last ten years, yet they are sporadic and uneven (Cooky et al., 2015).

Specific to fighting sports and as noted in chapter 2, the history of women's involvement is largely ignored and due to pervasive understandings of boxing and combat sports more broadly as being primitive and dangerous, coverage of women in fighting sports began with the sports craze of the nineteenth century (Jennings 2015). The figure of the women boxer took on two distinct framings. The first framing situates the boxer as a feminist figure using the sport to challenge gender differences and fighting for equality. It was this construct that led to one of the earliest recognitions that boxing has utility for women when it comes to self-defense (Boddy 2014). Contrary to this narrative, the second framing viewed boxing as anti-feminist, reducing women boxers to aspirant men. This was mocking, suggesting that women were engaging in "a kind of parody of masculinity" (Boddy 2014, 255).

Unfortunately, it is the latter discourse that has dominated, undermining the few women boxers who garnered media and public recognition for their sport, reducing them to spectacles fighting over "men," wearing sparse clothing to titillate, much like the carnival entertainment of the vaudeville (Toulmin 1999). Throughout the decades, there have been occasional stories of women boxers that have gained media interest, one of the most prominent being the 1995 coverage of Christy Martin, who as noted in chapter 2, was featured and appeared on the cover of *Sports Illustrated* (Hoffer 1996). Despite this and the serious athleticism of these women, the construction of women in fighting sports as being novelty catfights for the purpose of titillation still pervades.

Over the years there has been an increase in the number of women pursuing combat sports; however, there are relatively few who have made money from their sport, nor reached a level of notoriety associated with successful male athletes. Some worthy mentions include Laila Ali, Freeda Foreman, and Jacqui Frazier. Yet, these three women were catapulted into the media headlines due to their father's sporting reputations and cultural capital. Their father's reputations did not protect them from the same critical coverage labeling the fights and these athletes as a moral outrage and "perversion[s]" (Boddy 2014, 258). Add to this the further critiques of women's boxing that focuses on the threat women fighters pose to femininity. Thinly veiled concern for their bodies, specifically their breasts and faces, are voiced as cautions against violating widely established gender norms (i.e., that women should be pretty and attractive to men, not sporting black eyes) (Boddy 2014). This is compounded by stories and commentary that embrace the stereotype that women are too emotional and do not possess the requisite mental faculties to engage in boxing. They were not perceived to be aggressive enough.

Boxing journalist Katherine Dunn (2009) has argued that women vary considerably when it comes to the form in which they express aggression, and that this is largely dependent on culturally learned factors and not a result of their biology. Despite this insight, the real gains for increased media coverage and public acceptance of women in combat sports came with the inclusion of women in the UFC. Although many women paved the way for her rise (such as Gina Carrano and Cris Cyborg Justino to mention but a few), it was the 2011 matchup between then new-comer Ronda Rousey and Misha Tate, where the idea of women fighters began to become more normalized, that is, less of a novelty, although the elements of spectacle and titillation still persist.

The increased visibility of fighting women in popular culture was not lost on the participants in this study, which they too predominantly attributed to the inclusion and promotion of women fighters in the UFC. As reflected on by Matt:

It's definitely become, and it's weird because I think the rise of women's MMA has really helped with the rise of women's boxing. But, the rise of women's MMA hasn't been until very recently, people like Ronda Rousey . . . um and, you know, Cris Cyborg, and people like that. So, it wasn't until very recently that women's boxing has really gotten good looks at, you know, good publicity and coverage. Um . . . but back to Claressa Shields . . . Huge, huge, she's absolutely huge, you know gold medalist . . . Right and then, so you know Laila Alli, Muhammad Ali's daughter really set the stage because obviously she was Muhammad Ali's daughter. Everyone wanted to see her fight because he didn't have a son who boxed and they wanted so see the next best thing which was her. So she kinda set the stage and then there were other female boxers who kinda built off her and then allowed what Claressa Shields has done to be really what it is. You know she's done some really phenomenal things, which is really cool, um, but I think, I think women's boxing has become, or you know women's martial arts, women's combatives [sic] are overall getting much more popular. (Matt, Personal Communication, July 25, 2017)

In many ways, the inclusion of women in MMA has helped to normalize women's involvement in combat sports (Jennings 2015), and it has also helped to launch some women fighters to the status of celebrity in a way that had not been seen before.

Stuart Hall (1997, 64) argues that media's representation of society cannot be understood as a mere reflection, rather, it "implies the active selecting and presenting, of structuring and shaping." It is not surprising to find that media coverage of prominent women in combat sports impacted understandings in amateur and cardio-boxing gyms. Crediting MMA and the UFC for the increased societal acceptance of women in combat sports was a commonly held opinion. Evangeline said "yeah, I mean, yeah unfortunately, I mean I'm a big, still a big Ronda Rousey fan, I know she lost, but her skill was still incredible when she was in her prime" (Evangeline, Personal Communication, July 17, 2017). Hannah also credited the UFC for the acceptance of women in fighting sports, "Everybody's out for equal, equal, equal...but it is acceptable. I think that guys now even in the UFC and stuff see women, women are tough" (Hannah, Personal Communication, June 20, 2017). However, although Caroline agreed with this sentiment, she did note that "Um I think it has been a lot more accepting. But there's still a long way to go in the sport" (Caroline, Personal Communication, February 13, 2017).

The impact of such prominent female athletes and their portrayal in the media did not escape criticism, much of which centered on the objectification and sexualization of their bodies. For example, Evangeline exposed the ironies of Rousey's fame, "She was on the cover of Sports Illustrated and did like a nude photo shoot, which like all of them do for Sports Illustrated . . . ugh" (Evangeline, Personal Communication, July 17, 2017). In contrasting Rousey with Amanda Nunes, she said

> She's treated a bit differently than Nunes . . . yeah, I mean that's just inevitable, and that'll probably be a problem we face for a while. Yeah, I think a lot of people, a lot of people probably get off on women fighting . . . they love it, I'm sure tons of people don't tune in to see the skill of these women but just tune in to see women fighting each other. (Evangeline, Personal Communication, July 17, 2017)

The sexualization of Ronda Rousey was a prominent objection for many of the women. Anna saw Rousey as complicit in the image she portrayed, saying:

> Exactly like Ronda Rousey, nothing against how she fights but just how she portrays herself I'm just like why do you feel like you have to strip to you know make yourself known or like make a name for yourself when you clearly have done your talking in the ring. (Anna, Personal Communication, January 23, 2017)

The complicity of the actor in their own sexualization, however, does not necessarily mean they have lost agency. Art historian Maria Elena Buszek (2006) argues that third-wave feminism situates pin-up imagery as being a vehicle for the exercise of power. By focusing on individual expression and agency, it has been argued that pin-up imagery has "sexualized woman as self-aware, assertive, strong, and independent" (Buszek 2006, 8). This does not eradicate the sexualization of the women's form for the pleasure of men, this does not mean the woman is not confidant in her own sexuality, something that can coexist with other aspects of being a woman, that is, her race, age, professionalism, patriotism, desirability, and size (Buszek 2006). Combat sports scholar L.A. Jennings (2015) argues that this also includes her athleticism, as it relates to combat sports and sports more generally. Without having insight into the motivations of each individual athlete who agrees to be a centerfold or cover for a particular publication, it is difficult to assess whether they exist as subject or object, or a combination of both. It does, however, lead to a question posed by artist Barbara Kruger (1982, 210), "How do I as a woman and an artist work against a market place of the spectacle while residing within it?"

Conversely, Angelina's reflection on the topic situated her objections in the larger societal treatment of women, stating that:

> Um, yeah and I feel like there's this whole argument whether or not because, on the one hand Ronda Rousey has done a whole lot to make it acceptable for

women to be in that sport so that's great. But, immediately because she was like Danica Patrick, like a similar thing because she's relatively attractive, so we just have to turn her into a sex symbol immediately off the bat or like two months later um, but she wouldn't have gotten the kind of attention if she didn't have that. So, I mean it speaks to society, I can't really say, I mean I don't know that boxing is different than any other thing. I think while maybe a little bit different than car racing, I think that's already sexualized just because the blowing hair and all of that. . . . Maybe boxing just lends itself a little bit more because you're wearing shorts and a sports bra already. (Angelina, Personal Communication, February 16, 2017)

The sexualization and the objectification of women's bodies is not new, nor is it exclusive to sports.

Jennings (2015, xxiv) argues that "American culture is obsessed with the female body." Yet, this obsession takes on varying meanings dependent on the women and topic of focus. Women who openly defy traditional constructions of heteronormative femininity are often subject to harsh criticism while simultaneously being over-sexualized. Consider, for example, the popular trope of the femme fatale where a women's physical appearances, charms, and sexual appeal disguise their inherent dangerousness. Analyses of film noir have revealed that competent and intelligent women are portrayed in this manner to relieve and address men's desires and anxieties. This presentation was originally rooted in the changing gender roles post–World War II and reflected "Men['s] need to control women's sexuality in order not to be destroyed by it" (Place 1998, 49). These women are objectified and it is their dangerousness that amplifies the allure of an object of beauty. Another example are media portrayals of female criminality.

Consider how women have been portrayed in films centered on women in prison. The lineage of this particular genre is particularly seedy where "girls gone bad" story arcs were crafted to titillate male audiences. For example, consider that many of these films center on the vulnerability of young girls who are objectified and unapologetically sexualized—often through the depiction of sexual violence victimization/s, all experienced through a voyeuristic lens. For example, the tag line for the film *Caged Heat* (1974) was "white hot desires melting cold prison steel!" Many, if not all, of the movie posters for women's prison films feature scantily clad women that reveal their bodies (Caged 1950; Girls in Prison 1956; Caged Heat 1974; Caged Heat 2: Stripped of Freedom 1994; Amazon Jail 1982; The Big Doll House 1971), often in sexually vulnerable positions adorning expressions of distress on their faces. These exploitation films clearly construct the woman inmate as being both an object of desire and one associated with danger and violence.

Beyond the media, other deep-rooted myths that sexualize dangerous woman and amplify the narrative that tempting female flesh can be life-threatening, include religious tales such as that of Lilleth, Pandora and even Eve of the Judeo-Christian faith who tempted man with the "original sin" (Noddings 1989). Here, the role of gender and sex is a dominant consideration in historical and cultural logics of female deviance—that is, violations of heteronormative femininity. It is not surprising then that similar tropes and understandings make their way into combat sports, as there is a tendency for media to characterize and promote fights based on women's sexuality—that is, whether they meet normalized standards of beauty or not. This was evident in the all-female edition of the UFC show *The Ultimate Fighter*, where the attractiveness of the contestants featured prominently in the promotional material (Greenwell, Simmons, Hancock, Shreffler and Thorn 2017). Furthermore, it is not uncommon for audience members (the majority of whom are men) as well as fellow fighters to sexualize women athletes. Consider for example, MMA fighter Mike Brown who commented that paying to watch women fight was only worth his money if they would do so topless (Holland 2014). This not only sexualizes the athlete but undermines her seriousness as a competitive sportsperson.

The sexualization of women's bodies was objectionable to many of the women in this research, Julie argued,

Ah and it felt like the same type of thing, like you were saying, women yeah you can be smart, you can be scientists you can do all these things, but you still got to be sexy, you know. And that's still an important part of this for you, um and I think that, it was important to me, to try and remind people, no you don't, you can be smart, and sexy, or you can be smart and not give a crap about the sexy side of things you know, you can just, just focus on your career, and just focus on your science, or on politics, or on whatever it is that you do. And you don't have to be sexy for anybody. If you want to be sexy go for it. If you don't want to and it's not of value to you, then don't worry about it. I feel like the same thing is my take on representations of women in boxing and fighting. Um as you know, that's if you are a fighter and you also think that being sexy is of value to you and that's something you want to promote go for it, but I think we should also allow for women to be fighters without having to be sexy and for women to have all these other variety of skills, and of traits and characteristics, that are not just their physical appearance. (Julie, Personal Communication, February 5, 2017)

Julie's reflection on other institutionalized gender oppression that manifests through the sexualization of women reflects larger societal understandings of successful women, especially those who pursue careers in male-dominated fields like science and politics. Julie recognized that "being sexy" is not necessarily a bad thing unless it is something that is done to you—that is, women as objects. If a woman expresses herself exercising her agency through her sexuality, then she has transitioned from the object to the subject. However, the difference between object and subject is not easily parsed out when the athlete is launched into the public realm.

For women athletes, their physical attractiveness may have a greater influence on how they are perceived publicly. There has been considerable scholarship that has highlighted the misrepresentation of sportswomen by the media where despite their athletic prowess the coverage is centered on tasks or characteristics irrelevant to their identities as professional athletes (Goday-Pressland 2014). Consider that in an analysis of conversations on the social media platform Twitter, it was found that for male MMA athletes the focus was on their talent. Conversely, for female athletes, the conversations centered on both their talent and their physical attractiveness (Greenwell et al. 2017). For women participating in sports that are male-dominated (i.e., those still viewed as being inappropriate for women), studies have found that the media coverage is often contradictory and/or discriminatory (Hong 2012; Stone and Horne 2008). Despite this, there are some indications that coverage of women athletes might be becoming more gender neutral (Biscomb and Griggs 2012; Delorme 2014; Ross and Carter 2011), but the process is slow. This is especially so when coverage decisions are consciously related to the promotion and marketing of particular imagery that are reflective of organizations, institutions, and larger structures that are still male-dominated (i.e., media, sports, UFC, USA Boxing, etc.).

The commodification of sport relies on marketing techniques that have been found to be distinctly gendered, and physical attractiveness is a dominant factor that is considered by endorsers (Cunningham et al. 2008; Ross et al. 2009; Trail and James 2001). It has also been found that endorsers and promoters purposefully sexualize women athletes as a tactic to increase public interest (Grau et al. 2007). To hype up interest in a women's fight, the media will often frame the fight between two athletes based on beauty ideals with the woman who most closely meets heteronormative standards of femininity being framed as attractive and popular, and her opponent as less attractive or ugly (Jennings 2015). This was quite evident in the Carano versus Justino fight, where Justino was harshly criticized for her muscular physique and quickly labeled "The Beast" in the fight that was quickly dubbed "Beauty versus The Beast" (Jennings 2015). To this day, Justino has been subjected to a barrage of criticisms about her body and the questioning of her biological sex. This was compounded by her testing positive for anabolic steroid use in 2011, which resulted in her having her Strike Force title stripped. Employing such a catchy headline, while problematic in its reification of emphasized femininity, is reflective of the packaging, retooling, and repackaging of a product, that of the sporting spectacle and the athletes that make it possible, which is then sold to the public who consume these goods as entertainment (Austin et al. 2010). It is not surprising then that these framings of women athletes trickle down to amateur boxing circuits, fighting gyms, and even cardio-boxing spaces and influence how amateur and novice boxers are perceived and understand both others and themselves.

Dichotomizing women athletes into two categories based on physical attractiveness emerges in local gym spaces when discussions of professional fighters lead to a questioning of their use of performance-enhancing drugs, their sexuality, and even their biological sex. I personally overheard this several times in gym spaces where male gym-goers openly stated, "she's a man" (Fieldnote, November 2, 2018) or "she's got to be on something" (Fieldnote, November 2, 2018) in discussing Cris Cyborg Justino and Amanda Nunes. In addition, some of the women expressed that they were viewed as being more masculine because they boxed. Caroline said, "You know also the, many people think that if you fight, you're not very feminine" (Caroline, Personal Communication, February 13, 2017). The ideals of nonviolence and morality have been associated with femininity and participating in boxing violates these understandings (Davis-Delano et al. 2009). To reconcile that, Caroline is subject to the questioning of her femininity and could be seen as representing "gender-trouble" (Butler 1998, 103) as she embodies a deviation from the male sporting norm and she is challenging the traditional understanding of what represents a gendered body.

Gender trouble also emerged in gym-goer's reactions to women boxers. It was common to witness women who demonstrated skill at boxing being called names such as "beast," "scary," "mean," "terrifying," and "champ" both to their faces and behind their backs (Fieldnote, July 2, 2018). Interestingly, very few women engage in this labeling of others or name calling, rather it was a male prerogative. This labeling process, although not as overt as questioning a professional athletes biological sex, is reflective of a blurring of heteronormative gender expectations and acts as a vehicle for men to process women's participation in a traditional masculine sport and what is perceived as being a defiance of the socially and culturally prescribed gender norms (Channon and Jennings 2004; Follo 2012; McNaughton 2012). In my own observations it was not uncommon for male gym-goers to visibly react when confronted with a woman who not only demonstrated good boxing skills, but technique beyond their own capabilities. Some of the reactions included shocked expressions like "woah," "I didn't expect that" or declaring to others around them "wow, she's good" (Fieldnote, September 2, 2018). Other responses included increased interactions like fist bumping and slaps on the back, or even talking to the instructor/coach about the woman in question despite the woman being right there and often close enough to hear the conversation being had about them. The same reactions were not evident if a male athlete demonstrated high levels of skill. Here, the expectations of the body techniques associated with the female body have been violated (Johansson 1996), especially given the assumption that women are inherently good, moral, and nonviolent. Roth and Basow (2004, 259) argue that "those who wish to conceive of women as nonviolence/nonaggressive and morally superior ignore the fact that not all women have that luxury." It ignores that there are women in the world that do not abhor violence.

Increased attention from men in these spaces sometimes made women more aware of their gender and the impact their gender had on others around them. Faye spoke about the impact the male gaze had on women entering the ring,

> But I would say if I was actually boxing in a ring, I think you would definitely feel a lot more pressure because there's not as many around, the girls. And it is drawing a lot of attention, people want to see girls fight because that's never been anything like you said until recently. So, I think it draws a lot more attention which is like nerve-racking. (Faye, Personal Communication, December 15, 2016)

To be subject to the male gaze can be intimidating and intrusive, reducing the woman to a body object. Yet, women are socialized to expect or even desire this attention. It is not surprising then, that women are uncomfortable with the increased attention and surveillance from men when they are engaging in a behavior that historically and socially has been deemed inappropriate for them based on their gender. In addition, when beauty is held as being the predominant goal for all women, being subject to the male gaze can have damaging consequences and lead to a questioning of self as "sexuality necessarily entails intersubjectivity" (Cahill 2001, 81). To not be acknowledged by the male gaze can register as a denial of personhood. As previously established, sport is a male institution already placing women on the outside, reducing, or even silencing their presence (Crouse 2013). Women are either sexualized objects of desire or they are discarded.

Compounding this is the conceptualization of women boxers as novelty in the space of the boxing gym. This can manifest as increased scrutiny of the female physique, which can in turn, potentially deter women from entering these spaces. Anna noted how institutionalized this increased surveillance of the female form is in her comments about USA Boxing and the experience of a fellow boxer on the Olympic Team. Anna said,

> The Olympian in my weight class she's you know a model, a former model, so I get that why she would still wanna model and stuff but it's just like you know

you're really pretty and you're really a good fighter without having to objectify yourself or you know show off certain parts of your body and . . . and really that's kinda how women are viewed in the sport. Just in the, not even just in the world but in the actual sport, like community, um because you know the judges, USA Boxing, they wanna see, you know, a pretty girl, they don't wanna see . . . So, you have a lot of like homosexual women that are in the sport, and they will lose on purpose because like the judges are just like "no, we don't want that image for our sport" and . . . and I don't think that's right, I don't think that you, regardless of how you feel about that whatever, whoever, lifestyle that is or whatever their lifestyle is, you know, um how they dress or whatever, I don't think that's right. (Anna, Personal Communication, January 23, 2017)

Anna's comments on USA Boxing demonstrate the embedded nature of heterosexual femininity as being *the* requisite representation of gender by the governing body. Any deviation from this is rejected, or frowned upon, as according to Anna, it does not fit the image of women's boxing that USA Boxing is trying to cultivate. This had the effect of disappointing Anna as she was disheartened and frustrated by the sexism that still dominated not only the sport but also her direct experiences with the sport as she advanced in her career. She said,

As I was getting deeper into the sport and getting higher up I thought it would be more like "okay they're gonna recognize me for talent," and they do to an extent, but it is a lot of how are you looking. Like my coach you know talks about how like you know, you need to wear this dress to this and he's not trying to objectify, we're having to play in to what USA boxing wants, but it's just like wow I'm at a boxing tournament and I have to bring a dress. (Anna, Personal Communication, January 23, 2017)

Capitalizing on traditional ideals of heteronormative physical attractiveness was not limited to individual experiences, rather this was an overt marketing strategy utilized to commodify the sport for mass consumption.

SELLING BOXING: SEXUALIZATION
AS A MARKETING TACTIC

The public perception of women in combat sports is not isolated to the influence of professional athletes or associations, but also encompasses a wide variety of endorsers that range from super models, to gym franchises, to sportswear companies, to pop music, to lingerie sellers, to fast food companies, to mention but a few. Consider for example, Ronda Rousey was featured in an advertisement for the fast-food burger chain Carl Jr's. Dressed in a sports bra the advertisement switches from her eating a breakfast sandwich in slow motion, licking her fingers and smiling seductively, to clips of her hitting pads. The advertisement ends with the caption "A Knockout Breakfast Sandwich, with a Sweet Side" (YouTube 2015). Other examples include the Kardashians going to cardio-boxing gyms in their television shows, films such as *Girl Fight* (Green et al. 2000) and *Million Dollar Baby* (Eastwood et al. 2004), Ed Sheeran's music video for the song "Shape of You" (Sheeran et al. 2017) as well as a bevy of social media sites/pages that promote women in boxing pushing slogans such as "hit like a girl" (see allfemalecard/film, thegirlsgonestrong, bxingworld, 2kbxingofficial2). In addition, there are a slew of documentaries focusing on the rise of women in combat sports (see *Women Who Fight* (CNN 2017). *Fight Like a Girl* (Morley and Georgiev 2013), *The Ronda Rousey Story: Through My Father's Eyes* (Antico and Stretch 2019), *T-Rex* (Cooper and Canepari 2016), to mention but a few. There are a variety of tactics utilized here for the integration of women boxers into popular culture; however, the visual representation acts to normalize the idea of women in combat sports. Much of this media are factual, educational, or resource driven for women in the fight community. Consider, for example the hashtag WomenBox that provides videos of training, pad work, and boxing instruction, is for women and with content predominantly made by women. Hashtags such as these are body positive, inclusive, and encouraging to women looking to share or be part of a larger boxing community. This type of community building through online media coupled with documentaries contributes to overall perceptions among participants that boxing is less hostile to women than it was 20 years ago. Yet the problem of objectifying and sexualizing women athletes persists and is sometimes viewed as expected. As argued by Hannah "I think that any sport with women they always try to sexualize it anyways. That just sells that I think for you know…that's not always what we want to see but that's what other people want to see" (Hannah, Personal Communication, June 20, 2017).

Although there are many examples of this, one such campaign that received considerable attention during this study was a *Victoria Secret* lingerie campaign. This campaign featured models in their sports apparel, engaged in boxing workouts, touting the slogan "strong is sexy." Angelina spoke about both the benefits of such a campaign and the problems with it, she said,

Angelina: I remember also when about a year ago they [Victoria Secret] launched one of those ads and it was like all of a sudden there was all these girls that came in, over the course of like six weeks. And everybody's like, what is going on? There was some article or magazine that that said that boxing is the new barre or whatever, the new supermodel workout. And then they inevitably left because they were like only my arms look good. Well, yeah (said with sarcasm). (Angelina, Personal Communication, February 16, 2017)

Angelina liked that the advertisement attracted attention to boxing resulting in more women joining the cardio-boxing gym, but she was irritated that the version of boxing being sold to these consumers was solely about attaining the physique of a *Victoria Secret* model, a body type that is not genetically attainable to most women (Kilbourne 2010) nor reflective of the muscular physique of more noted women pugilists. Interestingly, the marked difference between women that box in real life and the promotional models for *Victoria Secret* was noted by Julie,

> But I'm not on board with presenting it as though that's how it should be, I'm not on board with pressuring anybody to do that while they box, and I'm really not, I don't like the idea of presenting boxing as though like that's how women box, you know because I don't think that it is. You see, um, legitimate professional boxers, you see female fighters, and they're not there to be sexy, their hair is tied up to keep it out of the way, they wear as little clothing as possible to make it, not a distraction and to make it so that it's easier for them, it's not about, you know, looking nice, while they do it, it's about having an advantage. (Julie, Personal Communication, February 5, 2017)

Julie perceived the *Victoria Secret* advertisement campaign as misleading and detrimental to women, but she did concede that it had the beneficial impact of introducing women to the sport. She concluded her thoughts on the topic by stating,

> So I cringe a lot of times when I see Victoria Secret models with boxing gloves, and the big satin boxing, you know, robe draped over them in a way that nobody actually wears it. And you know, I cringe when I see things like that, because that's not an actual depiction of boxing, that's using boxing for sex appeal. Um and that's not, that's not of utility when you actually boxing, so I think that it, in some sense it's disrespectful to the sport, it's disrespectful to the idea that women should be able to do these things without also the expectancy to be sexy. (Julie, Personal Communication, February 5, 2017)

As I have written about elsewhere (Collins and Rothe 2017, 2019), here there is a specific targeting of women in a fashion and beauty advertisement that plays on insecurities about their bodies. The anxiety is purposely manufactured promoting feelings of dissatisfaction and feelings of inadequacy about their bodies. The only way to resolve these feelings is to purchase the products offered by the corporation in the advertisement (Jarvis 2007). In this case, it would be to purchase *Victoria Secret* sports-apparel or under-wear and emulate the boxing workouts of their models. The targeting of women in these advertisements was made even more absurd by the launch of sparkling boxing gloves (something else that can be purchased) in pastel colors such as pinks and purples. As pointed out by Angelina, "There was another one [Victoria Secret Advertisement] where they have like rhine-stone covered boxing gloves. And I was like, the whole time I was just like, could you imagine getting hit with that though? That would be really bad" (Angelina, Personal Communication, February 16, 2017). Purchasing boxing gloves that counter their very purpose is an excellent example of sociologist Jean Baudrillard's (1998) magical thinking as the products propagated by the advertising industry are capitalizing on beauty ideals and are divorced from their meaning—boxing gloves are for hitting people, not a beauty or fashion accessory. Therefore, boxing is being utilized to advanced messages about beauty and fashion that are in accordance with the patriarchal status quo—that a woman must look a certain way—ignoring the basic principles of the sport.

Ironically, although there appears to be an inherent effort to make boxing more accessible and attractive to women by reducing the sport to a product for consumption, one that is then feminized through the celebrity endorsements, marketing campaigns, and women-friendly gear (i.e., pink gloves), a contra-dictory narrative emerged—one that classified some women as "too attractive to box" (Anna, Personal Communication, March 11, 2017). As a prominent discourse this was multifaceted and complex, considering that women are simultaneously being encouraged by commercial and cardio gym spaces to engage in boxing but also being told that to do so risks the physical attributes that are most valued by society (i.e., their face). This was a common utterance that often ran counter to the marketing techniques that sexualized and objecti-fied women's bodies to capture them as consumers of the sport. In fact, this supports the public bifurcation of women into those that are beastly or manly versus those that fit traditional ideals of beauty, the latter being worthy of protection from the violence of the ring. Women fighters that reinforce tradi-tional gender stereotypes and have characteristics of emphasized femininity, also have to navigate characteristics of femininity that paint them as weak and deserving of men's protection. Therefore, the marketing techniques of sexual-ization and objectification communicates a message that women should give combat sports a try, but in a limited fashion—one where they limit their chance of being injured or hurt. In this sense, *Victoria Secret*'s advertisement cam-paign is introducing the consumer to a form of boxing that is more palatable as it adheres to the societal gender hierarchy and promotes white middle-class ideals of beauty and fitness.

BOXING, BEAUTY, AND FITNESS

The reification of structural gendered norms and their consumption also emerged in the selling of boxing apparel and sportswear more broadly. Women boxers can purchase boxing gloves and wraps in a range of colors, but there were almost always some light pink gloves, headgear, mouth guards, and wraps available. This covertly reifies existing gender roles and norms as products are designed to reflect ideals of masculinity and femininity, that is, pink for a girl and blue for a boy. Yet, the broader meaning of these pink products is rarely noted, they become banal (Goold et al. 2013), fading out to the periphery (Miller 2010). Their very presence acts to reinforce the existing patriarchal structure. As argued by myself and fellow criminologist Dawn Rothe (2017, 7), "It is the banality or triviality of these products that lends them power, as through their pervasiveness they are rarely noticed or questioned, becoming part of the broader patriarchal status quo."

Adding a layer of complexity is that scholars have found that in navigating gender, women athletes are often encouraged to emphasize their femininity by actively differentiating themselves from men. This is often achieved through the adornment of feminine products, such as the aforementioned pink clothing, pink gear/equipment, jewelry, and make-up. Interestingly, women trainers that adhered to more traditional standards of beauty, such as wearing make-up, were reported to increase the comfort level of women gym-goers. Rebecca commented on other women's use of make-up saying "Uh, but I know some trainers that wear make-up and, you know when they train. So, I don't, maybe if they feel like they need to, I-I don't. I don't feel that way. It could be different for each person though" (Rebecca, Personal Communication, March 21, 2017). Caroline also commented on women wearing make-up during gym time, saying, "You know just looking, their hair's done…and their hairs long and their makeups done and I mean they look gorgeous but you know you can tell that it's meant to appeal to men" (Caroline, Personal Communication, February 13, 2017). It has been advanced that in order to negotiate the hierarchy of the gender order—one that privileges men and masculinity—women apologize for existing in these spaces by highlighting heterosexual characteristics (Delano et al. 2009). This is an active way to control or manage their deviant status as a woman that engages in combat sports (Lafferty and McKay 2004). Some women, however, were more critical of the use of such adornments in these spaces.

There were some women that made judgments about other women in the cardio-boxing space related to their appearance. Maggie said,

> But I think if you come in with like makeup on, I don't think you're serious about it. I mean I don't, because you're going to, it's like you're not wanting to

sweat then. It's like your wanting to find a boy or something, you know. So, I would definitely take somebody less seriously if they came in with makeup on. (Maggie, Personal Communication, December 28, 2016)

Wearing make-up in this instance was automatically assumed to be associated with seeking male attention, and it could be viewed as another example of women's compliance with emphasized femininity. Despite Maggie's questioning of these women's intentions, they are merely representative of gender socialization in a patriarchal society where women's capital is inextricably linked to their bodies, or parts of their bodies. Maggie conceptualized other women's capitulation to this gender socialization as not being acceptable in the boxing gym space as it detracts away from how seriously women are perceived as boxers. To be taken seriously, Maggie is suggesting that characteristics of emphasized femininity should be suppressed (i.e., women should aspire to fit within the masculine aesthetic of the sport). This is in line with research that has shown that achieving the perception of gender parity is related to the apparel or kit associated with the sport, something that can eradicate gender markings (Godoy-Pressland 2015). However, it should be noted that wearing the right clothes to be taken seriously could be construed as adopting masculine standards of the sport in question, and therefore strengthening the idea that *the* standard is that set by men (Duncan 1986).

Interestingly, it has been found that women boxers are often keen to demonstrate their femininity both in and outside the ring through performing their feminine identities, including the utilization of adornments (Mennesson 2000). Nowhere is this more apparent than in the case of women's sportswear. Sports clothing and apparel is a billion-dollar industry, bringing in 181 billion dollars in 2019 alone (O'Connell 2019). In the case of fashion and beauty, the female form is packaged and sold through the bombardment of advertisement, product placements, and mediated representations of women's bodies that due to their proliferation become normalized. By wearing makeup, jewelry, and other feminine apparel, existing gender roles are reified through their purchase and use. Maggie made several comments about the pressure she felt to buy and wear expensive brand sports apparel, she said,

So yeah, I definitely think it is like high brands. So, for Lulu for instance, I feel like if you don't have that on or have a very high brand on you get looked at. So, before Christmas I only had, like I did have a couple pair[s of] Lulu but I had just like two shirts you know, because my Mom and Dad and I would always say the gym is not a pageant. It's not somewhere you have to go to look beautiful, you're getting sweaty and going there to work out. (Maggie, Personal Communication, December 28, 2016)

Maggie had mixed feelings about the cultural pressure she felt to purchase Lululemon sportswear, but she also noted the redundancy of this pressure due to the physical exertion of the exercise regime. Yet, she like many of the women in the space, opted to wear tight fitting clothing, purchased from a variety of outlets that collectively promote the ideal physique for a woman.

Although not applicable to all women in these spaces, there was an overall trend with younger women with smaller statures who could be described as slim, wearing tighter fitting clothes than those who were larger and older. Some would argue that the type of clothing that women choose to wear is reflective of comfort and practicality independent of size. It is a matter of free will and choice, yet I would suggest that this choice is fictitious and reflective of a larger patriarchal capitalist structure that through the market dictates what is and is not "appropriate" for women to purchase and wear in these spaces. Rosalind Gill (2007) has argued that increased autonomy, choice, individualism, empowerment, and self-surveillance has been associated with the idea that we are living in a post-feminist world. This lends itself to corporate interests, such as sportswear companies, where women can be classified and see themselves as autonomous "empowered consumer[s]" (Tasker and Negra 2007, 2). This then places the empowered female consumer in a position whereby to exercise or demonstrate her power in the market place she purchases material goods. Women are encouraged to purchase what they want whenever they want (Gill 2007). In exercising their perceived choice to consume they are aligning themselves with larger structural gender norms. Here, in the case of sportswear, the choice to purchase is limited to specific types of workout gear, apparel that is form fitting, scant on material, designed to tuck-in, flatten-out, and smooth over any potential insecurities and blemishes women feel they may have. This choice is misleading creating a façade of empowerment that is touted as being feminist as women are only able to purchase what is made available by the neoliberal consumerist market (Collins and Rothe 2017). Under this premise, women have been made subject to the carefully constructed ploys of the market that dictate what they should look like when they are exercising (Stole 2008). By purchasing these clothes, women are adhering to hegemonic ideals of beauty and fitness, yet this ideal of women's health and fitness is not static.

Ideals of beauty and femininity change over time and place, but beginning in 2010, there was a movement in the health and fitness culture away from skinny toward a more muscular physique. This was often accompanied by head or tag lines declaring "Strong is the New Skinny," "Girls Gone Strong," or "Strong is the New Sexy." This shift was accompanied by empowering justifications of body positivity content. However, like the classifications of beauty that came before this, it served to exclude and belittle women who did not possess this physique. Whether the focus is on muscles, curves, skinniness, or fat, the overarching theme is that women should aspire to be physically beautiful (Jennings 2015); their social capital is linked to their attractiveness to men. Buying a workout shirt that says "hit like a girl" or "strong is beautiful" does not negate that the shirt is designed to fit the female form in a way that appeases the male gaze. The statement, exercise, or the participation in the sport is relegated to being second to the woman's appearance.

The proliferation of the desired female body image also influences the types of exercises deemed appropriate for women. Shari Dworkin (2004) in a study of women's utilization of weight rooms versus cardiovascular exercise rooms found that one of the reasons women avoided lifting weights was they did not want to become too muscular. The preference for the cardio machines was associated with the maintenance of a certain look or body ideal. I have personally encountered this point of view when seeking treatment for an acromioclavicular joint separation that resulted from training. To combat the pain and strengthen the muscles in effort to prevent surgery, my orthopedic surgeon referred me to physiotherapy. I had sought medical attention approximately four to five months after injuring myself, something I can only attribute to my own stubbornness and reluctance to admit that something was quite wrong—I did not want to have surgery. While I still experienced considerable pain and was unable to sleep on the injured side of my body, I continued to train (ill-advisably) but with limitations. So, when I started physiotherapy although in pain, it had decidedly improved since my initial injury. The physiotherapist was an older woman, maybe in her 50s, who would give me two or three pound dumbbells to use for my sessions. After a few sessions, I began to question the efficacy of such weights as very often I would leave the therapy session and go straight to the gym where my coach would have me doing rehabilitative exercises using 15 or 20 pound dumbbells, or have me utilizing cable weight machines with 40 or 50 pounds in weight. The two or three pound dumbbells seemed redundant and quite frankly a waste of my time. I asked my physiotherapist about this and she said that women should not use more than five pound dumbbells. I asked whether this was specific to recovery, and she replied that women should not ever lift heavier than that otherwise they would get too muscly. I was horrified, and we ended up in quite a lively discussion whereby she swore there was scientific evidence to support her claim. After this meeting I declined to go back and continued my recovery with my trainer at the gym. Here we have a working medical professional replicating gendered misinformation about weight training. It is, therefore, not surprising that there is a dominant cultural and social understanding that "bodies are carefully constructed through strategic selection and repetition of particular fitness practices" (Dworkin 2004, 132), and that these practices are gendered. This adherence to a socially prescribed body type was more apparent at one of cardio-gyms as compared to the others.

Related to the power of aesthetics and image signage, one of the cardio-boxing gyms also capitalized heavily on boxing stereotypes yet seemed to promote and prefer a certain consumer. This gym branded itself as a boxing gym promoting the stereotype of the heavily mediatized urban, street, working-class boxing gym but commercialized and packaged for the middle-class consumer. Yet, unlike the authenticity of a fight gym, the gym was decorated to appear this way and despite this curated image, there were very few actual fighters on staff. In addition to boxing classes, the gym offered a number of classes designed to replicate the roadwork that boxers do outside of boxing. Many of the trainers themselves had considerable experience as personal trainers specializing in a variety of different exercise techniques, but not boxing. From my perspective, and from that of others I talked to, this delegitimized their claim of being a "boxing gym." This was compounded by the lack of experience in fighting sports held by most of the trainers. Acknowledging the subjectivity of my personal observations, at the time I attended none of the female trainers sported muscular physiques, rather they were all young (under twenty-five years), lean, small, with no or little boxing background. I do not have an overly muscular form, but I do have a body type that is more reflective of boxing (thick legs, wider shoulders, and some muscle definition). None of the staff members looked like me, and although I am sure they were physically fit, none of the women promoted the physique of a fighter or the necessary skills to support their position as an instructor in a boxing gym. In fact, many of these trainers were in the same pads class as the members learning to box alongside us. As a consequence, when I stepped into this gym space, I felt uncomfortable and not welcome. I simply did not fit their target consumer audience.

The promotion of a beauty ideal seemed to be part of the commodification of this gym space. This ideal includes a range of images that are promoted by our consumerist culture, albeit this range is quite narrow. Although published some thirty years ago, philosopher Sandra Bartky's (1988) study is still quite relevant today. Drawing heavily on philosopher Michel Foucault's (1979) idea of bodily surveillance, Bartky (1988, 81) argues that women have docile bodies and engage in endless fitness and diet routines as not only self-discipline but as an "obedience" to the structures of patriarchy. The preferred body type for a woman cannot be escaped and young girls are subject to this conditioning from early childhood. Consider Disney princesses, Barbie, teen celebrities, fashion models, pop singers to mention but a few examples of the social promotion and adherence to the slim, petite, carefully groomed, white, middle-class standard of beauty. This adherence and promotion of this idealized femininity was no more apparent than when the gym was booked for a private group session for approximately fifty women who showed up one Saturday afternoon as I was finishing a pads class in the ring. Their entrance to the gym and my reaction is summarized in the following fieldnote,

> Waiting for our turn with the instructor, I stood in the ring as Cathy [another regular gym member] and I looked out in awe as the vast expanse of the gym began to fill with blonde women with a scattering of brunettes mixed in. They all were similarly adorned in coordinated workout apparel, tightly clinging to their trim, slender bodies. "What the fuck is this?" Cathy asked me, as she too looked stunned by the sudden swarming of the gym space by what seemed like as many as 50 faces, made up with make-up (even lipstick), wearing earrings, with their glossy hair overly styled pushed back into bouncing ponytails or hanging in waves down their backs. I laughed at Cathy's comment, but felt myself frown. I suddenly was self-conscious of my own disheveled and sweaty appearance, lack of make-up, standing sodden with sweat in my black mis-matched loose-fitting t-shirt and yoga pants. Catching the eye of a trainer I knew well, I beckoned him over to the ring, "what's going on?" I asked.
>
> "It's some sort of women's group, they're here for a private session with the head trainer, he's going to ask you all to get out" he said.
>
> "Get out? You mean like leave?" I asked, confused.
>
> "Yes" he said, then jokingly added "No boxers allowed" before laughing and wandering off. I was a little dumbfounded, and to be honest offended, that the gym I paid my membership dues to was closing early to accommodate a class of nonmembers. (Fieldnote, June 24. 2018)

In a later reflection on this event I tried to unpack my feelings, especially why I had such a strong negative reaction to what was really just other women trying out the gym. Beyond being ejected from the gym space without prior notification of a private event, my feelings were situated in my perceptions of the sport of boxing as being one that has historically been a vehicle for minority groups that exist on the margins to gain legitimacy and a stake in society through engagement with the sport. Ironically, I objected to the white-collar, middle-class appropriation of the sport for the purposes of financial gains, and despite my own status as a white-collar middle-class, educated professional engaging in the very behavior I found objectionable, being faced with the physical reality of that very thing was disturbing. For me, this was further compounded by my passion and seriousness for the sport and having trained quite seriously for several years, the presence of these women who emulated societal standards of the ideals of heteronormative femininity evoked feelings of resentment. I simultaneously feared their presence delegitimated the authenticity of the sport and my experiences, but also highlighted that I too may well be just another white, middle-classed woman reaffirming societal body ideals, playing at being a boxer. Especially as it is this bodily ideal that was promoted in this gym in a somewhat contradictory way considering this is not the body ideal of someone who wants to fight. Furthermore, I also recognized that not having the correct body for a specific shirt, or not fitting this stereotype of beauty as socially defined and promoted in this particular gym, can have adverse consequences creating pressures that have damaging consequences, such as eating disorders.

There were several women that confided in me that they struggled with healthy eating, and although hard to write about, I too share some of these issues. As someone whose Mum struggled with eating disorders and to this day still has a somewhat unhealthy relationship with food, battling with this issue can be consuming. In addition, as I was very overweight for a large part of my adult life, the pressures to adhere to socially prescribed ideals of beauty have caused me at times, to under eat, over train, and deny myself the requisite nutrition to sustain my training schedule. I also have found myself obsessively fixated on unhealthy goals such as attaining a specific weight on the scale, a certain dress or pant size, or being overly regimented when it comes to caloric intake. I also can be very unkind to myself and when I feel that I do not have control over my body, can get quite depressed. This is something that both my husband and coach are aware of, and they both make steps to assist and support me in pursuing and maintaining a healthy approach.

The National Association of Anorexia Nervosa and Associated Disorders (2020) reports that in the United States, approximately 30 million people of all genders suffer from eating disorders. This includes anorexia nervosa, bulimia, binge eating, avoidant/restrictive foods intake disorder, diabulimia, and other specified feed disorders. Although the causes of these disorders are multifaceted, discourses surrounding health and fitness, especially those populated by the media, promote unrealistic ideals of the female body. The fitness industry, including but not limited to diet, exercise, gyms, sportswear, and supplements, revolve around the notion that to attain this unobtainable body type, you need to consume their products or plans (Markula 2001). While the promotion of the ideal female body is not something that is exclusive to the fitness and exercise industry, gym spaces are rife with narratives that capitalize on the promotion of bettering the self. It is not surprising then that some of the women included in this study reported struggling with their relationship with food and fitness.

Promotional material, including posters and pictures on the walls, often featured women who fit within an ideal body type. This extends to features shared on social media platforms that identify the "client of the month" or clients who have achieved incredible transformations. Having lost 85 lbs myself, I was featured in one such publication and note the irony of me including a similar image in chapter 1 that is a before and after photograph of my own body transformation. In gym spaces such features include testimonies as to motivations for weight loss and the improvements that such changes make to gym-goers' lives. In isolation, such promotions are well intended with the view to inspire and congratulate, as well as garner prospective clients to sign-up for gym memberships. However, when viewed collectively with other promotional material and within the larger context of the populated ideal of a woman's body type, this too contributes to the larger discourse on health and beauty. Compounding this messaging was the use of quips and commentary from trainers and instructors that focused on food and weight loss. For example, it was not uncommon for trainers to relate working hard to earning a "cheat meal," or if it was a holiday to urge people to work harder to "make-up for everything they ate" over the weekend, even going so far as listing food types (i.e., hotdogs and burgers, or turkey and trimmings at Thanksgiving). These types of narratives cast eating food, especially certain types of food, as being detrimental to one's health with the only solution being to exercise and/or eat less. The narrative is not that you need to eat to live, but rather is twisted to one that necessitates exercising to being allowed to eat. The prolific nature of this narrative has the potential to contribute to some women's eating habits and can compound a negative perception of self.

Many of the women here were quick to note the "problem" areas of their bodies, or body parts they wished to tone-up, tighten, or change. Despite a move in the fitness discourse to one that promotes "strong as sexy" most of the women spoke more freely about losing weight, getting skinny, or getting beach body ready, opposed to getting stronger, packing on muscle, or bulking up. Maggie, for example, spent considerable time concerned about her body, she said, "In my arms, my stomach, what I like my whole body to look better, yes. It's just, I don't know my stomach really . . . if I could change one thing it would be that" (Maggie, Personal Communication, December 28, 2016). Maggie was very petite and slender, and from my perspective, I could not see the stomach she was concerned with. She later exclaimed that she was frustrated as "sometimes I just eat tuna all day, and I still don't see any changes" (Maggie, Personal Communication, December 28, 2016). When I probed for some clarification as to what she meant by "tuna all day" she confided that she would workout at the cardio-gym and eat a can of tuna for lunch and that would be the totality of her food intake for the day. This was alarming, but Maggie saw it as a normal and necessary part of weight-loss if she were to ever achieve the body she desired. Here, in a world where women are bombarded with images of the perfect body, struggling to accept the reality of the body they have can leave them feeling powerless. This then encourages them to engage in behaviors and thoughts that further devalue and even harm their bodies as well as their overall well-being.

The devaluing of women is not restricted to body image, rather there still remains glaring gender inequities when it comes to access to sporting careers for women, wages, media coverage, endorsement deals, and heightened inequalities for women athletes who also occupy other minority statuses—that is, race, class, ethnicity, LGBTQIA, or differently abled (Cooky and Messner 2018; Hargreaves and Anderson 2014; Sparkes et al. 2014). Throughout this book thus far, I have drawn attention to the advances made to the sport of boxing by Clareesa Shields, who has been heralded for laying the path for women coming up in boxing wanting to pursue a serious career (Schirmer 2017). Despite this acknowledgement, it must be noted that the devaluing of women athletes is institutionalized and deeply embedded. For example, consider that at the height of her career Ronda Rousey's pay was considerably less than her male counterparts. For example, in Rousey's 2014 fight against Alexis Davis (UFC 175), Rousey earned $120,000, of which $60,000 was her bonus for winning. This may seem like a lot of money but when compared with Chris Weidman's earnings of $450,000, who shared the main card with Rousey that night, it is considerably less. In fact, Lyoto Machida earned more than Rousey when he lost against Weidman—his payout was $200,000 (Yang 2015).

Similar patterns of gender inequality can be seen in vast gaps in earnings across most sports. In the 2015 World Cup, the United States' women's team earned $2 million for their win, yet the winners of the men's tournament received $35 million. The highest paid player in the Women's National Basketball Association earns approximately one-fifth of that of the lowest paid player in the National Basketball Association. Furthermore, in 2017, of the Forbes top 100 highest-paid athletes only one female athlete is featured, Serena Williams, and she is number 51. There have been efforts made to make prize money neutral; however, this does not account for endorsement deals that make-up a large percentage of professional athletes' income (Perasso 2017). As argued by Beatrice Frey, who is the sports manager partner at UN Women, "I cannot think of any other industry that has such a wage gap, really. Depending on the country context and sport, a man can be a billionaire and a woman [in the same sport] cannot even get minimum salary" (Frey as cited in Perasso 2017).

The differential treatment and devaluing of women was something that Anna spoke of with passion. She argued the following about her experiences with Olympic boxing,

> And I think that is what's really the women especially since we've, we got, the men got two medals this time, but in 2012 we we're the only medals. We had a gold and a bronze and the men didn't even medal at all and we we're the only gold in this Olympics so I think we're sitting back and like okay we're the most

talented athletes that team USA has right now, why aren't we getting more benefits, and really I don't even think. Like obviously we don't want the same benefits but a lot of the women are like just give us something to show you know that we are you know getting rewarded for our hard work cause we're working, my coach will always say that women train harder. We work harder, our technique is better. (Anna, Personal Communication, January 23, 2017)

The lack of benefits despite the teams' success was reflective of the persistent wage gap in sports that repeatedly undervalue sportswomen. Anna notes,

And so we really, women are definitely pushed aside and like the resources as far as tournaments go um the men are just stacked and as far as like jumpsuits, uh bags, shoes, equipment, all of that, and whenever I went to the Olympic training center whenever I was on team USA, um, they, you know we got a jacket and a jumpsuit, which was nice, we got some gloves, but like the equipment didn't arrive on time and it's like different little things were it's like okay, this definitely wouldn't happen if we were guys. (Anna, Personal Communication, January 23, 2017)

A brief examination of any sport would show similar disparities despite the prominence of the success of the women athlete involved. The wage gap and inequality when it comes to endorsements and resource support suggests that even though women in boxing and sports more generally are making gains, gender inequality is allowed to persist as the focus is on capital accumulation and an industry of carnival.

CONCLUSION

This chapter has examined the commodification of women's boxing as it relates to larger societal understandings of gender, beauty, fitness, and body. There have been some notable gains for women in combat sports, yet there still remains a deeply embedded gender hierarchy that undermines the athleticism of women athletes, reducing their success and prowess to gender norms, roles, and stereotypes reflective of heteronormative characteristics of femininity and masculinity. The last twenty years has resulted in greater normalization of fighting women, but the framing of them as the novelty spectacle still lingers, so much so, it is often capitalized on for the purposes of commodifying the sport as a product to be consumed. But in doing so, women are still navigating a number of binaries such as "beautiful/ugly," "strong/weak," and "feminine/masculine" (Jennings 2015), and to do so often means consciously subjecting themselves to the male gaze or actively engaging in emphasized femininity to just be permitted a place in the sport.

Chapter 4

Fighting Tough . . . but Not Too Tough

As mentioned in chapter 2, the cardio-boxing gyms purposely sought to make their spaces more attractive to women clientele, while retaining an element of authenticity by incorporating the stereotypical aesthetics of a boxing gym. Recognizing that one of the largest markets for recreational fitness are women, these gyms capitalized on the idea of boxing as fitness. In this chapter, the varying gym spaces are further unpacked as it relates to marketing, gender, hostility, and accessibility of these spaces to women. This includes examining how women viewed the class formats, the instructors, and their relationships with other gym-goers in these spaces. As expected, there were considerable differences between those gyms that offered cardio-boxing as compared to those that offered contact-boxing. These differences are situated within the larger societal structures of gender and sport and are related to the spatial boundaries that either invite women into these spaces or purposely exclude them. I will start with the more welcoming space of the cardio-boxing gyms.

CARDIO-BOXING GYMS

The classes at the cardio-boxing gyms all followed a similar format. An instructor would lead a class from the center of the room, surrounded by the class participants who each selected a bag to work on. A typical class in one of these gyms would start with a warm-up consisting of aerobic exercises such as jumping jacks, high knees, and squats, as well as stretching and shadow boxing. The class then proceeded with the instructor calling out punch combinations, usually starting with more basic punches and getting more complex over the course of each round (a three-minute interval, timed as such to mimic the length of a round in the ring). The instructor then weaves between the bags the gym-goers are hitting, correcting their form, and encouraging and motivating them to work harder.

As the focus is the utilization of the boxer's workout for the purposes of increased fitness, the class borrows from well-known rituals associated with being initiated as a boxer (Hoffman 2006). The three stages are as follows: (1) the air phase, which refers to shadow or mirror boxing where the movements associated with the sport are learned; (2) the leather phase, where the focus is hitting the bags; and (3) the adversary phase, where the boxer gets into the ring to take on a real-life opponent. The incorporation of the three stages into the cardio-boxing class adds legitimacy. This starts with the warm-up where the incorporation of shadow boxing mimics the air phase. Interestingly, only one of the cardio gyms had mirrored walls where the gym-goers could in fact practice and study their form during the class. Another gym had mirrors, yet the class was conducted in the dark with red and/or flashing lights making the utilization of the mirrors somewhat redundant. The third cardio-boxing gym did not have mirrors hanging in the gym space where the class was conducted. The choice of warm-up exercises also legitimates this workout as being authentically associated with boxing, as they too reinforce the body regimens of a boxer, that is, jumping rope (or pretending to), jumping jacks, and burpees are all exercises often associated with boxing.

The graduation from the warm-up exercises to hitting the bags replicates the transition a novice boxer goes through in working toward the ultimate goal of being inducted into the fighters world, "a liminal right" (Beuchez 2017, 76) that culminates when they have their first face-to-face encounter in the ring (Hoffman 2006). This moment of becoming a fighter has been written about at length by other ethnographers (Beuchez 2017; Garis 2000; Hoffman 2006; Wacquant 1995a) and will be further unpacked in chapter 6; yet, in the case of the cardio-boxing gym, this moment never arrives. There is no testing of the skills that have been acquired or negotiating their identities as fighters in the ring (Beuchez 2017). This creates an atmosphere where there is a mitigated risk associated with the type of boxing participants are doing as the potential for injury has been eliminated.

Attracted to the Idea of Boxing: Containing the Risk

The elimination of the adversary phase (Hoffman 2006) emerged as a theme in varying ways. It was revealed that many gym-goers wanted to further their skills by engaging an opponent in the ring. As expressed by Miriam,

> So, I did think about it a lot, but I think I would like, I thought about it a lot and maybe going into class early and asking one of the trainers to just spar . . .

and kind of just teach me how to do that and working a ring . . . because like I said I just punch the bag. So, I've always kind of like wanted to, you know, see what it would be like to be in the ring and work a round and [work] on moving and I just like never done it. (Miriam, Personal Communication, March 4, 2017)

This sentiment was echoed by Hannah who said "I think it would be cool. I would do it" (Hannah, Personal Communication, June 20, 2017). Others, such as Terry, were less certain in their aspirations to get in the ring, yet expressed a curiosity about taking it to the adversarial stage,

I guess I thought about it some. I don't think I would ever you know make it something that I want to do full-time or anything like that, but I mean I guess I would never be opposed to it, it doesn't make me want to hit somebody outside, you know just get angry and just find someone. But maybe, you know try boxing . . . other than just the bag for once. (Terry, Personal Communication, January 5, 2017)

This curiosity was quite common, but often came with reservations and concerns about the possible risks and subsequent consequences of getting in the ring. For example, although Hannah was adamant in her wish to try sparring, she also had reservations based on the impact her age could potentially have on her ability to participate,

Hannah: I'm a little old but . . .
Victoria: You're probably younger than I am.
Hannah: I'll be 40 in 10 months.
Victoria: I'm going to be 37 soon, so about the same.
Hannah: Yeah, I'm doing the countdown so. But yeah, I think it would be awesome. (Hannah, Personal Communication, June 20, 2017)

Hannah's enthusiasm was mitigated by her age, a feeling that adversarial boxing was reserved for the young.

Other reservations centered on possible health impacts such as wanting to protect themselves from potential injury. Concern was expressed about the impact sparring would have on employment as summarized by Julie, "Yea I mean, I just really didn't want to have any effect on my ability to think clearly and function everyday to the highest of my mental abilities, so um I never took it any further than for exercise and for personal training" (Julie, Personal Communication, February 5, 2017). The concern for long-term health consequences is one that has proliferated the media, especially as it relates to concerns for traumatic brain injuries (TBIs) (Rezzadeh 2019). However, this is something that occurs less frequently in amateur than it does professional boxing (Baugh et al. 2014), and is even less likely to occur in controlled settings where the focus is instructional.

Another reason that women shied away from sparring was the influence and opinion of others. For example, Agatha's husband influenced her decision-making,

Agatha: But I know my husband's pretty much against it.
Victoria: Does he say why?
Agatha: Um, I think he views it as a manly sport . . . Um, you know like when we . . . If I ever . . . We don't watch MMA . . . but I'll look at the YouTube videos of Holly Holmes and Ronda Rousey . . .
Victoria: Right.
Agatha: And he's like, you want to look like that?! For me it's not about what I look like type of thing . . . it's you know, being able to take this skill you learn and, you know, you've gotten fitness results from and make it something that you're able to get an accomplishment from . . . was my idea behind it . . . so maybe in the future [I'll spar] but right now, obviously not. (Agatha, Personal Communication, January 4, 2017)

Here, Agatha's partners' views and understanding of the sport, one shaped by popular cultural presentations and historically embedded notions of it being a "manly art" (Wacquant 2004, 14), informed his opinion, and by proxy hers, of it as an inappropriate activity for Agatha to pursue. The physical characteristics of women fighters like Ronda Rousey and Holly Holmes violate Agatha's husband's understanding of the cultural embodiment of femininity and masculinity. Both women are muscular athletes and as a consequence are contrary to socially promoted standards of beauty (although both women have been both objectified and sexualized as compared to other female fighters). This is rarely a conscious happening, and it is doubtful that Agatha and her husband are purposeful in their reinforcement of the culturally dominant understandings of gender embodiment.

It has been firmly established that bodies are marked, noted, or constituted for particular cultural requirements through the adorning of specific clothes, make-up, and hairstyles, yet other habits also demarcate cultural difference, such as physical movements. Culturally constructed narratives of gender advance beyond the adorning of a biologically given body (i.e., putting on earrings) to become part of our everyday gender schemas (Grosz 1994). The body is given values, it is "*made* body, by the hidden persuasion of an implicit pedagogy which can instill a whole cosmology" (Bourdieu 1990, 69). This is attained through simple suggestions that correct posture (i.e., sit up straight) or instill etiquette (chew your food with your mouth closed) that are so seemingly insignificant that they put "them beyond the reach of conscious and explicit statement" (Bourdieu 1990, 69). This process is gendered and becomes the common-sense reality of everyday life. These suggestions, beliefs, and experiences become a "state of the body" (McCaughey 1997), or a habitus that informs gender-appropriate behavior such as ways to walk, move, talk and be (Henley 1977; Young 1990). This includes sport, and especially in the case of fighting sports where a person performs physically, fulling displaying strength, muscular power, and taking advantage of spatial potential. These characteristics are more typical of the socialization of men and become the source of ideologies that then inform action as well as the larger social order. As argued by McCaughey (1997, 40), when engaging their physicality "Women tend not to reach, extend, and follow through because they are not as likely as men to have developed a relationship with their bodies as agents, as instruments of action." Women are therefore socialized away from physical competence; in fact, the achievement of "womanhood" is contrary to physical competence.

Sport, therefore, acts as a socializing agent, a means for men to achieve manhood through displays of physical achievement, confirming heteronormative gender norms as being a product of nature. When women do engage their bodies in a way that is counter to feminine socialization and they display their physical prowess, they violate social and cultural constructs of what it means to be a woman. While the unpacking of Agatha's comments has demonstrated the undergirding ideologies that inform resistance to women engaging in fighting sports, it also demonstrates the embedded nature of such understandings. It is unlikely that Agatha is relaying this information to me to demonstrate how her engaging in adversarial boxing would disrupt deeply embedded and widely accepted gender norms that pit physical strength against femininity. However, her reaction to her husband's comments, and reluctant acceptance of it, emphasizes the pervasive nature of these beliefs for women engaging the sport and how they manifest as a barrier for some women who would otherwise wish to have a go in the ring.

Here the cardio gym offers a way for women to engage the sport without the risk of adversarial boxing. The incorporation of real boxing rituals lends authenticity to the cardio-boxing gyms but mitigates any risk involved as it eliminates the third stage of becoming a boxer, the adversarial stage. It is fair to say that the majority of cardio-boxing participants, as well as a good percentage of those interviewed for this study (myself included), are middle class. The cardio-boxing gym provides a version of boxing that they can claim is real, in that it incorporates enough of the boxers' workout to signify that they know enough about the sport to be considered authentic in their discipline while remaining safe. There is no risk of harm or injury, or one-on-one testing of their skills in the ring. This means that constructions of boxing were not at odds with middle-class norms as the intensity of the workout regimen remained but the risk of injury or harm has been removed. However, this mitigated risk did impact perceptions of the authenticity of the experience as it related to the gender of gym members.

NAVIGATING MALE SPACES: HOSTILITY, SEXISM, AND THE PATRIARCHAL STATUS QUO

Manly Enough? An Infringement on Male Space

As indicated above, the cardio-boxing gyms capitalized on the common rituals associated with boxing and becoming a boxer and repackaged it into a group exercise class, something that is familiar and friendly, and especially welcoming to women. As summarized by Pierre, a trainer at one of these gyms,

> I think it's the group style atmosphere [that] is more attractive to a female base [as] they're more used to working in a group style setting. Ah like that . . . but ah it's a lot more geared towards the fitness weight loss, all that stuff, at the gym just because the endurance, high intensity. (Pierre, Personal Communication, August 14, 2017)

Attracting women to these spaces through actively creating softer spaces (i.e., choice in decoration, trainers, and emphasizing fitness and weight loss) has the desired effect of attracting more women members. The cardio gyms had a larger female clientele than male. "[O]ur thing is mainly women, we probably have 60 percent women . . . maybe 75 percent" (Jack, Personal Communication, March 7, 2017), with women in their 30s being a targeted consumer. As indicated by Agatha, "So as a concept [the gym] has moved much more feminine and kind of because they found um, that their biggest demographic was 35-year-old women" (Agatha, Personal Communication, January 4, 2017).

Furthermore, women at the cardio-boxing gyms made up at least 50 percent of the trainers if not more, and at one of the gyms the most experienced boxer was a young woman in her twenties. This same gym cycled through a number of different head-trainers of which only one was a woman. With the adversarial component of boxing removed in the cardio-gym spaces, it emerged that women boxing trainers felt their legitimacy as a trainer was sometimes questioned. In response to a survey administered by one of the boxing gyms,[1] it was suggested that certain exercises indicated to some male gym members that the gym "was more of a girls club because we were doing so many squats, we were doing um so many leg exercises . . . And he took that as being you know more a female thing" (Arthur, Personal Communication,

December 27, 2016). Here, characteristics of femininity, and misinformation about exercises that are supposedly more suited to women, shape the workspace and the perceived efficacy of women trainers.

The gendering of specific spaces in gyms is not new and creates a contradiction for women who traverse these spaces (Bryson 1990; Hargreaves 1994). Research has shown that the construction and reconstruction of gender in gym spaces is multifaceted and complex including women's navigation of their object status as it intersects with agency and subjectivity (i.e., women are not just oppressed objects subject to the power of the patriarchy) (Dworkin 2003). For the masculine sport of boxing, women trainers were subject to criticism when male gym-goers felt they promoted exercises that were "typical" of women's workout routines, ones they dismissed as being redundant for the sport of boxing. Having a wider appeal to women was generally viewed as a good thing; however, there were some consequences. Being more feminine in this instance had the impact of deterring prospective male members from frequenting the space.

The lack of adversarial boxing acted as a potential deterrent to prospective male members. Male members were more likely to seek out contact boxing and inquire about sparring when first frequenting the gym. For example, both Julie and Agatha, who worked at one of the cardio-boxing gyms, noted that they received more calls from men looking to spar or fight. Julie spoke of a typical inquiry from prospective male members, "They'd say that on the phone, that they were, you know, kind of not sure it was for guys because it wasn't actual fighting, wasn't actual sparring and then they'd get in there and they'd see girls kicking butt, and they'd be like oh" (Julie, Personal Communication, February 5, 2017). Jack also commented that "for some reason I guess I don't know what it is, they want to spar, that is always the first question" (Jack, Personal Communication, March 7, 2017). The draw to the boxing gym for men is likely related to the hegemonic representations of the sport in the broader society. As argued by Woodward (2007, 48), "the practice of the gym cannot entirely be removed from the wider cultural terrain or from the public stories that inform it." The public characterization of boxing as a sport is strongly shaped through the expression of hegemonic masculinity. Gender, as formulated through the physical and demonstrated through observable characteristics associated with femininity and masculinity, becomes the key source of identity. As noted in chapter 2, manhood is associated with power; "man *in* power, a man *with* power, and a man *of* power" (Kimmel 1994b, 125). Representations and narratives of boxing greats emphasize physical power, skill, and technique but also highlight the risk and danger of being punched. It is this danger that signifies masculinity, as to be victorious in such an exchange is, according to the popular narratives about the sport, to achieve manhood. It is, therefore, not surprising that men attracted to learning the sport inquire about the element of the sport central to the expression of hegemonic masculinity; that of sparring.

Catering to women and having an increased female gym membership led to a larger questioning of the authenticity of the space by male gym-goers. As indicated by Julie,

> The other regular kind of ambivalent sexism that I saw was men who would call um when I was working there, or they would come in and take classes, and I would just interact with them just to see how much, how they enjoyed it. And they would say, well but is it mostly girls who come here, you know it, it feels like the type of thing that would just be mostly women. Which again, kind of always struck me as, is that a problem? You know it's still, a very physical type of exercise, it's very taxing, it works you out really really well um . . . even if there are more women than men, that shouldn't have any bearing on your work out. And that shouldn't effect, the way that, you know, the workout benefits you. So there were, again it was never the sort of like . . . girls are worse at this than guys, or girls don't belong here, this is 'no women space.' Nobody outright said those things. It was just kind of a regular perception, that was you know, a bigger deal for women, or that in this specific context maybe because it wasn't sparring this is where women went. (Julie, Personal Communication, February 5, 2017)

This was not an atmosphere that was created by the cardio gym employees or space itself, rather this relates to larger cultural understandings of boxing, aggression, physicality, and masculinity. The absence of the adversarial stage of training coupled with the increased female presence deterred men who perceived themselves as being either more suited to the sport, or more serious about it. Interestingly, and somewhat ironically, the presence of women with boxing skills also acted to intimidate men, something that could be conceptualized as a threat to hegemonic masculinity and/or the male ego.

A good example of the presence of women in these gym spaces being perceived as intimidating to men is summarized by Agatha's retelling of something her husband had said,

> Um, I think a lot of men when they come in, they get intimidated by the fact that a lot of women in there can work harder and longer then they can . . . Um, and actually my husband had brought that up whenever I first started. Um, because I didn't . . . You know we are . . . We're mainly women, um, our club is. I don't know the exact numbers on it . . . But um you know, if you go in with your girlfriends and you know you look like an idiot in front of your girlfriend as you don't have any boxing [experience] that might be a reason you know we are primarily women. (Agatha, Personal Communication, January 4, 2017)

The ability of women to fight, and fight well, or even to demonstrate good fighting skill was something that some men found threatening. This manifested itself in different ways ranging from odd comments, invasions of personal space, and behaviors that conveyed oblivious entitlement to sites, space, and equipment.

Invasions of personal space were quite common in all types of gyms. At the cardio-boxing gyms, it often manifested as a complete obliviousness or disregard for people in shared spaces. For example, it was not uncommon for women to report that men gym-goers infringed on the space surrounding their heavy bag before and during a class. Before class, this often took the form of the man performing physical acts within the woman's proximity such as pull-ups on the metal scaffold to which the bags were attached, or wildly hitting or kicking the bag in aggressive performative displays. During the class, this took the form of men ignoring spatial boundaries which had the impact of limiting women's freedom of movement for fear of running into them. There is not a specific designation of space allocated to each bag, but when several 100 lb bags are hung from a metal scaffolding structure, there is an established cultural etiquette that you move with an awareness of those taking the class with you. Hitting the bag so it swings around madly knocking into other people was generally frowned upon.

This was not exclusive to the boxing bags, rather it extended to other equipment in the gym. As noted by Angelina,

> Just that men don't have any problem like expressing like ownership over a thing. Like over a machine or a set of weights even if they're not like using it. Whereas I noticed like women if they're using it, you know, [they] will throw a towel over there and be like you know that's mine. Women feel like, like not leaving it [the equipment] because if you do that's rude or whatever, or your towel will be enough to signal [you're using it]. And then you're definitely not going to have a confrontation where you say like "oh I was using that," because a man would be like "hey I'm not done," but a woman would never do that, she would just gather her things quietly and leave. (Angelina, Personal Communication, February 16, 2017)

This was quite a common observation made of the differential behaviors of men and women in gym spaces more broadly, and one I experienced myself. I cannot relay the number of times someone has taken a weight, kettle bell, mat, or medicine ball from an active circuit I have been working. In my experiences, the person has always been a man, and the interruption or taking of equipment was always done with no communication (i.e., no "hey are you done with that?")

Interestingly, Terry summarized the most commonly noted intrusive behavior that occurred during class time, "And there's this one [man] in particular that, like, I don't know if you ever noticed it before either, but he will like move around to different bags throughout the workout" (Terry, Personal Communication, January 5, 2017). This again was something that I too experienced on more than one occasion, but at its most acute the following interaction occurred during a cardio-boxing class,

> I was following the instructions from the trainer during one of the three minute rounds, when an older man decided to move away from his designated bag into the gym space, and throw the instructed combination on the empty bags surrounding him. There were six empty bags between my bag and his, and to my right was a large white man covered in tattoos, and to my left was a large Nigerian man I am friendly with. Both men appear quite physically imposing. When the older man got close to me, he threw the punch combination on my bag making it swing back and forth, effectively interrupting my workout. My reaction was to stop throwing punches and to stare at him, hoping he would see from my body language and expression that I was not happy with what he was doing and that he would leave me and my bag alone. He instead smiled and continued to throw punches on my bag. He then moved back to an empty bag, ignoring the bags of the two men on either side of me. I resumed my workout but could see in my peripheral vision that he was approaching again, and when he got close enough, he started hitting my bag. I stopped again but this time I said, "Can you not," a comment he then ignored and continued with his combination before moving back onto one of the empty bags. The third time he approached, I said "Stop with hitting my bag" to which he replied, "I'm just working out." I was beginning to get frustrated, so I snapped back "Me too, but my workout does not include you." To which he then moved off again. He returned a fourth time and when he started hitting my bag, I said "seriously dude, what's your problem?" He replied "wow, you're angry" and I then moved around the bag towards him and to be honest was so frustrated that I am not sure exactly what I said, but it was something to the effect of "there are so many bags, why do you insist on jumping on the one I'm using, and why mine and not anyone else's?" I am sure there was profanity mixed in and a serious scowl on my face, but I was so indignant that this man, who I had no prior relationship with, felt entitled to enjoy his workout at the expense of mine. And, I also could not help but notice that the two other gym goers in my close proximity working out on bags within his reach, were both large men whom he chose to leave alone. (Fieldnote, January 12, 2020)

When men's behaviors were challenged, the response often seemed to be surprise, sometimes coupled with an apology, but the above fieldnote illustrates that this is not always the case and me asking this older man to stop was not only ignored but labeled as "anger." This is likely related to broader heteronormative socializations on aggression. As discussed in chapter 2, women are socialized to shy away from aggression and embrace passivity. Here, I violated this socialization by challenging this man's infringement on my space in a direct manner. This, however, is not unique to the boxing gym.

As noted by Stephanie Coen (University of Western Ontario 2017) when interviewed about her study (Coen, Rosenberg and Davidson 2018) of gender in gym spaces, men and women self-policed their utilization of space. For example, she reported,

> A young woman told me she couldn't be authoritative in asserting her place and using the equipment because she might be perceived negatively. But she felt like if a man were to do that, it would be acceptable. It shaped how she engaged with the equipment in the gym. (Coen as cited in University of Western Ontario 2017)

While I chose to assert my place in the above interaction, this was not a typical reaction of all the women included here, as many women forfeited their space to the men who invaded it (Coen, Rosenberg and Davidson 2018). In fact, I too, having engaged this man, reflected later on the interaction and felt badly about my part in how it escalated, so much so, I contacted the trainer for the class to explain that I did not have malicious intentions. I also spoke about it at length with my husband, close friend, and boxing coach who all reassured me I had acted appropriately, the latter even said "he was lucky I didn't punch him" (Fieldnote, January 12, 2020).

Furthermore, beyond gender differentiations on the consumption of space, some of the women interviewed suggested the differential behavior of men and women was motivated by men needing to show off and to demonstrate their physical capital (Bourdieu 1984) through a practice of "instrumental peacocking" (Harvey et al. 2014, 462), whereby the man in question performs physical acts to attract attention. Although Harvey et al. (2014) conceptualize this as being related to political economy, whereby personal trainers utilize this technique to attract clients; in this case, it is being used to assert and display acts men associate with hegemonic masculinity, as well as to communicate ownership or rights to space. This behavior also manifests sonically, whereby men also were consistently louder than women. For example, Matt described the behaviors of some of the men demonstrating their physical capital noting,

> It was, you know, the constantly the one arm grab, the one arm pull ups, very loud. There were multiple people like that and it was the issue. It's like dude chill, like I can assure you that none of these women are here to look at you or

you know pick up guys, I can go . . . I'll put my life on it, they're in here to work out in what should be a safe environment for a more aggressive natured work-out and um so yeah that . . . peacocking is definitely an issue. (Matt, Personal Communication, July 25, 2017)

However, despite the peacocking behaviors, there were other instances where men were uncomfortable in these spaces because of the presence of women. At its extreme, men simply removed themselves from the cardio gym spaces occupied by women. For example, I personally experienced this on a handful of occasions in the cardio-boxing gyms, the most prominent being when I was paired with a brand new male member to go through a circuit class that required different boxing skills on a variety of boxing equipment such as footwork drills and hitting a variety of bags at different stations (i.e., heavy bag, upper-cut bag, double-end bag, etc.). After two stations, the young man abruptly left the class and the gym entirely. I continued my workout only to receive the following text message from the class instructor when driving home, "That kid was trying to keep up with you and gassed out he said haha. That's why he left lol" (Personal Text, July 12, 2018). This was not the first or last time I was partnered with a male gym-goer, who was deterred from continuing on with the activity when he found his skill level was not the same as mine. It is a somewhat odd and presumptuous expectation to have for someone new to the sport, especially when working out alongside someone who has been doing it for a number of years. This is not something I ever experienced with another woman or felt myself when faced with boxers with greater skills than my own. Interestingly, I would argue that the opposite was true of new women members or those with little experience. At one of the cardio gyms, a new member started to approach me regularly and we chatted a lot before and after working out. Having never boxed before, she struggled with form and skill, but she was extremely enthusiastic. She often asked me which classes I would be taking in the upcoming week so she could come to the same ones. She even told me that I inspired her to get better and pushed her to work harder. I too felt the same when I had the privilege to train with more skilled female fighters. One of my first ever sparring partners was so much better at boxing than me when I first started to spar with her, I felt honored to learn from her. To further unpack it then it could be argued that gender was central to this expectation. More plainly stated, this man expected to be as good at boxing trying it his first time, as someone who had been doing it for over four years because he was a man and I was a woman.

Another more pronounced example of this was brought up by Julie, who expressed frustration at men telling her, and more frequently than you would expect, that they wanted to spar/fight her. She said,

And they'd be like oh, you know, I can take you, because you know, I'm a guy you're a girl who knows what you're doing, so let's go at it. But yea, the "we should spar sometime thing" was always very strange to me and happened to me many times. (Julie, Personal Communication, February 5, 2017)

Julie did not engage in adversarial boxing, yet she was extremely proficient at both hitting the bags and the pads. She also had an athletic build and was into physical fitness. She, however, found these comments odd and speculatively wondered whether male gym-goers who had similar physical stamina and boxing skills were subject to the same remarks.

Julie: But the sparring comment, it was always, it was always presented in a way that made it feel like they thought my gender had something to do with it, you know like they thought that, yea, they wouldn't have said anything to me at all if I were a guy, or if I were a girl who had less skill, or worked less hard, um..

Victoria: Almost a little bit like it seems, and I might be reading too much into it, by saying that to you they're saying, you know, I'd like to fight you because I know, I think I can beat you in sparring, but it will look better because you have a skill set not like some of the other women?

Julie: Right. Yea, that's pretty how it felt. I mean it felt, it was always, it was frustrating for me when they would say it for me because it was always who were there for like their first or second class . . These guys who would come in, come in excuse me, and take one or two classes and still be trying it out, it was very much, kind of like a "I could take you type of comment." It felt like, you know, you've clearly been here working hard and I'm going to show you that I can still come in, and I don't know, again I don't know if it was more of like a stroking their own ego . . . type thing . . . um but again I don't think, I've never heard one of the male members say that they have those occurrences, like I certainly never saw these guys go up to male members. (Julie, Personal Communication, February 5, 2017)

In reflecting on these interactions, Julie believed they were gendered in nature and situated in a sexism that ignored both common sense and skill differentials. She said,

Julie: Um and it was, it was a very, and it was also silly, coz at the end of the day if we had sparred, it would've . . . I worked out next to these guys too, like they were not ready to spar at all, they weren't ready to spar a girl, a guy, a dog anything, you know. It was, they, so it was more of a . . . I think they felt like it was an empowering thing for them to say about themselves but it was very demeaning to me.

Victoria: Right, right of course.

Julie: Um and it very much came across that way. Um . . . and I would know, I mean I got regular comments from new people that I looked like I knew what I was doing and that you know, I worked really hard, and that, those comments never felt like they came from a place of sexism or anything like that, um it was just these specific comments always made by prospective male members that felt very sexist. (Julie, Personal Communication, February 5, 2017)

Here, societal power differentials between men and women coupled with the dominant social construction of boxing being for men is being replicated in the gym space.

The hegemonic gender ideology still promotes that men are naturally stronger than women. Popular sports including boxing are physical in their construct and based on attributes such as strength, toughness, and speed. As argued by Agnes Elling and Annelies Knoppers (2005, 258), "The strong association of competitive (media) sports with an athletic masculinism defined as active, strong, assertive, rational, and dominant—has long been used to legitimize the exclusion of girls and women from male-defined popular sports." As a consequence, many people including prospective gym members, view boxing as a male practice where men demonstrate their bodily physical and social superiority to women. As argued by sociologists Michael Messner and Don Sabo (1990), sport allows for the identification with a particular team, athlete, or group, as well as with hegemonic norms and values. But importantly, it also allows for the distancing from those norms, values, and characteristics that are counter to their own. In this case, Julie's proficiency in the sport provides a challenge to the hegemonic understanding of male bodily superiority in the sport of boxing. This leads to a reassertion of said superiority through the issuance of a challenge, one that knowingly and ironically cannot be answered in a non-contact gym, but allows for the challenger to feel reassured that they have gained back their gender positioning, that of being superior to a woman. The sexist and somewhat threatening challenge to Julie is a hostile display of male dominance, a behavior that emerged as being far more pronounced in gyms where sparring was encouraged.

BEYOND THE CARDIO GYM

Of the women interviewed in this study, just under half of them pursued the sport beyond taking classes in a cardio-boxing gym. This meant that they took instruction at gyms that allowed contact or found other outlets whereby they could learn adversarial boxing (i.e., personal training at someone's home). As unpacked earlier, there were many women interested in furthering their boxing experience. Some engaged in personal training that involved mitt/pad work and more intensive footwork drills. Others, however, joined sparring and contact gyms or acquired a boxing coach. I, too, found an opportunity to pursue the sport beyond the cardio gym and found myself in several different spaces including sparring in a boxing instructor's back-garden on a weekly basis and then frequenting four other gyms that allowed full-contact sparring, one of which identified exclusively as a fighting gym.

Fight Gyms

The atmospheres at the gyms that allowed and promoted sparring were very different for women as compared to the cardio-boxing gym spaces. They were less welcoming and existing members (usually male) actively guarded these spaces. This experience was summarized by Kerry Anne, who wanted to better her technique and increase her boxing skills, so she solicited the instruction of a professional fighter who offered personal training. At the time of the interview, Kerry Anne was in her mid-forties, a middle-class white woman, who was married with adolescent and adult children. Despite her enthusiasm, her experience of the fighting gym was not positive as indicated by the following exchange,

Kerry Anne: [the gym] is a completely different atmosphere for me, I perceive it that way, and part of that is because I've been at [cardio gym] since the beginning and you know I'm very comfortable there, and I'd never been to a true MMA type gym before, um but when I'd go there when I was meeting another trainer there, if he wasn't there after the first minute or two, I'd just wait in the parking lot . . . um I didn't like the level of attention I attracted even if it wasn't people approaching me necessarily, but I was very noticed in a way that I'm not at [cardio gym], um . . .

Victoria: When I go, I'm the only woman. Was that the situation?

Kerry Anne: Umhm uhm [nodding] . . . and and some conversations that went on longer than they needed to, or that kind of thing . . . yea, just an out of place of feeling, it's, so some of it was being approached or engaged a little bit more than I wanted to be, and more of it more often was out of my element type . . . yea. . . ." (Kerry-Anne, Personal Communication, July 26, 2017)

As indicated in the above quote, my own experiences echoed that of Kerry Anne's. In this gym space I too experienced feelings of being uncomfortable, not being welcome, and in a few instances some more overt hostility. Some of the behaviors included being subject to increased male attention (being subject to the male gaze (Trimbur 2013)), such as unsolicited conversations, remarks, infringements on my personal space, and in one instance a quite disconcerting and aggressive flirtation. This occurred during a personal training session where the man in question not only interrupted my workout session, but would not stop his overtures resulting in my boxing coach having to tell the other man to "back off dude, she's married" (Fieldnote, July 15, 2017) while physically placing himself between me and this man. The whole experience was made more disconcerting by the presence of the man's dog, quite a large pit bull mix he had brought into the gym with him. This, however, was an isolated incident in the more than 14 months I attended the gym. But had I not been with my coach, I expect I would have felt quite unsafe.

More typical of the space was the compounding of male gym-goers' behaviors that communicated that the space was not open to all. For example, it was common in one of the fighting gyms to be heavily scrutinized when entering the space, and on several occasions when I arrived before my coach I was confronted by other gym members and asked in varying ways to assure them I belonged (i.e., that I had a reason and a right to be there). Comments like "So [you] wanna be a boxer huh?" (Fieldnote, May 17, 2017) said with amusement were typical, and on more than one occasion a male gym member took it upon himself to enter my personal space to ask "who you here for?" or "you know someone here?" (Fieldnote, August 3, 2017). This is the only gym space in which I experienced these types of confrontation and some may argue that this is evidence of concerned patrons looking to help a new member. Yet, although this happened more frequently in my first few months, it happened throughout the duration of my time at the gym. While these questions appear somewhat reasonable and benign on the surface, for full understanding such interactions should be placed in the larger context in which they occurred. From my perspective, I had arrived somewhere I had been going on a regular basis, sometimes four times a week, to walk into the space where members already occupying said space stop what they are doing and stare. One person detaches themselves from the group (a group I am not yet part of, or was ever really made part of because of my gender), walks directly up to me, often infringing on personal space boundaries, and asks some amalgamation of "what are you doing here?" This self-appointed gym guardian was always male, physically bigger and taller than me (I am five feet two, and one hundred and fifty pounds), often covered in sweat and not wearing very many clothes (typical training attire in this space that did not have air conditioning). The overall effect was me being confronted with quite an imposing person both physically and as it related to spatial boundaries. The situation would quickly resolve with my mentioning the name of my coach (a vouching process), or if he arrived during the interaction. This would then sometimes result in a fist bump, a sheepish comment such as "oh, I was just checking on ya, as you looked like you knew what you were doing," or even an introduction with a hug (whether I wanted a hug or not). However, I think it is important to re-enforce that the clear message was that without someone vouching for me in a process that legitimated my presence, I was not welcome in this space.

Gyms as gendered spaces have been written about at length (Coen et al. 2018; Johnasson 1996), with considerable studies arguing that sports as an institution provides spaces and sites where masculine hegemonies can be enforced and maintained (Bryson 1990; Cahn 1994; Hargreaves 1994; Messner 1988). Yet, these spaces are complex as they provide the site for the contesting and renegotiation of these hegemonic gender scripts, as women are not simply objects that suffer through the oppressive harm of patriarchy, rather they provide spaces for bodily empowerment and the embracing of women's physicality in the creation of new social and cultural identities. Despite this, the historical legacy of the sport remains and in the space of the fighting gym here, it is still very much a designated male space. Interestingly, in a spontaneous conversation that occurred in one of the fight gym spaces, one boxing coach spoke about how introducing women, especially women who fit a certain outward appearance—skinny, white, blonde, and pretty— had caused some tension with other coaches at this gym. In expanding his own personal training business, he had recently acquired more than a handful of new women clients primarily from one of the cardio-boxing gyms where he also taught classes. Some of the women wanted to improve their skill and technique and others wanted to give adversarial boxing a try. The introduction of these women to this space upset other coaches, as they were not "proper boxers" (Fieldnote, November 3, 2017) or were not viewed as "taking the sport seriously" (Fieldnote, November 3, 2017). They felt that this undermined the legitimacy of the training space. According to this trainer, his most vocal critic was an older African American man who trained predominantly African American and Latinx fighters including at least two black and Latina women. When pressed for why including these women was causing such offense, the coach struggled to articulate the reasoning, settling on "he is old school" as an explanation (Fieldnote, November 3, 2017). Although based somewhat on conjecture, I suspect that the presence of white, predominantly middle-class women, myself included, upset social and cultural understandings of the authenticity of the facility as well as who had the right to access the space and the sport more broadly.

Boxing as a sport has historically attracted men from working-class back-grounds, often mirroring immigration patterns as economics intersects with race and ethnicity. As noted by Wacquant (2004, 41) in discussing patterns in Chicago, boxers were predominantly "Irish, then of central European Jews [descent], Italians, and African Americans, and lately of Latinos." While the boxer of the popular imaginary is often portrayed as coming from the most disenfranchised of the lower classes, the reality is that they are working class where boxing and fighting sports more broadly provides a vehicle for socio-economic stability. As argued by Budd Schulberg, author of the 1947 novel *The Harder they Fall,* boxing can be viewed as,

> a magnifying glass of our society. It is hardly accidental that out of the poor Irish immigration of a people being brutalized by their British overlords, we have a wave of great Irish fighters . . . As the Irish moved up into the mainstream there was less economic need to use the prize ring as their way out and up. The wave of Jewish boxers followed exactly the same pattern, and so did the Italians. The almost total domination of the ring today by African-Americans and Hispanics speaks directly to the continued economic deprivation and discrimination of large sections of our inner-city communities. (as cited in Bodner 1997, xi)

Boxing has a long history of being the sport of those on the margins of society, where those who exist on the periphery can carve out a space where their identities can be contested, and power relations and inequalities can be dissected and understood. As argued by Benita Heiskanen (2012, 26–27) in her in-depth analysis of amateur boxing in Austin, Texas, "When boxers advance from the ostensible obscurity of the barrio to the centerstage of the ring for the duration of the fight, they also take control of the geography of the canvas to forge a niche of autonomy and a space for the movement for themselves." This leads to a reflexive questioning of the structural assignment of their "place" in society; that of the margins. A similar understanding of the sport was organically summarized by Matt, an amateur fighter at the gym,

> I think you know some people who many have come up, like [in] inner city New York or whatever who've always had to fight to even walk down the street, you know there was an everyday struggle that they risk the run of getting beat up every time they walk down the street. It brings out that dog in you, you know, that back against the wall feeling, pitted in a corner you know, where no one wants to be. So, I feel like the people who wanna compete and want to take it to the next level are the people that have, for whatever reason, have that dog brought out in them. Um and at some point have felt you know trapped or backed against the wall, cowered down, whatever. (Matt, Personal Communication, July 25, 2017)

Women, especially, white middle-class women, spilling over from a cardio-boxing gym, provides an intrusion or a challenge to the fighting gym space and its purpose.

Furthermore, and as written about by Trimbur (2011), this renavigation of spatial boundaries also intersects with economic interests as trainers supplement their incomes or even start small personal training businesses with the income generated from offering classes and instruction to novice boxers.

In this gym space, a younger trainer, arguably from a different generation, saw his skills and expertise as marketable to gym-goers who would not otherwise have entered that space. Trimbur (2011) notes, however, that training white-collar or recreational boxers has implications for the trainer/ client relationships that are situated in structures of race and class. Adding the economic exchange of payment leads clients to select the components of their workout. For many clients, they pick the most prominent and exciting elements of boxing such as pad-work. This was not unique to this trainer as many semi-professional and professional fighters also trained people on the side. For example, one more traditional fight gym in town[2] opened its doors as the main training facility for a charity event where fraternity and sorority members from the Flagship University volunteered to fight in amateur matches referred to here as "The Boxing Event" (please see chapter 8 for more information). The "fighters" were permitted to train at the gym in the weeks leading up to the event lending an authenticity to the tournament. The gym was described by one of the competitors in the following way. "It's just kind of this hole in the wall place with one ring, and there's like three heavy bags, and it's like little kids are even training there, but it's so like, legit…you just feel like, Muhammed Ali would have been there" (Penelope, Personal Communication, November 1, 2016). Other trainers took on novice boxers who had signed up for amateur competitions like the national *Rough N Rowdy* events or *Tough Man/Guy* competitions. However, the older coach's vehement displeasure with the younger coach for introducing novice women boxers to the space caused more upset and a heated argument that almost got physical. The implication being that women, especially women of a certain race and class, had no business being in these spaces and to permit them to do so is making a mockery of the sport and the other coaching occurring in the space. For this "old school coach," this was independent of the work ethic of the women involved, largely centered on perceptions situated in race and class, and independent of the potential financial gains to the individual trainer involved or for the gym itself; signing these women as members.

Before examining adversarial boxing and sparring in greater detail, my conversations and informal chats in gym spaces revealed a rather novel happening, that of an "all women's fight club" that, at the time of writing, had organized Fight Nights. The unearthing of this club indirectly provided the catalyst for my advancement in the sport and serves as an interesting place for further analysis as it was revealed to be a women's only space. Having mentioned it to one of the trainers at one of the cardio-boxing gyms, I was strongly discouraged from attending due to the potential for injury. He then offered to teach me to spar personally in lieu of me attending the fight club. I was, however, able to track down the organizers of the club to garner some clarity on its emergence and its purpose. The following chapter departs from the central goals of the book to delve into the less commodified world of women's Fight Night. Although not boxing by any traditional definition, it did involve many of the participants in this project who were seeking out a way to try adversarial boxing.

NOTES

1. I did not have access to the data from the survey, rather the results were summed up in conversations with staff and trainers.

2. Not a gym explicitly included as a space in this study, but one that came up in interviews and discussions in gym spaces.

Chapter 5

There Are Only Three Rules of Fight Club, "No Spectators, No Social Media, and No Boob Shots!"

INTRODUCTION

As noted in chapter 4, the cardio-boxing gyms did not venture past sociologist Steve Hoffmans' (2006) first two stages of boxing (the air phase and the leather phase). The only exception being the special training programs that were offered at additional cost advertised to get people "ring ready." As expected, participation in these programs were resource driven and as a direct result they were offered irregularly with low enrollments. Despite this, many of the women included in this study expressed a desire to test their boxing skills and sought opportunities outside of the cardio gym spaces to do so. While the traditional routes of seeking out private lessons or a fight/contact gym appealed to some of the women, evidence emerged of a less traditional option; that of a women's fight club. Although this revelation might be discarded by some as not constituting "real" boxing, it did provide an opportunity for exploration beyond the traditional ethnographic focus of the boxing gym and as an exploration of a pre-commodified more authentic expression of fighting sports. The purpose of this chapter is to provide an exploratory overview of the unsanctioned women's fight club. Drawing on the concepts of emphasized femininity (Connell 1987), alternative femininities (Schippers 2007), gender maneuvering (Schippers 2002), edgework (Lyng 2005), and precorporation (Fisher 2009), this chapter examines the women's motivations for carving out a space that empowers and supports, as well as resists hegemonic gender structures.

WOMEN'S FIGHT CLUB

Rumors of a clandestine all women's fight club emerged early on in this research. There were whispers of it in the cardio-boxing gyms and several women reported having attended the group. The following conversation with Angelina, a member at one of the cardio gyms, is typical of how women were introduced to this event.

Victoria: How did the whole fight club thing come about?
Angelina: Yeah it was weird, ugh so you know Maggie?
Victoria: Yes.
Angelina: It was her. She had a friend. She knows like everyone in this whole town somehow . . . um and it was an acquaintance of hers who basically was like I'll put you on the list to get this text message, where [it is] going to tell you where to show up. (Angelina, Personal Communication, February 16, 2017)

The women's fight club was a closed group where people were invited through friends and acquaintances. The organizers of the event confirmed that "It's our friends, we don't do social media, so its' mostly been just like mass text" (Sasha, Personal Communication, July 26, 2017).

Having been invited, the evening followed a general format.

Sasha: Yea, so uh the basic structure for our Fight Nights. We have headgear, mouth guards, gloves . . . They're MMA sparring gloves so they have like the big pad on the knuckles, and so it's not like they're really hard boxing gloves. So, we do 30 second fights, there's no winners, no losers. Random draws, 30 second fights, no social media . . . no pulling hair, no boob shots. (Sasha, Personal Communication, July 26, 2017)

In an interesting mimicking of the Chuck Palahniuk (1996) book and later Hollywood movie *Fight Club* (Linson et al. 1999), there were rules that participants had to abide by. In the book, there were infamously eight rules of fight club,

Welcome to Fight Club. The first rule of Fight Club is: you do not talk about Fight Club. The second rule of Fight Club is: you DO NOT talk about Fight Club! Third rule of Fight Club: if someone yells "stop!" goes limp, or taps out, the fight is over. Fourth rule: only two guys to a fight. Fifth rule: one fight at a time, fellas. Sixth rule: the fights are bare knuckle. No shirt, no shoes, no weapons. Seventh rule: fights will go on as long as they have to. And the eighth and final rule: if this is your first time at Fight Club, you have to fight. (Palahniuk 1996)

The women's fight club had three rules; "Yea, our three rules for Fight Night were, um if you come you have to fight because we didn't want it to be spectator sport . . . Yea, like yea um no social media . . . Yea, and then no boob shots" (Bailey, Personal Communication, July 26, 2017). The mirroring of the movie coupled with the secrecy created an element of excitement and attraction. This was something that was capitalized on by the organizers to create an atmosphere, describing it as "a sacred event" (Sasha, Personal Communication, July 26, 2017) where they played loud music such as "ACDC, DMX, and a bunch of others, rowdy music" (Sasha, Personal Communication, July 26, 2017). They even had a "fog machine and a stack of TVs all doing white noise" at one of the events (Sasha, Personal Communication, July 26, 2017), and Christmas lights at others (Bailey, Personal Communication, July 26, 2017). Furthermore, the venue for the event changed each time. "It's been in a bunch of basements, some attics, some yards. Um but never the same location two times in a row" (Sasha, Personal Communication, July 26, 2017). When asked about the changing location Sasha said, "it's part of the charm to be at some random house you've never been to and you go into like the basement" (Sasha, Personal Communication, July 26, 2017).

In further conversations, it was unearthed that although the book-turned movie provided the inspiration for the rules and perhaps the desired ambiance, this came via a documentary that aired on HBO titled *Hidden in America: Underground Fight Clubs* (Yu 2012), Bailey said,

When I was pregnant with my daughter, who is now four and a half, um I was doing my Masters' research, I was doing all my classes and I ended up taking my final exam for my Master's thesis like a week after she was born. So it was just like a lot of stuff happening, right, and then I found myself just like home with her, and I had nothing going on, just being a Mom, and in that kind of time in my life I didn't really enjoy that infant stage, you know, and so I would be up at 3am like nursing her, and I would watch TV or whatever, and I saw this HBO documentary on. Um, it's like a nerd fight night, you know, and it was these guys from Silicon Valley and stuff and they would, they have this Fight Night, and theirs was like really intense. It was like, they were like hitting each other with keyboards and like chains, and like weapons . . . but it was people that would never, suspect would do that, just by their vocation, and so I was just like we gotta do this. So I think we went out one night, and I was like talking, talking her ear off about it, and she was "I don't know" and then I think we went out again, or I talked to somebody else about it, and I was like we've got to do this man this is going to be so much fun. I have like this aggression I need to get out in like a healthy way. (Bailey, Personal Communication, July 26, 2017)

Commenting on the influence of the Hollywood movie *Fight Club* (Linson et al. 1999) had on underground fight clubs in the United States, sociologist Michael Kimmel said,

> I think it was meant as a critique of the culture in which these guys were living. You know, you live in a box, you work in a box, you go to work in a box, you come home to a box, you eat out of a box, you watch a box, it's like your life is completely circumscribed, your life is completely inauthentic. (Kimmel as cited in Yu 2012, 6:00)

The documentary's evidenced success of normal or everyday people engaging in aggression in this way legitimated the possibility of this working for Bailey. This intersected with a time in her life where she was experiencing some significant life changes.

Here, Bailey is struggling with accepting the heteronormative gender script she has been dealt that provides she relinquish aspects of her personal identity and career aspirations to be a full-time mother. Within the context of our larger gender system this is broadly normalized with little consideration for the impact this sacrifice can have on some women. She later said in a conversation with Sasha,

Sasha: Yea, there's like, I remember when you wanted to do this, you were talking about the aggression that you had, you were like, I'm not mad at my baby, I'm mad at my husband. You know you were like, "I don't have aggression towards my child, it's like aggression towards a partner," that you need to really . . .

Bailey: And towards a feeling of like a loss of my life . . . like of my career life which was very important to me in that I just spent two years of my life busting out a Master's degree only to have it like stop and now like nobody would talk to me about anything except for how my baby was doing and constantly asking me like "how are you?" And you can't just be like "I'm feeling really horrible today" you know? (Sasha and Bailey, Personal Communication, July 26, 2017)

Operating from a position of subordination within the larger gender system, Bailey challenges traditional constructs of femininity by initiating nonconventional behavior; organizing a fight club.

The involvement of women in nonconventional activities has been written about extensively as it relates to art, music, sport, and gangs (Holland 2004; Klein 1997; Messerschmidt 2002; Mullaney 2007; Wilkins 2004). Much of this literature has found that women retain aspects of femininity while they engage alternative/subversive femininities that exist within different subcultures. As noted by Connell (1987, 187), the term "emphasized femininity" is more appropriate to more accurately describe femininity that received the most cultural support and is therefore legitimated by society. This is heteronormative femininity that complements and accommodates the interests of men and emphasizes characteristics such as motherhood, sexual receptivity, fragility, passivity, vulnerability, and acceptance of marriage. Bailey's idea to form a "fight club," is rooted in her situational frustration and feelings of having to subscribe to emphasized femininity. It is a vehicle for the rejection of the expectations and characteristics that are instrumental to emphasized femininity as well as the power differential that accompanies them. This is supported by her own justification and motivation for forming the fight club but also through the ousting of men from the fight club space.

MEN ARE NOT ALLOWED!: MAINTAINING A "WOMEN'S ONLY SPACE"

The involvement of men in the women's fight club did not exist beyond the acquisition of safety gear such as the MMA gloves, head gear, and mouth guards. There was also mention of men associated with the women who frequented the Fight Night events giving unsolicited instruction on how to throw a punch, but even that was rejected. In recounting this experience, the women expressed amusement openly laughing at the men's efforts. When asked why this was funny, the general feeling was that it was patronizing and not relevant to the women's reasons for being engaged with the fight club. "It was like I wasn't willing to invest the time into punching someone properly, I just figured out what worked in like the moment, so when it got to Fight Night I totally forgot what they said" (Bailey, Personal Communication, July 26, 2017). Again, the women are rejecting emphasized femininity that complements hegemonic masculinity; they are dismissing and confronting these expectations, and creating what gender scholar Mimi Schippers (2007) might term "alternative" femininities. Schippers argues that through a process of face-to-face negotiations, the traditional power relations between hegemonic masculinities and femininities become something different; male dominance is disrupted as such negotiations "do not articulate a complementary relation of dominance and subordination between women and men" (Schippers 2007, 98). If successful, these forms of alternative femininities are resistive, something that was reinforced by the rules of fight club.

The exclusion of men from the Fight Night space was one of the rules that was rigidly adhered to despite Bailey declaring "they always want to come" (Bailey, Personal Communication, July 26, 2017). This rule was cemented early on in the development of the group following a singular event where they allowed two men to fight.

Sasha: There's one time when we let two dudes fight. It was after we were all done. We had all of our extra curricula fight stuff. I think it was one of the first two [Fight Night events]. And so, one of the guys that lived in the house asked to come down . . . and they fought, and we like ended it immediately . . .

Bailey: Ah man . . .

Sasha: because the energy was so . . .

Bailey: It was . . . different . . .

Sasha: intense, it was awful. I was like I hate watching this.

Victoria: They take it very seriously, their masculinity. . . .

Bailey: I mean we take it seriously, but they were. . . .

Sasha: Well half and half.

Bailey: Well yea, half and half . . . I take it seriously because I really like, try to get better, but whatever . . . and like you know, but the guys were like, they got . . .

Sasha: Brutal . . .

Bailey: yea, too brutal.

Sasha: And being watched by a group of women too so that didn't help with their . . .

Victoria: Strange dynamic?

Sasha: Yea, so that's never happening again, never opening it out. We were just being courteous as they lived in the house, but we lost that courtesy, we don't care, you can't do it. (Bailey and Sasha, Personal Communication, July 26, 2017)

The men violated the spirit of the event and twisted it into something brutal. Despite the physicality required to participate, the increased aggression and intensity of their engagement violated the implied boundaries of the event. The violence displayed by these men was a hypermasculine display, perhaps another form of peacocking (see chapter 4 for further discussion) meant to show dominance to an all-female audience and reassert the power differential associated with hegemonic masculinity and emphasized femininity. Recognizing this, the women were quick to stop the interaction and reject not only the behavior but men more broadly, resisting the imposition of the hegemonic gender hierarchy that accompanied this interaction. As Schippers (2002) has argued in an analysis of subcultures for alternative rock music, the women engaged in a face-to-face interaction that disrupted the localized heteronormative gender patterning, challenging and restructuring the acceptability of gender relations within their group; they engaged in purposeful gender maneuvering to create an alternative femininity.

Interestingly, when gender maneuvering is successful, the construction of an alternative femininity can be viewed as a form of successful resistance as it is purposeful in its disruption of heteronormative gender relations within the localized space. However, when it is not purposeful and/or unsuccessful, it creates what has been termed "pariah femininities" (Schippers 2002). These femininities are those that do not fit within the accepted characteristics of emphasized femininity. They are not lesser forms of femininity, just less accepted because of their masculine content. When women embody traits such as aggression, defiance, authority, or physical violence, they are not accepted unless they can be discarded or dismissed through a process of stigmatization or feminized. These femininities "constitute a refusal to complement hegemonic masculinity in a relation of subordination and therefore are threatening to male dominance" (Schippers 2007, 95). In this case, the exclusion of men from these spaces entirely coupled with the reasons offered for this decision supports the framing of women's Fight Night as being situated in resisting the heteronormative gender structure opposed to a stigmatized violation.

There were several further justifications for the exclusion of men including, but not limited to, creating a space to empower women, camaraderie and bonding, and the advancement of the argument that learning what it felt like to hit someone and be hit was a necessity especially as it related to women's safety. Women who attended the group as well as the organizers spoke about empowerment; "it makes you feel so good and so confident" (Margo, Personal Communication, March 17, 2017), and "we felt a million bucks the next day, and people would text us [to] talk about how much fun they had" (Sasha, Personal Communication, July 26, 2017). It was also expressed that like with traditional boxing spaces, women who participated were inspirational to others making the activity more accessible. Bailey said, "I think seeing other people in the Fight Night do different things and like oh I can do that too, or you know or something like that" (Bailey, Personal Communication, July 26, 2017). Here, by controlling the resources, access to the space, as well as the networks that supported them, the women have created a site for hegemonic gender resistance.

Contrary to the rest of the chapters in this book, the fight club does not represent traditional sport or boxing as we know it (i.e., as it has not been corporatized and commodified). Instead, it represents fighting in its most raw form, a space distinct and separate from the other options available to women wanting to pursue combat sports. However, in a world where our fantasies and desires are manufactured through the ever-present, sustained bombardment of advertisements, it could be that the formation of this group is not as truly separate and distinct from the big box gyms and the commodification of the sport as it first appears. Rather, it may merely represent a fad, one that has been shaped by the influence of capital on the larger culture, whereby these women seek out a seemingly authentic cathartic experience limited by the parameters of capitalist culture, what Mark Fisher (2009) would term precorporation. More plainly stated, women's fight club might not be quite as unique as it feels to its participants. Framing it as being outside or counter to "mainstream" or as an "alternative" pastime or space for women engaging fighting sports does not designate it as such. Rather, it too represents a scripted or preformed understanding of what "alternative" is, and, therefore, it is reduced to merely a style of expression within the larger capitalist mainstream society (Fisher 2009). This argument is strengthened by the fact that women's fight club has its roots in popular culture as in its original form it is reminiscent of endeavors associated with men's pastimes and heightened masculinity (i.e., bare-knuckle fighting and underground cage fighting). Yet, this does not negate the importance of the club to the women involved, nor as a site for sociological inquiry as to gender and alternative femininities. For example, rather than directly emulate and covet the aggressive and uncontrolled physicality associated with such histories, much like the roller derby of Finley's (2010) analysis, the rules of the group including the nature of the interactions, were negotiated by the women themselves. But it brings to the fore the question of whether the fight club is representative of the emergence of an alternative femininity that challenges the heteronormative status quo, or merely is another example of the feminization of yet another male pastime, one that is precorporated?

WOMEN EMPOWERING WOMEN: GENDER MANEUVERING THROUGH PHYSICAL FEMINISM

Although men were excluded from the fight club spaces, the women involved practiced inclusivity as it related to the women who attended. For example, it was open to women over the age of 21 and accommodated those with medical issues including old injuries and conditions such as multiple sclerosis. An example of an accommodation was demonstrated when 65-year-old Mila wanted to participate. "Mila said she had a bad shoulder and so it was like oh, well who wants to do a like one arm fight, and so whoever volunteered they did just like one hand behind their back and she did it like that too" (Bailey, Personal Communication, July 26, 2017). Emphasis was placed on prior knowledge of health conditions or difficulties and the participant voicing these concerns. This fostered an environment of inclusivity that was generally associated with the wish to nurture camaraderie and in-group empowerment.

When asked to describe the events, one of the women used the words, "catharsis and camaraderie" (Margo, Personal Communication, March 17, 2017), as well as "getting some shit off your chest" (Sasha, Personal Communication, July 26, 2017). The catharsis came in the form of the fights themselves as they evoked and allowed for the expression of a range of emotions, some of which are not traditionally associated with emphasized femininity. This included anger, sadness, aggression, frustration, and even gleefulness. Yet, when the fight was over there was a general understanding that these feelings have been expelled through the physical, something that was heralded as being productive. The embodiment of emotions that women are not traditionally allowed to express through aggressive physicality also led to an openness of expression in verbal exchanges that followed the fights.

Important to the organizers were the conversations and bonding that occurred after the events. At the end of the evening the women often had in-depth and meaningful discussions. Sasha reported,

> Yea, I mean the release you can get and great conversation afterwards. So like it wasn't bar talk, it wasn't small talk, it was you got right to the meat of stuff pretty quickly after you just punched someone in the face, you could talk about stuff, and you were way more open in the way that you reveal things that [you] usually didn't tell a total stranger. (Sasha, Personal Communication, July 26, 2017)

The intimacy of the discussions was related to the closeness of engaging physically with another person. The physical connection was presented as a precursor to securing deeper emotional connections. Possible explanations for this could be related to the emotional geography of the women's only space promoted and created during Fight Night. As noted by Joyce Davidson, Liz Bondi, and Mick Smith (2005, 3), emotional geography is an "attempt to understand emotion – experientially and conceptually – in terms of its socio-*spatial* mediation and articulation rather than as entirely interiorized subjective mental states." Cathy Van Ingen (2009) argues that emotional geographies allow for the exploration of in-depth and rich emotional experiences through and in particular spaces. These experiences can be both situational and partial and it is the body that becomes the site for the feeling of said emotions. Experiencing emotion as a process is dependent on the social interaction in which the person is located (Denzin 2009). During Fight Night, emotion is an embodied experience that is both expressed through the physical then again through verbal discussions and connection.

Topics of conversation included feminism, what it means to be a woman, aggression, and women's safety. Aggression and its expression were considered as it related to its validity; " I mean violence and aggression is just as valid as laughter and crying, and it's something that is a biologically wired in our bodies, and it needs release" (Sasha, Personal Communication, July 26, 2017). The fight club space was thought to provide a healthy place to expel this aggression. However, this was not a shared experience across those who attended.

Angelina, while seeking out the experience to primarily test out the skills she learned at the cardio gym, reported Fight Night to be disorganized and potentially unsafe. During our conversation about the event, she became very animated at the injustice of being hit on the top of the head in what she perceived as an inappropriate matchup.

Angelina: Because it was like, it was the first person I ever hit, and I was like I don't want to hit you like at all. Um, but then I fought someone who was about 5'10 and she just punch me right in the top of the head. Like . . .
Victoria: Illegally, so it's not like boxing rules either?
Angelina: No, so it's like well there's no kicking . . . And boxing type anything . . . you're not even supposed to even like [hit] each other in the face. It's like the rules are such to minimize basically someone accidentally hurting someone else, I think. Because I don't know what they're doing, because most the people there don't know what they're doing. Um, but it's just like everybody gets caught up in a whirlwind, because they don't know what they're doing. (Angelina, Personal Communication, February 16, 2017)

From her perspective, the lack of rules, properly informed supervision from an experienced boxing coach, and overall chaotic nature of the event were problematic. Of heightened concern was the way the matches were made, namely, a drawing process.

Angelina: So basically, you put, you drew a number . . . And your matching number, there's two of each . . . was who you are going to fight. Um, it was like . . .
Victoria: So, it wasn't based on weight class or anything?
Angelina: No, and that was the part that I, it was the only part that I disliked because I did it three times and once I actually fought Maggie [her good friend], so that was weird. (Angelina, Personal Communication, February 16, 2017)

Angelina's concern for fairness and safety were situated in her experience in the cardio-boxing gym and her knowledge of the sport. The organizers acknowledged they had no experience in boxing or fighting sports more generally, which Angelina felt contributed to a feeling of chaos and disorganization. Despite this, however, the organizers stressed that they were careful to ensure that no one got hurt. Specifically, they argued that they monitored the space itself to guard against accidents (i.e., someone crashing into a wall or a sharp corner) and shut down the fights if they felt they were getting out of hand. For example,

Sasha: There's one girl, let's just call her alien, and she . . . came up and I asked her if she has ever fought before and she said no, and we get her in the ring, and pair her with another girl who actually did have some fighting experience. But the alien . . .

Bailey: She said she didn't.

Sasha: She said that she didn't but once she got in the ring it was obvious that she did, afterwards we talked to her coz she was yoga, she had a lot of yoga background, so she was just pure muscle but also, didn't disclose she'd been watching boxing for the past 15 years of her life religiously, and I don't think she trained professionally but I think that she'd been practicing and so she like took one punch . . .

Bailey: And there was a general consensus that nobody wanted to fight her.

Sasha: Yea, I mean she just went really hard and like and put someone's like [Sasha made a knocking noise].

Bailey: It was crazy.

Sasha: Yea.

Bailey: It was probably the most intense I think it ever got.

Sasha: Yea.

Bailey: And we were just like . . .

Sasha: And we stopped it.

Bailey: Immediately. (Bailey and Sasha, Personal Communication, July 26, 2017)

The organizers seemed to be very conscientious about safety and the potential for someone getting hurt. In addition, and despite her concerns, Angelina participated three times in Fight Night and said she would have returned had she heard about another event. So, seemingly the fight club was tapping into something that many women felt was missing from their overall boxing experience or served a purpose more generally.

It was also suggested by the fight club organizers that it behooves women to experience the physical expression of these emotions in the safe space of fight club opposed to learning about aggression and violence in real life. As summarized by Sasha, commenting on a post-fight discussion, "we talked about women throwing their first punch of their life at someone and feeling way more equipped to maybe possibly defend themselves if there was some, if someone approached them on the street" (Sasha, Personal Communication, July 26, 2017). The underlying theme of women's safety, especially as it relates to the threat of men's violence against women, is demonstrated in Bailey's comment; "There's definitely an intimidation factor when it comes to that kind of stuff, and my response is always would you rather be prepared, or more prepared than unprepared to fight for your life in a situation" (Bailey, Personal Communication, July 26, 2017). The women felt empowered and more able to protect themselves if they were attacked. For example, Margo said "Walking on the street at night knowing that, especially that night, or the next day when you're walking by yourself knowing that no one can touch me" (Margo, Personal Communication, March 17, 2017).

The pervasiveness of potential violence included the threat of street harassment from strangers. For example, Sasha felt that,

> I feel like a lot of predators prey on those weaknesses. I feel this with men as well, a lot of gay men, we talk about fighting a lot too, and like going into an urinal and having the confidence, not having to fake it you know, just to . . . I think 60 percent is confidence, maybe even more. Like having that confidence will prevent you from harm, there are some people who are crazy and then some people where you are just being targeted, but if it's just a random thing and you're walking on the street and you're feeling yourself, it's less likely than someone whose on their phone. I don't know they can just smell it, it's like a literal sense to fear, it is one thing that you can conquer. (Sasha, Personal Communication, July 26, 2017)

In a similar way to the women who engaged cardio-boxing (i.e., hitting a heavy bag), empowerment manifesting as physical confidence was viewed as a vehicle for the subversion of the heteronormative scripts assigned women (i.e., as passive, weak, and dependent). Interestingly, Sasha summarized this very point

> Women are trained not to know their power and they're taught that someone else will fight for them. And I mean, and we have had a lot of awful things happen to our girlfriends throughout the last 15 years. So, it's like no one's going to protect you and you might not be able to protect yourself but give yourself a chance. (Sasha, Personal Communication, July 26, 2017)

In reality, violence against women is one of the most pervasive human rights abuses across the globe (United Nations Population Fund 2014) and has been termed an epidemic in the United States (National Organization for Women 2020). It includes a range of behaviors such as domestic violence, street harassment, stalking, femicide, and sexual assault that impact women from all walks of life. It is, therefore, unsurprising that stories and experiences of victimization shape women's motivations to better equip themselves with fighting skills. This perspective suggests a pragmatic realism where the participants feel that practicing physical engagement during Fight Night, experiencing being hit and hitting others, serves to normalize and ready women for the eventuality of a real-life attack. As Sasha argues,

> It's like, now you've thrown that first punch, now you've actually had to defend yourself, someone's hit you and you've hit them back, like it'll always be you know, unwelcome and absurd if it happens, but at least it won't be your first time if you ever have to fight back. Like if you've fought. (Sasha, Personal Communication, July 26, 2017)

The idea that for women to better deal with the threat of men's violence, they need to be more versed in violence themselves undergirds this justification for fight club. This highlights a popular feminist critique of formal self-defense programs that are targeted at women victims of gender-based violence. Namely, it has been argued that philosophically, violence as the solution to violence is unacceptable. As argued by Russell, McCarroll, and Bohan (2007, 5), "Women need to be safe from violence without having to learn self-defense, and we must develop better means of conflict resolution than physical violence." Yet, this critique makes no differentiation between aggressive and defensive violence operating on the assumption that all violence is equally wrong. Furthermore, this criticism is bolstered by claims that argue educating women in defensive tactics does nothing to curtail the violence committed by men against women (Russell et al., 2007). However, scholars who argue the benefits of self-defense, to my knowledge, have never made such claims about its applicability (see Hollander 2007; McCaughey 1997). This stance also neglects the feelings of confidence, self-assuredness, and empowerment that the women who have experienced Fight Night claim to achieve. In much the same way the participants felt empowered from taking cardio-boxing classes, participating in Fight Night interrupted dominant discourses about gender embodiment where previously socially prescribed behaviors, those learned through bodily enactment, can be unlearned and others learned (i.e., acquiring the skill of being able to properly throw a punch and not freezing or being shocked if you are punched).

I do want to note however, that there are significant differences between cardio-boxing and Fight Night. As explored in chapters 2 and 4, cardio-boxing mimics the boxers' workout and two of Hoffman's (2006) three stages of training necessary to get to the adversarial stage of the ring. It is a regimen of endurance and skill building that capitalizes on the bodily discipline necessary to acquire and retain a boxers' physique and athleticism. This is contrary to the experience of fight club where there is no precursor to involvement beyond showing up. It does not require or mimic the regimen of the training process, the learning of skills, discipline, or achievement required of a boxer. In fact, the creators were not shy about their lack of professional training or experience with fighting sports. Therefore, fight club and their Fight Nights are firmly situated outside of the sport of boxing and can be more readily likened to unsanctioned underground fight clubs.

In the documentary *Hidden in America: Underground Fight Clubs* (Yu 2013, 2:10), the rationale offered for the engagement in such ventures is offered that "Some believe that modern society has stifled our urge to test ourselves with our fists," a drive they suggest is located in a primal need for violence. As Michael Kimmel argues in the film, "You want to go out into the woods, and you want to tear some, some animal you know and eat their

meat raw or something, you know you want to do something that feels real"
(Yu 2013, 6:15). Similar sentiments were offered here as an explanation.
For example, in speaking about how fighting in fight club made her feel,
Sasha said "It kind of makes you feel like a badass if someone says that to
you, I just feel like it's a so much more dynamic thing" (Sasha, Personal
Communication, July 26, 2017). However, much of the albeit limited
scholarly work on fight clubs as a sociological phenomenon look to the crisis
of masculinity in the United States as a motivating factor if not *the* catalyst
for their emergence (Faludi 1999; Friday 2003).

It is argued that white middle-class men, having experienced a continued
loss of prosperity since the 1950s (Faludi 1999) that promotes a narrative
of emasculation and victimization (Friday 2003), look for alternative ways
to reframe their identity. These men, unable to reproduce the hegemonic
masculine roles promoted by the generations that preceded them, are left
anxious and waiting for confirmation of manhood; one that is no longer
attainable. As argued by Kimmel (in Yu 2013, 28:46)

> There are many, many cultures that require some kind of rite of passage where a
> young man is tested. He has to prove himself. In virtually all cultures, its older
> men who design the ritual, figure it out, plan it, execute it, and are there on the
> other side to say "yes son, you've made it, you are now a man, you're a member
> of this culture".

Sociopolitical and historical change has negated the normativity of white
middle-class masculinity, and it has become a simulacrum (Hartt 2014). This
paradox plays out in the film *Fight Club* (Linson et al. 1999) in an irreconcil-
able way through the juxtaposition of the two characters: the narrator and the
character Tyler Durden. The narrator represents the contemporary man, one
divorced from traditional ideals of masculinity—what Brian Hartt (2014, 2)
refers to as the "not man." However, Tyler represents the traditional man of the
past. Both characterizations represent each side of the paradox and are equally
unachievable; they represent the fractured identity of the whiteman's political
self. Looking for an authentic experience that leads to self-transformation,
they seek out the experience of fight club. As summarized by Kimmel (2012),

> Here's what's really interesting about fight clubs, the idea that you feel some-
> thing that's real, that's authentic, that's immediate, that's visceral, you don't ever
> get that in our culture anymore, you don't feel anything. Our society provides us
> so few opportunities for anything that really feels meaningful. (Yu 2012, 43:36)

Seeking out authenticity and meaningful interactions was also evident in the
section of women's Fight Night referred to as "extracurriculars."

EXTRACURRICULARS

There was a section of the evening reserved for fights that did not follow the previously established format. These fights happened at the end of the evening when the randomly drawn matchups had finished. In addition to accommodating special requests, like the aforementioned one-armed fight, this allowed for participants to consensually engage in fights that were not so controlled, permitting behaviors outside of the previously agreed upon parameters such as kicking. These matchups were optional and normally occurred between friends and were entered into in the name of fun. However, it must be noted that the risk of injury increased during this time because of the lessening of restrictions. As noted by Bailey, "I mean like I think with the blackeye that we got while goofing around, has been like the worse that's happened" (Bailey, Personal Communication, July 26, 2017) and this occurred during an extracurricular fight.

The existence of the "extracurriculars" section of Fight Night seemed to have a twofold purpose; first, it promoted inclusivity for those who could not otherwise participate; and second, it provided space for those who wanted to further push their experience beyond the bounds of normality. The women have formed this group to engage in risk-taking behavior, albeit with protective parameters and very little real chance of being injured, as a means to provide refuge from the formal institutions (i.e., work and family) that they felt did not fulfill their needs (Lyng 2005). This is in line with the commentary made in the movie *Fight Club* and with Kimmel's aforementioned analysis of underground fight clubs in the United States. Therefore, although at the surface level women's engagement in these risky behaviors may garner shock and be characterized as alarming, they have not really created something new. Rather, influenced by the larger capitalist culture, they have coopted an existing idea that has been propagated in the popular imaginary, something that could be characterized as a permissible form of rebellion as it does nothing to change the status quo (Fisher 2009). Therefore, benefits of engagement in Fight Night are at the interactional level, whereby the women themselves benefit from group cohesion and the excitement of engaging in risky behaviors.

The seeking out of high-risk behaviors as a form of escapism has been examined by scholars of edgework (Hamm 2005; Lois 2001; Lyng 2005; O'Malley and Mugford 1994). Edgework is a conceptual framework offered to theorize risk-taking behaviors. Sociologist Stephen Lyng (1990) in his seminal article argues that people engaged in risky activities do so as it allows for an exploration of the boundaries between order and chaos, resulting in social and psychological benefits. There is a considerable scholarly literature on the influence of edgework on voluntary risk behaviors that include high-risk sport or adventure leisure activities (Laurendeau 2006; Laurendeau and Gibbs Van Brunschot 2006; Miller and Frey 1996). In its original formulation, Lyng (1990) argued that the edgework was a form of escapism in which the confines of modernity were rejected and resisted. Engaging in risk activities is a way for people to access their true selves, or what social theorist George Herbert Mead (1934) would term the "me," in an era where the alienation of paid labor makes this more difficult (Lyng 1990). In more recent theorizations, Lyng (2005) has argued that edgework can also be understood as a vehicle for skill development as it relates to the greater need to function and perform in a postindustrial society that is characterized by institutional environments that are increasingly specialized and risk-conscious. People are therefore "pushed and pulled to edgework practices by opposing institutional imperatives" (Lyng 2005, 10).

Through the lens of edgework, the participation in women's fight club is about an escape from their everyday lives. As argued by sociologists Lori Holyfield and Gary Alan Fine (1997) citing fellow sociologist Ralph Turner (1976, 358), "Today, adventure discourse surrounds the self. The undiscovered 'real' self'." For these women, the voluntary risk-taking and adventure of fight club exists outside the approved societal bounds of heteronormative gender, resists institutional dictates to which they are subject, and rejects the more formal engagement of fighting in a designated commercial space, one that is still predominantly masculine, that is, that of a gym. However, it must be noted that while the authentic realism of fight clubs may be about the revelation of self, prior analyses of similar groups then narrows the focus to masculinity and its crisis as *the* explanation for the formation and participation in such groups. As a holistic explanation, this ignores the complexities of gender and neglects to decenter the analysis. This is in line with a central and repeated criticisms of edgework (Miller and Lyng 1991; Chan and Rigakos 2002; Donnelly 2004; Walklate 1997), namely, that there is little research that extends beyond the "unique experience of White, middle-class, adult males, whose edgework activities have been studied most extensively" (Laurendeau 2008, 11).

For women, there exists a conflict, yet this conflict is not paradoxical in the same way that is so oft discussed in analyses of men's fight clubs including its fictional representation in the movie *Fight Club*. It is not about a crisis of masculinity in late modernity. Rather, the traditional gender roles associated with the feminine, or Schippers' (2007) emphasized femininity, provides one of the catalysts for the formation and participation in the fight club. The women here are resisting the normative heteronormative gender script that demands they be nurturing, passive, weak, and protected. Motherhood, its expectations, sacrifices, and demands, provided the motivation for seeking out the physical release provided by Fight Night. Furthermore, motherhood has become part of the larger gender order whereby work performed by women is devalued (Duffy 2007). Women get paid considerably less than men for equal work (Mandel and Semyonov 2006), perform the majority of domestic work, the second shift (Collins 2015), and are repeatedly prevented from holding positions of power, what has been termed "the glass ceiling" (Masser and Abrams 2004). This is contrary to men's experiences as they are not subject to the same repeated and institutionalized devaluation.

Interestingly, when familial/domestic duties and responsibilities have been discussed as it relates to men's fight clubs, they were done so as it related to "aging out" of risk behaviors because of an adverse effect on their engagement. For example, one man interviewed in *Hidden in America: Underground Fight Clubs* (Yu 2013) argued he was closing down his fight club due to his increasing age and his shift in focus to his wife and children. However, in women's fight club, the burdens and shifts to increased domestication were a major catalyst for the formation of the group. As Sasha argues "There was also a pattern that emerged, where new mothers were the most ferocious" (Sasha, Personal Communication, July 26, 2017). The crisis here is not that the social no longer matches the rite of passage to womanhood, as is the case with men's fight clubs, rather it is that the social *does* promote these narrow and restrictive understandings of what it means to be a woman.

Sports sociologist Peter Donnelly (2004) addresses some of the criticisms of edgework by going beyond explanations for voluntary risk-taking that are grounded in relationships to labor and instead takes a constructivist approach. This explanation argues that the motivation is about finding a broader sense of self, a more general identity. Through the engagement with certain behaviors and groups, there are emotional and material rewards that result (Laurendeau 2008, 47) including the valuing of "character, a shared identity, and comradeship." Women therefore, sought out an alternative to "the 'other,'" something "to be resorted to by those seeking to escape from, to resist, or to transcend mundane, modern rationality" (O'Malley and Mugford 1994, 198). The "extracurriculars" portion of Fight Night provided an opportunity for women to further push their boundaries by testing their mental and physical limits (Lyng 2005). As argued by sociologist Jennifer Lois (2005), this allows for a narrowing of focus where extra information is blocked out providing a spontaneous cognitive experience. One example of this spontaneity and testing of boundaries manifested following a political discussion at a Fight Night event that was held close to the then approaching 2016 political election. Having consumed alcohol throughout the evening, and completed the randomized matchups portion of the night, it emerged there was a Trump supporter in the crowd. In retelling this story Sasha and Bailey acknowledged this was unusual, but it provided the catalyst for the following to transpire.

Sasha: So, we did a Democrat versus Republican fight . . . in the nude.
Bailey: We had to bare it all. The idea was . . . no clothes on.
Victoria: So, no clothes on, just . . .?
Sasha: No clothes on . . . that was hilarious.
Bailey: Not my proudest moment.
Sasha: Well, the Democrats won (Bailey and Sasha, Personal Communication,
   July 26, 2017)

Seemingly, the participants here felt freed from all social constraints where the situation "filter[ed] out much of the reflexive, social aspect of the self" (Lois 2005, 121). The authentic self, as perceived by the participants of fight club, was multidimensional and not exclusive to gender constraints and structures. This was further highlighted by the understanding that not all women chose to participate in fight club because of their rejection of traditional gender roles. Some sought out the group to test their skills, ones they had acquired through engaging cardio-boxing.

CARDIO-BOXING MEETS FIGHT CLUB

The collision of the two worlds, that of commercialized cardio-boxing and fight club, emphasized the differences in understanding of the event and its purpose. As previously mentioned, some participants like Angelina were motivated by their cardio-boxing experience to attend a Fight Night. However, the highly structured cardio-boxing experience did not necessarily prepare them for the evening of fights nor did it necessarily benefit them socially. While openly acknowledging their lack of fight experience, the organizers commented on the participation of a woman who attended an event for the first time who seemingly had cardio-boxing experience. In relaying their perceptions of the participant, Bailey and Sasha made the following comments

Sasha: This one girl, I don't know her name, but she did [cardio]-boxing, and
   came with all of her gear. And she was like a bigger girl too.
Bailey: She was very tall and very like muscular.
Sasha: Yes.
Bailey: Like I want to say thick boned, you know.
Sasha: And she had a bag, so she started wrapping her knuckles and like freaking
   everyone out, coz you know we welcome all experience levels, because we are
   not experienced ourselves, but when this person went into the ring, she got like
   a really tiny girl with her.
Bailey: It was me, I fought her.

Sasha: Oh, you fought the [cardio-boxing] girl?

Bailey: Yes, I was terrified. (Bailey and Sasha, Personal Communication, July 26, 2017)

The perception of the cardio-boxer as being someone with experience and skill intimidated other women and elicited feelings of fear about engaging her in a fight. This was compounded by the woman's physique as she had a body type that did not fit within the parameters of traditional femininity; she was more muscular. Despite this, however, the reality of transitioning from the highly commercialized non-contact boxing—hitting the bag—to hitting a person, did not go smoothly.

Sasha: Well she never made contact with another person before, she only ever hit a bag, and so . . . so once she started doing her moves, then it all fell apart. Because once you get hit in the face . . .

Bailey: Its' disorientating. Its' funny, because like what Sasha was saying about the [cardio-boxing] girl, was that she had this experience and she was really well prepared, but when it actually came down to being hit and hitting someone that's like a moving object, who has a brain, and is like trying not to be hit, it was a whole different story. (Bailey and Sasha, Personal Communication, July 26, 2017)

Much like the women discussed later in chapter 6, there is a large difference between looking the part having embraced the commodified version of the sport and executing the skills necessary to hit a real person (Nash 2017).

CONCLUSION

This chapter has examined the emergence of an all-women's fight club that periodically held unsanctioned Fight Night events at covert locations throughout the community. The motivations for the organization and participation in the group were complex and varied. The freedom and cathartic experience of engaging in physical confrontation elicited excitement in the women who participated, spurring feelings of clarity and resistance to the heteronormative gender structure that had recently disrupted their senses of self. For some women, this disruption centered on the pressures of motherhood and feelings of a loss of self. Yet, for others this group offered a sense of camaraderie and cathartic release, where expressions of aggression were not only accepted but celebrated. Others sought out the group for the purposes of testing skills they had learned in cardio-boxing gyms and to experience the next level in the boxing regime. The exclusion of men made it a more desirable space for such skill testing than seeking out and joining a fight gym, spaces that they perceived as being predominantly occupied by men. Although the inclusivity of this group helped foster this space as being women friendly, it did however mean that there were very few true boxers in the group (i.e., people with fight experience beyond that of street fighting). This is not a criticism, rather it provided an opportunity for a glimpse into an unsanctioned fight group that was very loosely, if at all, associated with the regimens of commodified boxing in both the fight gyms and cardio gyms. I would argue that the seemingly lack of space in fight gyms, or lack of friendliness perhaps, contributed to the success of this group.

In addition, this chapter addressed the ever-present specter of men's violence against women that also pervaded the group. This shaped the understandings of the necessity of experiencing violence, something that the women felt is better learned in their women's only space opposed to when confronted with it inevitably happening in the street or other realms of their lives. Stories of victimization and self-defense played into the justifications for engaging each other physically and for the reclaiming of power, something that women are socialized to suppress. This narrative of self-defense will be later explored in chapter 7, but first I return to adversarial boxing in the more traditional gym spaces of the cardio and fight gyms.

Chapter 6

Sparring Like Men?

Gender Maneuvering and the Emotional Work of Getting in the Ring

INTRODUCTION

This chapter focuses exclusively on the engagement with the sport in the ring as it relates to bodily regimens, inter-gendered sparring, and coaching relationships, exploring the challenges women face when engaging in adversarial boxing and navigating the relationships necessary to do that safely in male-dominated spaces. Drawing on the work of scholars such as Lucia Trimbur (2013) and Meredith Nash (2017), the spatial and bodily dynamics of contact boxing is examined as it relates to paternalism, sexism, and navigating ego. The chapter also examines how gender is used and exploited as a teaching tool by coaches and the excess emotional work women boxers expend to navigate paternalism and ambivalent sexism in an effort to be taken seriously. The chapter highlights the importance of coaches as gatekeepers who have considerable power to include or exclude women from these traditional fighting gym spaces.

SPARRING LIKE MEN?

Just under half of the women interviewed for this project attempted adversarial boxing in some form, whether this was through their participation in the previously mentioned fight club (see chapter 5), through the recruitment of a boxing coach, or taking classes at a fight gym. The women represented a diverse group comprised of varying ages, backgrounds, and skill and engagement levels ranging from those that tried it once or twice and decided it was not for them, to professional boxers who were actively pursuing careers in the sport. Therefore, the depth of experience was varied, but there was a shared acknowledgment that sparring/adversarial boxing was a chance to test the physical and psychological skills necessary to advance into the next stage of boxing (Paradis 2012). In describing how/why they made the decision to try adversarial boxing, some of the women reduced it to happenstance (i.e., the intersection of chance and circumstances). For example, Anna became involved in the sport at an early age as it was a pastime her brother pursued.

> Um and so I went in the gym for like a year and a half just watching Robert and really not having any desire to be in boxing and um I, there, really was never like at first, at least any pull for me, or enticement for me to try it. I was really like I said, into softball and basketball and I was good at those sports. I didn't wanna add anything new and then my coach, uh my first coach and then my parents kinda encouraged me. My coach more so than my parents but they were like you know you you're athletic, you could just try it out. My coach, um my first coach knew that I was athletic and into sports. He was like come on just try it, like your brother does it and you got that natural ability and so I remember I went and did this summer camp and I felt so silly, punching the air and doing shadow boxing. I was like this seems so dumb. And then um, you know, I just picked it up pretty easily. When something comes naturally you just want to do it more and more, so I got more into it. (Anna, Personal Communication, January 23, 2017)

This, however, was not a typical experience of the women included in this study, as the majority made informed decisions to pursue the sport.

My segue into adversarial boxing followed approximately 18 months of cardio boxing and working with personal trainers on the pads. I began to favor one specific instructor, Nate, who I sought out for further instruction, but this was still very much situated within the cardio-boxing gym space (i.e., no contact). For several months preceding my decision to try sparring, I contemplated doing it, trying to determine my motivations for why I would want to pursue a sport that risks being hit in the face and head. I was still conflicted when I heard several rumors about an instructional contact-boxing group that met weekly in a local community center that some of the cardio-boxing gymgoers were attending. Shortly afterward, I also began to hear rumors of the all-women's fight club discussed in chapter 5. During one of my training sessions (non-contact boxing) with Nate I brought up the topic asking whether he had heard of the groups or could make any recommendations about how to take it to the next stage. His response was unexpected, arguing that if I wanted to learn to spar/fight, it would be better for him to teach me himself than to attend an improperly supervised fight group where I would risk injury. Within a week I found myself strapped into head gear, wearing a mouth guard in Nate's back garden (Fieldnote, May 4, 2016).

As briefly noted in chapter 2, my first sparring experience was very similar to the experiences of other women included here and as documented elsewhere (McCaughey 1997; Nash 2017). Nate started by telling me to punch him in the face. He dropped his arms and bent down a bit (he is a very tall man, standing over 6 feet tall), making no effort to defend himself. Despite being there for a boxing lesson, knowing that hitting him was an instrumental component to the lesson, it felt wrong. I asked him several times "Are you sure?" (Fieldnote May 4, 2016). I also laughed uncomfortably at the situation. After reassuring me that he truly intended for me to hit him in the face, I did punch him, but then immediately apologized. I felt bad for punching him despite him instructing me to do so. As noted by Nash (2017, 744), "'Looking' aggressive was different to actually being aggressive." In retrospect, in that moment I was having to suppress 35 years of being socialized into thinking that women should not initiate violence (Trimbur 2013). I realized the depth of my own subscription to the heterosexual narrative, that even though I considered myself an empowered feminist woman equipped and ready to engage the sport of boxing, when confronted with the reality of engaging my own aggression or initiating a physical attack I reverted back to "the ideology of heterosexual virtue [that] forms the cornerstone of the designation of women as nonviolent" (Allen 1986, 21).

As argued by Martha McCaughey (1997, 21), "women's fighting challenges a fundamental association between women and goodness," something that has been discursively constructed and emphasizes passivity as a core component of femininity. The pervasiveness of this sexist discourses in the media, polity, family, and other institutions, that construct women as being unable to or ill-equipped to exercise their physical agency in the same ways as a man, leads to an institutionalized de-skilling (Hoagland 1988) that manifests at the individual level. Women learn *not* to fight, *not* to be aggressive, and *not* to initiate violence. My feelings of wrongness or deviance that manifested in punching Nate can be explained by the intense social pressures that inform gender, specifically femininity, that I had just violated in initiating a physically aggressive act. Other women reported similar experiences when first getting in the ring. Angelina said,

> It's really weird. It feels like they have to be joking because it's just, and then like even when that was a thing I kept getting yelled at to hit the person . . . because I had no problem, you know, like doing my defensive [moves], but I had to be like literally reminded that I was supposed to be throwing punches. Because it was so like not in the back of my mind or in my mind anywhere . . . that was what I should be doing. So pretty much the entire like first fight was a bunch of people yelling at me telling me to throw punches. (Angelina, Personal Communication, February 16, 2017)

Here Angelina is comfortable with defending herself but resists initiating an attack. Again, we can revisit the dominance of the heterosexual discourse mentioned in chapter 2, that teaches women from a young age that their bodies are not their own, that they are objects to be admired and appropriated by men. Women have been taught the appropriate response to physical aggression is submission and that they are not supposed to fight back or hit first (McCaughey 1997). Angelina felt comfortable deflecting punches, that is, using her physicality to remove herself from harm, but struggled with being the aggressor. Lucia Trimbur's (2013) study of the women in Gleason's gym found similar patterns where women boxers felt uncomfortable hitting other women or waited for their opponent to hit them first to justify a counter punch.

Being hit for the first time was a similar experience, although I found the thought of it to be worse than the reality. Penelope expressed a similar experience,

> You can't prepare for it, I don't think, you have ideas, but coz like there'll be things where you'll like, you like fake hit someone, you know, but then when they're actually full force hitting you back, you, it's scary, and so, I think even the first few times I did it with Nate, I was just like "oh my god why I am doing this?" But now, it's just, I kind of gotten used to it, I guess, it sounds really bad coz it's like it's awful being hit. (Penelope, Personal Communication, November 10, 2016)

Although the shock of hitting and being hit was there initially, some of the women, myself included, found their "fighting spirit" (McCaughey 1997, 89) where these behaviors became normalized and part of the training regimen.

THE IMPORTANCE OF TRUST: COACHING AND SPARRING IN MALE-DOMINATED SPACES

As I became more involved with adversarial boxing, I found myself regularly training (four to five times a week) at a gym that allowed sparring, as well as continuing to attend a cardio-boxing gym several times a week. As you would expect, there were significant differences in the training regimens implemented at the gym that allowed contact boxing as it related to intensity, expectations, and requirements. Unlike the cardio-boxing gym (see chapter 4 for further information on the format of the boxercise classes), the workout was more holistic, including cardio, strength training (including lifting weights), skill trainings, pad/mitt work, footwork drills, partner drills, bag work, and sparring sessions. The fight gyms and their coaches projected an image of "toughness," a finding that mirrors what Meredith Nash (2017) found in her study of Tasmanian boxing gyms As in Nash's (2017) study, it was common to hear coaches yell phrases such as "[p]ain is weakness leaving the body" (Fieldnote, August 20, 2017), "don't you dare give up," and for them to call out or make fun of the last trainee to complete a specific task—sometimes punishing the whole class for a perceived lack of effort (Fieldnote, July 2, 2018).

In keeping with this presentation of toughness, one of my first workouts in a fight gym space was presented as a "real boxers' workout" (Fieldnote, November 30, 2017), as I was invited to accompany another woman boxer in her training. As this was at the beginning of my venture into these spaces, I was totally unprepared for this session. It became evident quite quickly that despite my years of cardio-boxing and my one-on-one sparring lessons with Nate, my conditioning was poor and although I endeavored to keep pace with the other boxer, my presence slowed her down. I took this as a challenge and looked to her for motivation. This work ethic seemed to endear me to the coach despite me "need[ing] a lot of work" (Fieldnote, November 30, 2017), something he joked about several years later; "You were a challenge Victoria, do you remember when I had to drag you to the bench because your legs went out after doing the bike!?" (Fieldnote, December 14, 2019). I do remember. My legs had given out feeling like jelly after I finished a some-what minimal workout on the stationary bike. I had very inelegantly slid off the bike seat onto the gym floor. Although I was embarrassed at the time, my coach had physically picked me up, legs dragging, and deposited me on a bench. He then reassured me I was doing well. However, for some people the challenge of more traditional boxing was not a motivator as some women found it defeating and either became overwhelmed or gave up. Coaches often took this as an indicator that they were "not serious" (Fieldnote, January 14, 2018) and, therefore, withdrew some of the boxing-related opportunities and reverted back to more basic personal training workouts that would be pleas-ing to the gym-goer—especially when they were paying clients.

Interestingly, the emphasis on individual work ethic, although not explicit, was where boxers, especially new members at the gym, were expected to invest time beyond personal coaching and classes to improve their condition-ing and form. Therefore, the expectation was that some of the components of the regimen were done independently of your coaching sessions (i.e., doing your "roadwork" [Wacquant 2004, 63]). It was not uncommon for my coach to assign homework or weekly challenges where he would text reminders or positive messages intended to encourage progress during the week. In other instances he would require evidence that the task had been completed. For example, periodically he issued the "100 burpees before breakfast" chal-lenge (Fieldnote, February 27, 2019) where he required all his trainees (and sometimes just me) to complete a set of 100 burpees before starting their day, every day for a week. This was in addition to the normal training regimen. As a proof of completion I was required to send him short videos of me completing the task.

In fight gym spaces the requirement of demonstrating a workout ethic was not specific to one coach. It was not unusual for me to witness coaches refusing to engage new members as they had still not perfected their punching form or barking orders for them to continue on with their shadow boxing until "they got it right!" (Fieldnote, February 12, 2018). My coach was less abrasive and because of this excelled in working with women who tended to shy away from the more confrontational coaching styles. This did not mean his expectations were lessened, rather that his delivery was less abrupt. He tended to tease to motivate opposed to bark insults at his trainees. While he too said things like "pain is weakness leaving the body" (Fieldnote, November 30, 2017) and "we need to get you into [fight] shape" (Fieldnote, September 2, 2018), he also often joked "don't be a punk!" (Fieldnote, November 2, 2018) if he felt you were slacking. Weirdly, and as I discussed with him at a later time, my internal reaction to these statements was to work harder as I did not want him to think I was a punk! In retrospect this is a seemingly ridiculous sentiment taken out of the context of the boxing gym. But this need to please was, and still is, associated with the value I placed in gaining his respect. In agreement with Wacquant (2004, 86), I felt the need to "prove myself" in the ring and in every way "prove myself" capable to my coach.

Over time, I developed considerable respect for my coach as a fighter and instructor as well as built a relationship characterized by trust. This was common of the women who regularly got in the ring. Anna spoke about her relationship with her coach,

> Well I think that the trust is really in your coach. So your coach is supposed to um . . . um where like he's not gonna let you get in the ring with anyone, regardless of whether it's sparring, fighting whatever, that he thinks . . . can hurt you or you could potentially, you know, get put in harms-way. So I put a lot, most of my trust in my coach and like how he's trained me and if he lets me get in the ring with somebody then you know he trusts me to be able to perform well and so that's where my trust goes. And then as far as like, if, cause I would never, I guess why I say that is because I would never spar without my coach. (Anna, Personal Communication, January 23, 2017)

Similarly, I would not spar or get into the ring without my coach being present or advising me on the situation. At 5 foot 2 inches, independent of gender, I often found myself to be the smaller or at the very least the shorter opponent in almost every partner drill or sparring interaction I ever had. This often created an anxiety of the unknown spurred by what I felt were physical disadvantages—height and reach. Yet, if my coach asked me to spar someone, even if the person was considerably larger than myself, I would trust that this was in my best interest and I was going to learn or gain something from the experience.

As argued by Trimbur (2013), some of the women at Gleason's gym justified the engagement with the sport, specifically the initiation of a fight, by shifting the responsibility from themselves onto their coach. In this instance, the coach provides an authorization for the punches, reducing the anxiety or feelings of conflict associated with being the physical aggressor. The irony being that a woman engages in physical aggression only with the permission of a man (if you have a male coach). Although elements of this argument ring true (such as looking to your coach for authorization), I am unconvinced that this a gendered happening, especially as there are some, albeit few, women fighters with women coaches where the same process manifests. For example, Emelia had a woman coach who she also looked to for authorization in the same way, describing her coach as someone who "knew women, she understood how women worked" (Emelia, Personal Communication, July 17, 2017).

Alternatively, Trimbur (2013, 99) found that some of the women of Gleason's gym reconciled their initiation of the violence through "the creation of a fictive space that has different rules and boundaries than the gendered system outside of it. In this space, women possess the right to hit *a priori*." This explanation seemed to resonate with some of the pugilists here, myself included, noting that entering the physical space of the ring granted the permission to hit and be hit. For example, Anna said of her experience,

> Yeah but I, so going back to you know just being in the ring with somebody who you are matched with as far as you know, with skill wise, you're both trying to help each other, I've had to multiple times be like you know you can hit me. It's okay. And my coaches even um had to be like you know she's gonna hit you really hard if you don't fight back. (Anna, Personal Communication, January 23, 2017)

This fictive space (Trimbur 2013), surveilled by coaches and guided by rules and regulations, granted women permission to not only engage physically but to test their skills. As argued by ethnographer Jérôme Beauchez (2017, 80), sparring is not combat, as its purpose is not to obliterate your partner but to "build with him[/her] an agonistic pedagogy that both parties accept and seek to preserve." It is instructional. A means to learn, negotiate, and renegotiate the physical and psychological techniques of boxing (Beauchez 2017). This relies on a balance, a negotiation of terms that are understood by both parties that includes respect, deference, and a "negotiated order" (Strauss 1978, 5–6). In a good sparring session, this balance is upheld independent of gender. Yet, this balance is not always observed and is especially precarious when men and women spar together, that is, when the gendered system outside of the ring is brought front and center in the ring.

PRIDE AND MASCULINITY: SPARRING WITH MALE PARTNERS WHILE NAVIGATING EGO

Feminine Fighters

Due to the dominance of men in the sport of boxing, it is not surprising that at the amateur or novice level, there is a scarcity of women engaging in the sport and therefore, available to spar. Over the course of almost three years of adversarial boxing, I have engaged dozens of opponents in the ring, the majority of whom have been men. This is not to say I have not sparred with women and over this time period I had three regular women sparring partners. However, as was the experience of most women pursuing adversarial boxing interviewed here, the majority of sparring was done with men and although many of these experiences were mutually beneficial, there were some patterns that emerged that are worthy of further discussion.

The first notable pattern related to appearance, specifically being under-estimated due to gender and femininity. In the world of boxing the body is important. As noted by Oates (1987, 5) "like a dancer, a boxer 'is' his body, and is totally identified with it." Wacquant (1995a,b, 1998, 2004) has noted the importance of the body as an instrument for boxers as it is both a weapon and a site for the acquisition of capital. He argues that the,

> boxing gym in which they spend much of their waking time as a social machinery designed to convert this "abstract" bodily capital into *pugilistic capital,* that is, to impart to the fighter's body a set of abilities and tendencies liable to produce value in the field of professional boxing. (Wacquant 1995a, 66–67)

As argued by interdisciplinary scholar Elise Paradis (2012), the body also has value in its display as boxers are consciously aware of their presentation of self. They want to appear tough, trim, hard, and taut, conveying the message that they are ready to fight (Wacquant 1998). More generally, there are specific blueprints within different sports that implicitly dictate the ideal, or necessary body type for success, what Paradis (2012, 91) drawing on Bourdieu's concept of doxa (logics specific to the field), refers to as "*doxic* schemes." In boxing this includes a muscular physicality and an aggressive focus that rejects aesthetic and bodily traits associated with femininity. Although there are many weight classes in boxing as well as many body types (i.e., shorter, lithe and wiry like Manny Pacquiao through to the larger, less muscular physique of Andy Ruiz Jr), there are archetypes such as Muhammad Ali, Mike Tyson, and Anthony Joshua that become representative of what it means to be a boxer and have a boxers' body. These archetypes also inform understandings of legitimacy in both boxing spaces and in the ring.

Although I have a complex relationship with my own body image, I feel it is a fair descriptor to say I present as being quite traditionally feminine as it relates to dominant understandings of middle-class white women in the United States. I have long blonde hair, blue eyes, wear make-up (not at the gym), and I am quite short. Unlike Nash (2017), who noted her muscular physique smoothed her transition to acceptance in the gym space as it communicated "pugilistic capital" (Wacquant 1995a), I would not describe myself as muscular. I do have some muscular definition in places but also carry weight in my stomach and chest. On initial inspection my body does not communicate that of boxer or pugilist (see Figure 6.1).

Other women reported similar experiences related to their appearance. Anna said, "So when I first started it was more of the 'you're too pretty to box' kinda reaction" (Anna, Personal Communication, January 23, 2017). This was echoed by some of the other gym-goers who in casual conversations sometimes queried why "pretty" or "good looking" women would want to box (Fieldnote, December 1, 2017). The expectation that attractive women should not be able to or want to engage combat sports was common and communicates a woman's value is primarily associated with her physical appearance and attractiveness to men. To risk that by boxing is to risk her societal worth (i.e., her face) and being no longer aesthetically attractive to men.

Being one of the women in the gym space, it was difficult for me to ascertain whether the men categorized women into groups based on their appearance such as Trimbur's (2013, 101–102) "diesel fighters, "gym hos, and "skanky females." Due to the relatively low number of women engaging adversarial boxing, it was harder to assign women to specific typologies. For example, Sonya, an African American fighter, who stood over 6 feet in height, on initial inspection would have been classified as a "diesel fighter." She wore baggy clothes, was taken seriously due to her stature by other gym-goers, sparred with both men and women, and also had a bit of a temper if she was pushed harder than she felt reasonable both in training and in the ring. In addition, as a lesbian woman she was not shy about her sexuality (not that she should be). Therefore, in accordance with Trimbur's (2013) "diesel fighters," she challenged the heteronormative gender codes and norms and may have been perceived as having an ambiguous gender identity. However, on deeper inspection her choice of gym attire was not about being accepted in the gym space but about her own comfort and related to her expression of self as a gay African American

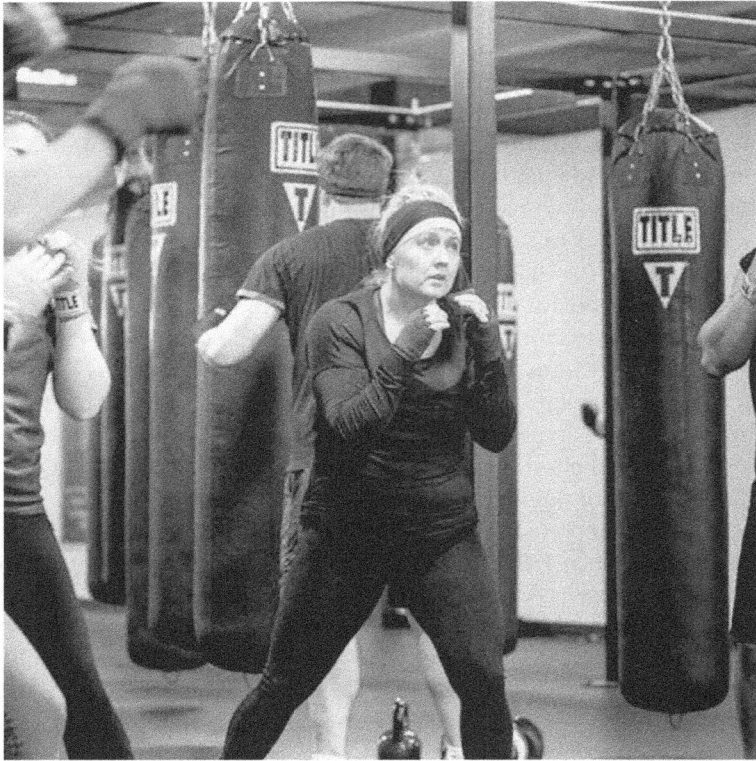

Figure 6.1 Not Having the Typical Body Type for Adversarial Boxing. *Source*: Photograph by Scott Kulaga.

woman in the United States. In addition, she was quite social, talking and joking with lots of the gym-goers, yet it was not flirtatious in nature as in the case of Trimbur's (2013) "gym hos." She also was episodic in her training due primarily to financial constraints, and some of the gym-goers would often say of her "she could be a great boxer if she was more serious" (Fieldnote, April 4, 2018). These latter characteristics are more closely aligned with the "gym ho" typology, but this also illustrates that Trimbur's (2013) typology of women boxers was less clearly delineated in these spaces studied here.

Furthermore, men in these fight spaces did not seem to put as much emphasis on clothing as Trimbur (2013) found. Rather, the focus seemed to be primarily on work ethic. As noted by Matt,

If you come in there wearing a full face of makeup and you're "lolly gagging" around the whole time, that's gonna piss me off because you know it's instruction time for guys who are taking, want this to be a lifestyle, and you're in here you know prissing around or whatever. But again, that same person can come in there with a full face of makeup or whatever and be the hardest worker in there. And so, it's all about work ethic and not just presentation. So, if you've got a good work ethic and you're willing to work and willing to learn, I can accept that no matter what shape, size, color it don't matter. A will, a will to work and a will to get better is really all that it takes for me to want you there. If you wanna learn I want you there. If you're in there, you know for social time go to a [cardio-boxing gym]. (Matt, Personal Communication, July 25, 2017)

Due to a number of reasons that differentiates these spaces from Gleason's gym, I also did not see any evidence of "skanky females" (Trimbur 2013)—women just there to watch the men train and fight—although they could have been there just not when I was training.

Although I took the sport and my training very seriously, I too did not fit neatly into the "diesel fighter" category. My gym attire varied but did include yoga pants/tights, as well as long sleeve and short sleeve t-shirts, some form fitting and others not. I was not particularly social beyond my regular sparring partners and my coach, although if approached I was never rude; I was definitely not a social butterfly, but this is not a character trait I hold in my life outside the gym. In fact, I was often teased by my coach for appearing unfriendly to other people he trained, the only explanation I can think for this was my inability to see distances without my glasses leading to the perception I was snubbing people if I did not respond to a wave or acknowledgment. My feminine appearance coupled with my clothing choice confirmed my heteronormative gender status making me "safe" (Nash 2017, 743), as I was not outwardly bucking or challenging the patriarchal dictates of appropriate white middle-class femininity. Yet, due to my feminine appearance, it was not uncommon for expectations about my skill level to be lowered.

But She's a Girl!: Underestimated in The Ring

A common experience reported by the women in these spaces were reactions, especially those of male gym-goers, to their skills and abilities. There were two different types of sparring relationships that presented different challenges when the sparing was inter-gendered; (1) when skill level was evenly matched, giving the sparring a competitive as well as instructional focus, and (2) when one partner was at a noticeably much higher skill level than the other, and therefore the purpose for sparring was purely instructional. In the first situation it was not uncommon for women to report the reluctance of a male sparring partner to hit them or when they did, they noticeably held back. As indicated by Anna who reminisced,

Um they kinda, I'm looked at when they don't know who I am, like oh I'm going up against this girl. I'm not gonna go hard. I've dealt with that so much in sparring like oh well I'm just gonna go really easy and then that's when I kinda feel like, not necessarily, I feel like maybe that's when I feel like I need to prove myself, honestly, as a woman. (Anna, Personal Communication, January 23, 2017)

This reluctance to hit manifested in many of my sparring sessions where not only were partners shy about hitting me, but when a punch was thrown it was done slowly and with little impact on contact. Caroline expressed similar frustration at her experience,

But, um, I sometimes feel like I still don't get taken seriously. I'm trying to think of how, like I should word this. I met a lot of guys who fight . . . and um, like I have to work so much harder than other guys to gain others' respect you know? And that can be a little aggravating. (Caroline, Personal Communication, February 13, 2017)

This hesitancy to engage a woman boxer in the ring is situated in an adherence to broader gender scripts that are related to understandings of masculinity and vulnerability (Nash 2017). Drawing on the work of Cover (2015), Nash (2017, 745) argues that in an already hypermasculine space, the male sparring partner has to engage in a reframing of the dominant gender structure "renouncing their gender privilege." This undermines the larger social construction of women being in need of physical protection from violence due to their inherent fragility. Having women as adversarial partners in the ring requires men to actively ignore any social conditioning they have been subjected to that dictates they must never hit a woman, something that is an ingrained societal taboo. Nash (2017, 745) argues that "a man pulling his punches is demonstrative of his need to re-secure an unstable masculine identity by foreclosing on other possibilities of gender relationality." This also manifested itself frequently in my sparring session, and at its most extreme resulted in me being goaded into hitting someone in the face who chose not to defend himself. In support of Nash's (2017) analysis, having been confused by this behavior, one of the coaches present during the session suggested that my male sparring partner quickly realized I could outbox him, so, in order to save face and hide his skill deficit when people were watching, he actively allowed and then encouraged me to hit him. By doing this, he was not only controlling the action in the ring and the accompanying narrative but also reasserting his masculine dominance and reestablishing his place in the gender order—tough enough to invite direct hits to the face and body.

However, Nash's (2017) analysis does not fully account for some more pragmatic aspects of inter-gender sparring, namely, the renegotiation of the balance necessary for both parties to have a mutually beneficial sparring session. In my experiences, my considerably smaller stature would have meant that had some of my male sparring partners, those who stood over 6 feet in height and weighing close to 100 lbs more than me, not held anything back and then caught me with a punch, I could have been seriously hurt. Beauchez (2017) argues a confrontation between two boxers, especially those of differing skill levels, requires adherence to the rules. If these rules are violated then it interrupts the negotiated order of the sparring session. Anna spoke of dealing with violations as being a normative part of the women's boxing experience,

> As far as the other person, like I said, there was a couple times with older guys and it's you touch them and like I said they're like oh gosh I'm getting embarrassed sparring so I need to keep her honest or whatever and I've dealt with that. (Anna, Personal Communication, January 23, 2017)

The rules of sparring are not overtly stated, rather they are learned through bodily engagement and gym culture; they are implied. For example, a boxer with greater skills than his/her opponent must not demonstrate their superiority with malicious intent or brutality. Instead, the sparring session can serve as mechanisms for practicing other skills such as defense techniques, movement, or counterpunching. Likewise, the less skilled boxer should not then take advantage of the superior boxers' benevolence and throw dirty or cheap shots. Therefore, in a truly beneficial sparring session the pulling of punches represents an adjustment period whereby the two boxers are sizing each other up, adhering to the tacit rules of engagement, and finding the appropriate balance for both parties. Gender, whether it manifests as differential size, skill, and strength factors, or feminine characteristics, is an instrumental part of this adjustment period. The problem arises when the punches are pulled despite the skill level and when gender alone is used as *the* sole influencer of sparring behavior. As argued by Anna, "obviously if I were to fight the top male in my weight class he would be stronger, faster, but, so I'm not by any means saying that women are just as strong" (Anna, Personal Communication, January 23, 2017). Gender informs all aspects of social life, so it, of course, actively informs sparring interactions. If it is acknowledged, adaptations can and should be made. Good sparring partners, independent of gender, manage to do this effectively and quickly at the initiation of the session. However, not all sparring partners complied with the implicit rules of engagement which then led to violations.

For as many male sparring partners that held back, there were those that did not. As Anna notes here,

Then I've also dealt with the opposite where it's like they, I hit them and they feel that, and then they try to kill me and so then it's like okay, that's where it's like okay you are still a guy. Nobody's questioning your masculinity, um, and so there is a balance. (Anna Personal Communication, January 23, 2017)

For some men, the possibility of being out boxed by a woman posed a threat to their presumed masculine dominance and in some instances led to increased aggressiveness that upset the balance or "negotiated order" of the sparring session. In three years of adversarial boxing I have experienced the consequences of this in different ways such as the sudden use of illegal moves (such as being grabbed around the neck and lifted off my feet), the session being abruptly ended early by the boxer leaving the ring, being shoved hard enough to be pushed over, comments made expressing shock, stopping the session, crying foul to coaches (i.e., "Can she really do that?" (Fieldnote, December 22, 2019)) and even more subtle manifestations of frustration and tension through shifts in body language and facial expressions. There was one instance though that was of note as it perfectly demonstrates the complexity of this issue.

We were doing partner drills and I was training with Ryan. Our coach had me throw specific punches and Ryan had to block them, we had to alternate back and forth between throwing and blocking punches. Within a few iterations, I could tell that I was better at boxing than Ryan and his punches became harder. His body language also began to change as he became more forceful and more serious. I kept glancing at my coach to see if he noticed, but nothing indicated that he was concerned, so I tried to block it out. But I could feel myself becoming less comfortable and more anxious. After breaking for a few minutes, my coach told us we were going to "light spar" (meaning the sparring was supposed to be controlled and instructional in nature). Ryan came out of the gate throwing hard punches and I could feel myself begin to mentally shut down. I was able to block or slip most of his punches but the few that got by my defenses unnerved me. Ryan's vibe was not friendly, rather the increasing aggressiveness that started during the partner drills seemed to have escalated considerably. I began to make silly mistakes. I was worried he really wanted to hurt me. After taking a punch that knocked me to the ground my coach stepped in and shut the sparring down. Ryan, rather cockily, swaggered about for a bit before asking if I was okay. Ironically, I was disappointed in myself for feeling anxious and concerned when I knew had I just stayed calm I could have got the better of Ryan. I spent over 20 minutes with my coach going over the session and dissecting what had happened. I even cried in frustration about my performance. I told my coach something was off about Ryan and I did not feel comfortable with him, but at the time could not verbalize why. (Fieldnote, June 13, 2018)

On reflection, Ryan had violated the negotiated order and balance of the sparring session. There was a "breach of the background expectations" (Garfinkel 1967, 55). Sociologist Harold Garfinkel (1967) argues that only when there is a violation do the moral underpinnings of an order become clear. So, when a tacit rule is infringed upon, it is fully revealed, no longer existing in an implicit state. The tacit rule here was that size and power differentials should have been observed and mitigated while still remaining at an intensity that benefited both boxers.

The following week my coach revealed that Ryan had told him, "Yea, I wasn't going to be beat by a girl, so I pulled some dirty moves" (Fieldnote, June 20, 2018). My coach confided that hearing directly from Ryan confirmed my suspicions but that I should not worry about it as he "took care of it" (Fieldnote, June 20, 2018). He also expressed shock at Ryan's motivation for behaving that way and for his blatant ownership of such sexist viewpoints. When I asked him to explain what he meant by "took care of it" my coach informed me that having found out what Ryan did, he had got into the ring with Ryan and taught him a lesson in respect. He even said that as he was doing it, he told Ryan "this is for Victoria!" (Fieldnote, June 20, 2018). Here, Ryan's masculinity was threatened by engaging a woman in the ring, one whose skills not only rivaled but bettered his own. His behavior in the sparring session was an attempt to reassert his masculinity, something he feared was being threatened by having lesser power in the ring being faced with a more skilled sparring partner and this was further compounded by perceptions that women are the inferior gender.

Nash (2017) reported a similar experience in her analysis whereby a man she calls Troy violated the implicit rules that undergird sparring. As a consequence of her interaction with Troy, she found herself sitting on a bench bloody and overwhelmed. Her male friends at the gym not only offered words of comfort, but another boxer "Jason" "dismantled Troy as payback" (Nash 2017, 745) for his behavior in the ring in the same way Ryan was handled here by my coach. Nash (2017) suggests that the comforting and the retributive sparring session were indicative of reaffirmations of hegemonic masculinity as the men were able to offer care to a heterosexual woman. I agree with Nash's (2017) assessment, but suggest there is more to unpack. The heteronormative script that is being enacted here is that of a protective paternalism (Lafferty and McKay 1994). Social scientists Peter Glick and Susan Fiske (1996) argue that protective paternalism is the notion that men should provide for and protect women who they depend upon. The ideology underpinning of this notion is that women should be cherished and protected in a manner that provides affection and thoughtfulness. Yet, these behaviors are inherently sexist, albeit benevolent, as they reinforce the subordinate positioning of women underscoring their reliance on men (Dardenne, Dumont and Bollier

2007), as well as provide justifications for limiting or restricting women's behavior (Padavic and Reskin 2002). Protective paternalism has been found to be more prominent and accepted across genders in romantic as opposed to other types of relationships; however, this form of paternalism can extend to other relational aspects of social life. Here, the proximity of the relationship between coach and boxer, one that can be characterized by an elevated level of trust and intimacy, allows for and even justifies the enactment of paternalism whereby the wronged party must be protected and the person committing the wrong punished. I would argue this is especially true when the coach is a man and the boxer is a woman.

Sports sociologists Lafferty and McKay (2004, 263) made a similar observation in a study of Australian boxing gyms, reporting a coach saying of women in his gym, "If they do want to box at least I know I'll look after 'em properly and I'll do the right thing." Lafferty and McKay (2004) suggest that this approach can provide a disservice to women boxers. Women may not receive the same amount of ring time, or when they do, they are faced with sparring partners who have been told by coaches to pull their punches or hold back. Despite this explanation, I did not process the actions of my coach toward Ryan as benevolent sexism, although there were other occasions that I would more readily classify this way such a highly skilled fighter wanting to teach another boxer a "lesson" when I received a black eye in sparring. But, as it applies to the situation with Ryan, I felt validated and valued as a fighter that he would take it upon himself to "correct" behavior on my behalf. Reflexively this could potentially be related to an attributional ambiguity that would make it difficult for me as the target of the behavior to determine if it were, indeed, discriminatorily paternalistic (Jackman 1994). Especially if the behavior in question is situated within the larger coach/trainee boxer relationship and the wider, yet implicit, codes of conduct that guide sparring interactions. My feelings about the interaction and subsequent happenings, although complex, also include elements of anger, frustration, and even gleefulness at the comeuppance that Ryan ultimately received. Much of this is grounded in my perception, and that of my coach, that Ryan did not fight fair.

Of note, later there emerged several rumors about Ryan engaging in hypermasculine and aggressive behaviors on a more regular basis. One story of note asserted that on entering the gym space one evening, he targeted a professional MMA fighter and tried to instigate a fight by insulting him. Having rebuffed Ryan's attempts to start a fight several times, the fighter acquiesced and jumped in the cage with him. Being at very different skill and experience levels, the professional fighter played with Ryan before efficiently and quite brutally beating him in the ring in front of the rest of the gym-goers (Fieldnote, January 30, 2019). It seems that Ryan's issues with aggression and overt displays of masculine domination were indiscriminate and he had a problem adhering to the implicit rules of adversarial sparring despite being repeatedly "checked."

Keeping Men Humble: Gender as a Lesson in Humility?

The idea of "checking" or "keeping fighters humble" emerged as a theme of interest. Generally speaking, grand violations of the implicit yet specific habitus of sparring were processed as both an interactional aggrievement against the wronged party as well as a social aggrievement against those occupying the gym and the space itself. However, although aggression and ego were instrumental to the *doxic* schema (Paradis 2012) that was often applauded in these gym spaces, these characteristics were socially policed when the boxer did not have the requisite skills necessary to support such behaviors. Echoing sociologist Travis Satterlund's (2012) finding that middle-class boxers found displays of ignorant hypermasculinity stupid, ego and bravado were regularly "checked" by coaches and more experienced fighters who felt it "better to learn here, than in a fight when it matters" (Fieldnote, January 30, 2019).

On several occasions and in varying circumstances, I was asked to spar to help with the process of "checking" another boxer. In all instances it was at the request of my coach, but the purpose varied. For example, a more common occurrence was that a prospective trainee, often transitioning from a cardio-boxing club, wanted to spar. The majority of these interactions did not involve "checking," rather, my presence was no more than a body needed to assist a newcomer in their introduction to adversarial boxing. However, there were a few occasions when the newcomer fancied themselves as being quite good at boxing and therefore I was instructed to "provide them with a reality check" (Fieldnote, March 2, 2019). This "reality check," however, did not translate to a beat-down, rather, it was a measured display of skill that exposed the prospective boxers' vulnerabilities, inexperience, and lack of proficiency. This technique, more often than not, led to the prospective gym member signing with a coach to get further instructional time and was beneficial to all parties involved. However, there were a few occasions when I was more overtly used as an instrument for "checking" and keeping someone humble. One of the most memorable is detailed below:

> "Put your big gloves on Victoria" my coach yells from the cage. I am early for my training session at the fighting gym and he is in the main cage with another client (sometimes we use the cage when the ring is occupied). A male client, one who is training for a "tough man" competition is bouncing on his feet and hitting the pads my coach is holding. A little nervous I fight my anxiety at the unknown (this was not what I was expecting this morning) and I wrap my hands, warm up quickly and climb into the cage. The other client towers over me. He is a large

white man, about six feet tall, with a long beard. "Victoria this is Matthew, I want you to throw punches at him," my trainer says before turning to the man saying, "don't let her hit you, work on your defense, you're not throwing back yet." The man, my opponent is visibly tense, eyeing me with what I perceive to be skepticism and amusement. We touch gloves and it's on. (Fieldnote, April 2, 2017)

I was later informed that the purpose behind me being asked/told to spar with Matthew was to provide a reality check as the tough man competition was in less than a few weeks and his coach was not confident he was ready. As predicted by the coaches, I was much quicker than Matthew and his defense was weak. This was repeatedly pointed out to Matthew by his coach, who yelled things such as "you gotta be quicker than that!" and "don't let her hit you" "she may be small, but she's fast man" "keep your hands up" and "you gotta adapt" (Fieldnote, April 2, 2017). The commentary and his lack of defensive skill frustrated Matthew, so much so, that he became visibly upset and even more predictable in his movements. Yet, his coach did not relent.

More explicitly, afterward I was told that his coach wanted him to realize that if I could hit him easily, especially given our size differential and my gender, he was destined to fail if he were to face a skilled opponent of the same size and gender. They wanted to test him both physically and psychologically of which my stature and gender were an instrumental part. Unlike the situation with Ryan, the asymmetricity in the power dynamic of sparring was to my benefit and was purposefully used as a teaching tool to help humble a novice fighter the trainer felt was not ready to fight. The lesson seemed to be delivered with a mix of pride and good-natured amusement on the part of Matthew's coach that can be interpreted in two contradictory ways. In my experience, the pride was in that I could hold my own or best a significantly larger opponent in the cage. Demonstrating to all those present in the gym space that my skills had earned me a level of legitimacy as a boxer. Yet, the presence of amusement and the delivery of a lesson in humility to Matthew was in part compounded by my gender and physicality communicating to him that not only did he struggle in the ring, but he was beaten by a girl. Through this lens, my legitimacy as a boxer was mitigated by my gender and although I did well in the cage that day, my status as a fighter and my ability to effectively perform the physicality necessary of boxing could not be divorced from my gender that still acted as a dominant signifier, that is, I did well for a *woman* boxer.

CONCLUSION

This chapter has explored some of the many challenges to adversarial sparring that I and other women in this study experienced. Due to the limited number of women who engage the sport at this level, whether amateur or professional, there seems to be a growing acceptance of women in the sport. This, however, does not erase the challenges and barriers that women experience when navigating gender, both theirs and others, in the masculine space of the boxing gym. As has been established in prior studies, the technique, skill, and bodily capital necessary to engage the sport is not enough to become a woman boxer. Rather, gender has to be negotiated and navigated in these spaces as it does in all aspects of life (Merz 2000; Nash 2017; Owton 2015; Paradis 2012; Trimbur 2013). The hypermasculine world of boxing requires considerable emotional work that includes making men comfortable with women boxers (Satterlund 2012). The gender politics at play in spaces that promote adversarial boxing are complex and as noted by Nash (2017) require more than just increasing the number of women accessing the sport and the opportunities afforded them. Instrumental to change are those who are gatekeepers to the sport, specifically coaches who greatly shape the experience of women in the sport. Of importance, is the emergence of heightened gender scripts that playout in these spaces, but as expected reflect those that dominate society more broadly. It is some of these scripts that I turn to in chapter 7 specifically, as they relate to understandings of gender, violence, and self-defense.

Chapter 7

Violence, Safety, and Self-defense

Unpacking the Narrative that Boxing is Self-Defense

INTRODUCTION

A repeated motivation for women's engagement in the sport of boxing, cardio or adversarial, that emerged during this research revolved around the potential or experienced threat of men's violence against women. Some women sought out and engaged the sport following a violent attack, others did so because of the threat of gender-based violence that pervades their everyday lives. The pervasiveness of men's violence against women in the United States has been well documented (Chen et al. 2020; DeKeseredy et al. 2017; Fisher et al. 2000; Renzetti et al. 2017; Warshaw 2019) and includes a range of behaviors such as rape and sexual assault (Spohn et al. 2017), domestic and intimate partner violence (DeKeseredy et al. 2017), stalking (Logan and Lynch 2018; Logan and Walker 2017; Spitzberg and Cupach 2014), and sexual and street harassment (Forell 2005; Kissling 1991; McDonald and Charlesworth 2016). According to Smith et al. (2017), in the United States, 23 million women have been raped, 45 million have experienced some form of abuse at the hand of a partner, and 19 million have been stalked. Global rankings also highlight the threat of violence against women with the United States rated the tenth most dangerous country for women in 2018. Being the only Global North country to make the top ten list, the United States' ranking was largely due to it being considered high risk for sexual violence, which includes "domestic rape; rape by a stranger; the lack of access to justice in rape cases; sexual harassment and coercion into sex as a form of corruption" (Thomas Reuters Foundation 2018). Furthermore, it has been long acknowledged that prevalence rates and incidence statistics do not include the many harms that go unreported (Morgan and Kenna 2018) compounding an already pervasive threat to women and girls' physical, sexual, and emotional wellbeing.

Considering the scope of the problem of violence against women in the United States, it is unsurprising that women included in this study expressed that concern for their personal safety was a catalyst for pursing boxing. In addition to the very real micro-level threat of violence, narratives of self-defense emerged in boxing spaces, promotional materials, discourses, and larger socio-cultural understandings of the sport. This chapter examines and unpacks the relationship of women's amateur boxing to gender-based violence and self-defense as the sport is packaged, commodified, and now sold to predominantly middle-class, white female consumers as a means to not only improve their health and fitness (i.e., boxercise) but also as a tangible way to defend themselves against a would-be attacker.

SELF-DEFENSE: A BRIEF OVERVIEW

There is a nuanced and limited literature on women's self-defense (Cermele 2010; Hollander 2009; McCaughey 1997), the most prominent contribution being Martha McCaughey's (1997) book *Real Knockouts: The Physical Feminism of Women's Self-defense* that dissects the attitudes and understandings of self-defense as a useful tool for women to resist men's domination. Sociologist Joyce Hollander (2009, 574) notes that there is a "curious scholarly silence on women's self-defense." This is largely related to notable criticism launched by feminist scholars that fall under one of the following three critiques: (1) when faced with a male attacker, women are not physically capable of resistance therefore any training in self-defense simply drains resources that are better designated; (2) self-defense training places women in increased danger as it creates a false sense of security, leading them to act recklessly or seek out/enjoy violent confrontations; and (3) suggesting self-defense as a resistance approach leads to victim-blaming, whereby the focus shifts to why a woman being attacked was not successful in defending herself, or did not take self-defense classes in anticipation that she would be attacked (Hollander 2009). While recognizing the inherent dangers of compounding victim-blaming in situations of rape and sexual assault within the broader social structure of patriarchy, these criticisms are more oft founded in speculative theorizing opposed to empirical research (Cermele 2010). Despite this, few researchers have persisted in their examination of this topic, focusing on the potential effectiveness of physical resistance—more broadly conceptualized—as a means to counter violent attacks perpetrated by strangers and acquaintances (i.e., sexual assault and rape) (Bart and O'Brien 1985; Levine-MacCombie and Koss 1986; Quinsey and Upfold 1985; Ullman and Knight 1992, 1993). Furthermore, much of this research has found that self-defense as a means of resistance is successful (Brecklin 2008; Ullman 1997, 2007; Ullman and Knight 1992, 1993).

Beyond debating the merits of the pragmatism of self-defense as resistance (see McCaughey 1997 for an exhaustive overview), the narrative itself carries considerable power. Narratives of self-defense, especially as it pertains to violence against women, follow socially recognized scripts that not only designate the actors but also their expected behaviors. For example, in the case of rape, the roles of the victim and rapist are typically defined (Marcus 1992). As argued by psychologist Jill Cermele (2010), generally the script starts with avoidance, whereby the focus is on ways in which women (the victim) can best avoid rape (do not venture out alone, at night, in a short skirt, and other such prevalent rape myths), and the script ends with engaging professional assistance whether it be the criminal justice system, medical, or advocacy services. What is less clear is what happens during the attack itself and "the absence of such information implies that while rape can be avoided and survived, it cannot necessarily be thwarted" (Cermele 2010, 1164). The rape script, albeit brief and oversimplified as relayed here, is *the* socially accepted understanding of rape and one that pervades throughout society. Self-defense, therefore, provides an alternative script, one where the rape does not end at the perpetrators' whim or with intervention from the outside, but with the victim's successful resistance that challenges the pervasive understanding of gender and violence.

While Cermele (2010) examines the role of self-defense as an alternative to the aforementioned rape script, here the focus of inquiry is the pervasiveness and commodification of such scripts as they are coopted into a broader self-defense narrative within the sport of boxing—one that utilizes socially accepted scripts that designate men as perpetrators and women as victims (Marcus 1992). The narrative capitalizes on common understandings of masculinity and femininity where women are automatically socially constructed as being weaker than men and offers commentary on the relationship between gender, violence, and capitalism. This is especially visible in the growing popularity of pugilistic sports (or versions of said sports such as boxercise), where self-defense is a dominant narrative utilized as a tool to sell an exercise product to female consumers.

IS BOXING SELF-DEFENSE?

According to the Brooklyn Center for Anti-Violence Education, women's enrollment in self-defense classes has significantly increased over the last three years (Hobson in Goldberg 2019). Offered explanations for this increase have attributed it to varying social factors such as the emergence of the MeToo Movement, rise in hate crimes, and the election of Donald Trump (Goldberg 2019). There is, of course, considerable variation in how self-defense is taught with some courses offered being relatively inexpensive (sometimes free) and lasting a short period of time, and others are offered through martial arts programs, on university campuses and/or rape crises centers whereby 24 hours plus of class time is required (McCaughey 1997). McCaughey (1997, 58) identified four different types of traditional self-defense programs, "padded attacker courses; firearms courses; martial arts or martial-arts orientated self-defense courses; and fitness-orientated courses." Although there are considerable differences, the general goal of all the courses is to better equip participants, primarily women, with the skills necessary to thwart a physical attack. For example, padded attacker courses "offer women a chance to experience full-force fighting, as self-defense instructors believe that most successful assaults occur not because women aren't strong enough to fight men but because women facing an assailant often freeze up rather than fight" (61). However, cardio-boxing classes do not emulate violent attacks, rather the focus is learning the techniques of the sport through practicing punches and defensive moves against an inanimate object (i.e., a boxing bag).

It is important to note that none of the gyms included in this study offered self-defense classes. However, the fight gym did not shy away from the power of defensive tactics largely due to the necessity of defense skills and techniques for full-contact sparring. However, this chapter focuses on cardio-boxing gyms, and although there are elements of defense techniques taught (slip, parry, u-dip, duck, block, fade), there is no opponent to practice against. Therefore, even though some of the techniques might be similar to those taught in martial-arts-oriented courses—that is, standing punching and kicking techniques—there is no practicing these techniques with a real-life person. Therefore, the cardio-boxing classes can be most likened to the fitness-orientated courses in self-defense where the movements are emulated in an exercise-driven program (i.e., like jazzercise but with self-defense moves), yet without contact with a partner or explanation as to how to best implement these moves in an actual attack. There is also no emotional or psychological work provided, elements which are necessary to process and deal with being confronted with an attack. Therefore, there are clear differences between self-defense orientated programs and cardio-boxing, differences that although acknowledged became convoluted in the gym spaces visited as part of this project.

Most of the employees and gyms were careful to distinguish what they did from self-defense. As indicated by Agatha, "we're pretty careful to say we don't provide self-defense...Because there's a very specific way to teach self-defense versus what we teach" (Agatha, Personal Communication, January 4, 2017). And Julie, who was a long time member and also an employee at one of the gyms, emphasized what I would argue is one of or *the* fundamental difference between self-defense classes and cardio-boxing/ kick boxing. "So, I think that for, I think it's very different from traditional self-defense in that we're not training with somebody coming at us" (Julie, Personal Communication, February 5, 2017). Yet, interestingly, Julie did not dismiss it as being completely distinct from self-defense, rather she said,

> I think that is still makes you much more capable of . . . having the skills you need in that situation. So I wouldn't say that it is the, you know if you want to get into it, specifically to learn effective self-defense that's probably not your fastest route. But if you . . . you know, if there are other reasons to do it, and then this is also I think one of the side effects, so you know, again, you learn to move quickly, you learn to punch fast, you learn to punch in a surprising way you know, part of it is to not be predictable. Um and I think you know, in case, when you are in that situation, when you have boxing training you don't have to think about how to punch, you got that part down. You just have to think about how do I get away you know, and then you got a lot of the skills that you are going to need for the physical side of it, and it's just thinking about, you know, how do I, how do I escape, how do I make sure that I get away from this dangerous situation. So, I don't think that it should be billed as self-defense, as I don't think it is traditional self-defense, but, I do think that a lot of women felt like that was a side effect of it, that they were more prepared were they to ever to find themselves in that position. (Julie, Personal Communication, February 5, 2017)

The idea of learned skills becoming the immediate response to a real-life attack was a common understanding among participants and trainers. For example, Evelyn suggested that attending cardio-boxing classes "develops muscle memory...you, you're more likely to keep your hands up and [it] kind of helps with your reaction time, you know being able to fade, slip, like what if someone [attacks you]" (Evelyn, Personal Communication, July 15, 2017). This is likely due to the empowering effects that women experienced (see chapters 2 and 4 for a more detailed discussion). As noted by Arthur, a seasoned trainer who differentiated what they did at the cardio-boxing gym from self-defense, who also endorsed the skills they taught as being useful for gyms members in defending themselves,

> Ah, I think that it definitely gives you the skill and confidence to . . . to feel like you can defend yourself now. Obviously if you want to actually learn that stuff now you can take some self-defense classes . . . there are proper ways to do that. But you know if somebody's like trying to take some money or something away from you, at least you can throw a punch, right? (Arthur, Personal Communication, December 27, 2016)

Another trainer at one of the gyms also blurred this distinction, "if you do want to start fighting people, then you know you'll have your cardio up and your standard defense moves, you have your foot movement down, you'll have your basics" (Lucas, Personal Communication, January 7, 2017).

Despite attempts at distancing self-defense from boxing, it was a script that emerged frequently in many of the spaces and was often specifically directed towards female gym-goers. For example, during classes, there were many motivational quips thrown out by predominantly male trainers such as "He got your purse, what you gonna do!" (Antonio, Personal Communication, July 9, 2017) and "You never know when you might get into a fight, on the street or at a PTA meeting!" (Arthur, Personal Communication, December 22, 2016). As previously noted, some of the cardio-boxing gyms had large female gym membership and specifically catered their classes to women. Jack, a trainer at one of the cardio gyms felt that incorporating real-life situational narratives in the courses he taught was beneficial to the gym members, he argued "I usually try to uh, make my classes for that context like you don't want, you don't want nobody to grab you so that's why we gotta be fast with our punch" (Jack, Personal Communication, March 7, 2017).

Defense as a narrative, therefore, was incorporated as a tool to empower and increase women's confidence in their physical selves. It contributed to the commodification of the boxers' workout as being something useful to women beyond physical fitness. Although not expressly marketed as being traditional self-defense, the enduring understanding for many people in these spaces was that learning to box would help as "if you were punched you would know how to like either block or hit back if you had to" (Hannah, Personal Communication, June 20, 2017). It must be acknowledged that the narrative of self-defense capitalizes on common understandings of masculinity and femininity where women are automatically socially constructed as being weaker than men. It also offers commentary on the relationship between gender, violence, and capitalism.

Sociologist and philosopher Zygmunt Bauman (1987, 166) argues that "Men and women are integrated into society as, above all, consumers." This extends beyond market logics to aspects of everyday life. As a consequence, "every item of culture becomes a commodity [and] . . . all perceptions and expectations . . . are trained and molded inside the new 'foundational' institution – that of the market" (Bauman 1987, 166). Boxing is no different. Bauman is also careful to emphasize that consumerism extends beyond the material to include the symbolic, something that constructs self, identity, and relationships with others. Here, we see larger social relations—that of heteronormative gender as it relates to the very real threat of men's violence toward women—manifest in marketing and sales techniques in boxing spaces. Memberships, classes, and "ring ready" programs are marketed and sold to women reinforcing individualized scripts of self-defense and protection from future violence. But as boxing gyms are a microcosm of the society in which we live, it is not surprising that women, independent of their level of engagement with the sport, consume and reproduce the narratives of self-defense. Given that we live in a time where we had a sitting President that openly bragged about sexually assaulting women, the self-defense narrative as a marketing tool offers a pragmatic and accessible (not for all) means for women to claw back some of their control and power. This understanding of the sport was further reflected in some of the experiences women had that shaped their decision to seek out boxing as a pastime as opposed to other group activity classes such as cycling, yoga, barre, and/or crossfit, to mention but a few.

PAST VIOLENCE AS A MOTIVATOR TO LEARN BOXING SKILLS

Although the official line from cardio-boxing gyms was that they did not offer self-defense classes, some of the women mentioned having a past experience with male-perpetrated violence as being a catalyst for inquiring about classes. In these cases, the commodification of defense directly intersected with the threat of men's violence against women. One participant said, "I went through a divorce um, which when me and my ex-husband split he had put me in the hospital, and that brought me to the [cardio gym] and ever since then I couldn't leave" (Rebecca, Personal Communication, March 21, 2017). Another recalled a frightening attack, "Yeah, I wish when I was attacked that I had been boxing because I probably would've at least tried to defend myself better. I got thrown through glass by a guy, by [a] man" (Hannah, Personal Communication, June 20, 2017). In addition, several trainers said that women specifically sought out the boxercise gyms because of an attack or as a method to reclaim some of their confidence and power. The following conversation with Jack illustrates the types of experiences that brought women into the gym.

Jack: I've heard a lot of them mention self defense [women] . . . and like, is this, if I take these classes will I know how to defend myself? And my answer's yes. And I had two girls come in that had been beat. One girl downtown . . . she was downtown

Victoria: Yeah?

Jack: And a guy asked to dance with her, and I don't know how drunk he was, she said no and I don't know the whole context, but she said she said no and he hit her.

Victoria: Wow.

Jack: Broke her jaw . . . and nobody did anything . . . Um like a girl, her friends did something. Found some guys or something [to help]. So, she came in, and she came with her friend, her friend said she had gotten hurt, she had a boyfriend last year that was beating her. So, she wanted to come in here for that too . . . um and the cardio gym is good coz it's not, it's not like you walk in and it's full of bruteness and getting beat up.

Victoria: Right.

Jack: It's ah, it's a nice way you can start in, start with self defense, so, everyone needs to know how to defend themselves so that's why I try to throw it in there, uh through the context stuff. (Jack, Personal Communication, March 7, 2017)

Here, a violent incident coupled with a history of intimate partner violence led this woman to seek out the boxing gym.

In an analysis of the impacts of recreational boxing programs on women and transgendered survivors of violence in Canada, Cathy Van Ingen (2011) argues that boxing has many therapeutic benefits. One such benefit was that boxing allowed for the physical expression of anger. As noted by Joyce Carol Oates (2006, 63), "boxing is the only sport in which anger is accommodated, enabled." While I agree that the boxing gym provides an appropriate venue for the emotional exploration and expression of anger and aggression, behaviors that are considered taboo for women, it remains problematic to conflate the learning of a pugilistic sport with the acquisition of traditional self-defense skills.

The goal of traditional self-defense programs is to better equip women with the physical and psychological skills necessary to defend against a violent attack, with the focus most often being a sexual assault (Follansbee 1982; Kelly 1988; McCaughey 1997). The programs also provide for the empowering of women to trust their own situational awareness and instinctual feelings/reactions to a potential threat. Health educator and victim advocate Nina Cummings (1992, 185) argues that the main goals of self-defense programs are,

(1) to identify the realities and myths regarding sexual assault and violence against women; (2) to provide information that will support the basic attitudes and attributes of self-defense, including assertiveness, awareness, self-reliance, confidence, and physical fitness; (3) to establish ways for students to learn how to identify threatening and high-risk situations; (4) to provide skill-building activities that incorporate mental, vocal, and physical self-defense techniques; (5) to provide strategies for specific situations that may occur on campus; and (6) to provide information about resources available to women who have been or may be abused or assaulted.

There is, of course, considerable variation in the types of programs provided with some extending beyond relying solely on the physical body to incorporate weapons and firearm trainings (McCaughey 1997). However, the overall goal is specific to resisting an attack and often includes components that extend beyond the physical to include the psychological, emotional, and behavioral. Although some of the benefits of engaging boxing may be the same (i.e., increased confidence, assertiveness, and reclamation of control whether perceived or otherwise), the goals of boxing and pugilistic sports more broadly do not center around deflecting a sexual assault by any means necessary.

Fighting sports, including boxing, are just that, a sport. There are techniques, rules, and skill development centered around winning a bout that is guided by rules and regulations, restricted to the use of certain punches with other moves deemed illegal, with the contest playing out under the surveillance of a referee. At the risk of stating the obvious, beyond fists there are no weapons or improvising with the tools that may surround a person. The difference is nicely summarized by an established boxer who stated,

> It's another thing to actually hit someone and like without the glove and that's another thing in and of itself. But then there are no rules. You could, you could do anything you know? Bite, pinch, like all these different things that you don't think about and even me as a boxer think about like kick-boxing or another form of fighting in, in as far as in a sport sense, that is it just blows my mind. I'm just like oh shoot I have to think about all this other stuff that you know I have to defend [against] and so yeah, that's why I think it's best if it stays in the sport world. (Anna, Personal Communication, March 11, 2017)

As indicated here, there are some obvious differences between the two despite the dominant understanding that cardio-boxing increases self-defense capabilities. It perhaps is easier to understand this conflation when metrics of success for both cardio-boxing and traditional self-defense rely on self-reports.

Measures of participant success in traditional self-defense training have utilized metrics that rely on self-reports of increased assertiveness, confidence, self-efficacy, self-esteem, and reduced anxiety and fear (Brecklin 2008). By these measures, engaging cardio-boxing would be considered a successful self-defense program. As summarized by Hannah, "I've definitely been in situations where I'm like if I was to be like, I got these combos in my head you know. So, it can see you or give you that security" (Hannah, Personal Communication, June 20, 2017). However, when other metrics are used, such as significant decreases in sexual assaults, there is little evidence that self-defense programs have any impact (Anderson and Whiston 2005). Reviews of self-defense programs exclude martial arts trainings, providing rationales that highlight the differences in skills that are taught. For example, some studies have argued that traditional martial arts courses teach skills that are disparate and impractical for women faced with a decision where they would have to defend themselves (Searles and Berger 1987; Searles and Follansbee 1984). Other criticisms suggest martial arts are geared toward men, exhibitions, and competitions (Haven 2004). Psychologists Amy Angleman, Yoshihiko Shinzato, Vincent Van Hasselt, and Stephen Russo (2009) suggest these understandings of martial arts can be misleading and are often reflective of larger cultural understandings that are presented in the media.

Women's interest in self-defense and fighting sports is reflective of cultural shifts that inform its construction in the public domain. For example, in the 1990s, there was a cultural shift in how women's self-defense was not only portrayed but consumed. This coincided with the rise in attention to women's rights and the dangers of sexual and intimate partner violence. Prior to the 1990s, the predominant representation of sex and violence in the media had eroticized and romanticized a women's inability to defend herself against a sexual attack (something that in no way has been eradicated). This has served to not only normalize sexual violence but promotes the idea that women enjoy forced sex. Beginning in the 1990s however, film and television offered several examples of strong women who were able to defend themselves including characters in the movies *Thelma and Louise, Aliens, La Femme Nikita* and *Blue Steel* to mention but a few (McCaughey 1997). Other more recent examples include the television show *Jessica Jones* and the films *Wonder Woman, Kill Bill,* and *Atomic Blonde* where women successfully defend themselves from violence perpetrated by men. In addition, there are a number of films where the utility of martial arts is demonstrated undermining the misconception that they are indeed gender specific. For example, consider the film franchise *Charlie's Angels,* where women characters use traditional martial art techniques against significantly larger male opponents. This movie highlights the importance of technique and skill over size, as well as suggests that women using traditional martial arts as a means for defense is becoming more socially acceptable.

In a comparison between traditional martial arts programs and self-defense programs, Angleman et al. (2009) conclude that despite some of the aforementioned misconceptions about traditional martial arts programs, there is not enough research comparing the two to make any significant conclusions. They do however, highlight that traditional martial arts programs can teach necessary skills that may aide in thwarting an attack, namely, "proficiency in physical skills combined with an ability to execute these skills under duress" (Angleman et al. 2009, 92). They also emphasize the benefits of one-on-one instruction and trying your skills against varying opponents opposed to being restricted to the group structure of a standard self-defense course. Angleman et al.'s (2009) assertions would support the utility of cardio-boxing as being beneficial to women if they were attacked; however, I want to caution that despite boxing being a fighting sport, there is considerable debate as to whether boxing can be considered a traditional martial art (Ivanov 2020). In addition, cardio-boxing, as studied here, is group-exercise classes where the emphasis is cardio fitness and not necessarily the development of increased proficiency in boxing skills and techniques beyond taking on the opponent of a heavy bag. As a result, it was not surprising to find that there seemed to be a disconnect for some members about their own proficiency and ability to defend themselves as compared to how other more experienced fighters viewed them.

REALITY OR FANTASY? THE UTILITY
OF BOXING AS SELF-DEFENSE

Many participants felt that the boxing skills they acquired at the cardio-boxing gyms increased their feelings of safety. For example, Agatha said "Yeah, I think it's liberating. Especially for me and um, you know it gives you that self-control and I'm able to now comfortably walk out on the street and so like if I was to be attacked I would be able to defend myself..." (Agatha, Personal Communication, January 4, 2017), and Lana who reflected, "I didn't really realize until I thought about it that I feel an awful lot less scared to be alone" (Lana, Personal Communication, August 4, 2017). Having a better sense of security and self is not necessarily a bad thing, and it would be difficult to quantify how much of it can be attributed to newly acquired boxing skills opposed to general feelings of empowerment and improved bodily confidence. I too noticed considerable differences in myself after I started attending cardio-boxing classes related to my posture, feelings of confidence, and having increased power over my physical self. Having engaged in adversarial boxing, however, I am not convinced that my cardio-boxing experience really prepared me for the experience of being hit, or hitting someone else (as discussed in chapter 6), and I feel I would be remiss to present cardio-boxing as an effective self-defense program in isolation. My feelings on the topic are more readily reflected by more experienced pugilists who were skeptical of this perception and argued that being better able to defend yourself as a result of taking "bag classes" bordered on the absurd. Pointing out that anyone can be brave or fight back when the opponent is a stationary object, one experienced pugilist boxer called these novice boxers "heavy-bag heroes" (Lucas, Personal Communication, January 7, 2017).

Commentary from more experienced pugilists centered on what they characterized as a disconnect between feelings of better preparedness when faced with a potential attack because of engagement with cardio-boxing, and the reality of what that might mean. This dissonance was effectively summed up by the following conversation I had with Marie,

Marie: It makes me feel like I guess if I was out somewhere and had to use it or something I could . . .
Victoria: Okay.
Marie: You know I would be able to protect myself better.
Victoria: Okay, so you feel, would you say it's fair to say you feel a bit more secure?
Marie: Yes, yes for sure.
Victoria: Okay.
Marie: Definitely.
Victoria: And have you ever hit somebody before?
Marie: No. (Marie, Personal Communication, June 18, 2017)

Without undermining Marie's feelings of security and her reclamation of her physical self, it must be noted she was representative of the majority of women who exclusively engaged cardio-boxing, that is, they reported feeling better able to defend themselves having never entered the ring, thrown a punch at a person, or having been hit. This is in line with sociologist Lori Holyfield's (1999) commentary on consumer adventure where she argued that many people want the appearance of risk and the emotional dividends that result, without any real test of their skills when confronted with actual danger (i.e., stepping in the ring or utilizing these skills to defend against an attack). It was this that those more deeply engaged with the sport (actual amateur and professional fighters) took issue with. The more experienced fighters clearly made the distinction between cardio-boxing, adversarial boxing, and self-defense. For example, a professional fighter said the following about the cardio-gym.

> And I'm like you guys aren't even real boxing. You just out there cat fighting. Hitting the bag which you know it's, that's what it's for, it's a workout but, I don't know. They set people up for failure. Cause some people in there . . . take that stuff to heart and I hope they don't have to put it to the test one day. They're gonna be surprised you know. No one in there really knows how to slip a punch. No one really, they never practice." (Antonio, Personal Communication, July 9, 2017)

Another amateur MMA fighter agreed, making the following comment.

> [T]hey have this huge head because they hang out with, you know, the fighters and everything and then they'll get in the ring to spar or something and they

shut down and it's like, it's like you're well, you're just talking all this mess about you know how good you've gotten whatever, why'd you lock up? [freeze in the ring] And he's like, well I just got nervous. Okay, so what are you gonna do in the street? Okay, so are you gonna just get nervous and lay, and lay down or what? So the false sense of security is definitely an issue and that's something my coach talked to me about you know, it's no different than like you see these karate dojos and stuff like that um that are providing this false sense of security because you know they're taught to, they're taught for scenarios not whatever comes at you, so you know some of these self-defense martial arts . . . it's like if somebody has you, you know armed locked out choking you, you're gonna do all of this. You know, it seems like how many times in a street altercation have you seen someone come at you like this, you know, that they, they're basically like we call them uh Hollywood martial arts because they're made for Hollywood movies, like movies and stuff like that. (Matt, Personal Communication, July 25, 2017)

The more experienced fighters had the beneficial experience of transitioning from Hoffman's (2006) leather to the adversarial phase of boxing. They had experienced the reality of hitting and being hit, the process of fight or flight, and were more likely to emphasize that self-defense and boxing have different approaches, pedagogies, and end-goals. The inability of cardio-boxers to practice on a person creates the potential for problems. As indicated by an amateur boxer who also taught classes at one of the cardio-boxing gyms, this has the potential to create a false sense of security. "The only problems I see is giving people this false hope. Uhm, of uh, yeah, you could hit this bag so you can totally hit someone else if you needed to. Which is completely not true" (Lucas, Personal Communication, January 7, 2017).

Boxing, both cardio and adversarial, was more clearly distinguished from those skills privileged in self-defense by those with greater involvement in the sport. However, it must be noted that although some more experienced women pugilists made similar comments, it was male combat fighters that more quickly questioned its efficacy as a self-technique. Therefore, the situational positioning of men on the gender hierarchy could have made them more likely to adhere to tropes about femininity and protectionist rhetoric that women should be reliant on others, perhaps men, for protection from physical threats and danger. This is despite research that has found that when women do physically fight an attacker they frequently attempt ineffective strategies (Bart and O'Brien 1985; Kleck and Sayles 1990; Koss et al. 1988; Zoucha-Jensen and Coyne 1993). In teaching women self-defense techniques when the focus is on upper body strength, women are less effective than when the emphasis is on hips and leg muscles (Madden and Sokol, 1997). It has also been argued that the most successful strategies, that is, those that increase the chance of escape—emphasize a combination of physical resistance, yelling, and running away when possible (Bart and O'Brien 1985; Ullman and Knight 1992, 1993). Boxing, especially cardio-boxing, does not emphasize any of these techniques, rather the focus is on mastering the punches through repetition and elevating the heart rate to burn calories for exercise. There is no emotional situating or recreation of attack scenarios.

Although the experience was not typical, there were a few women who predominantly engaged in cardio-contact boxing that reported having an experience where their newly acquired boxing skills helped them defend themselves. One such story that was shared came from gym member Savannah, as detailed in the following conversation.

Savannah: Um, I used to work at [bar name] two summers ago, I was a bartender . . . This night I wasn't there, I was at you know where [bar name] used to be?

Victoria: I've heard of that. I sort of know where you mean, I think.

Savannah: Well, I had gotten off work early and my friends were there, and I went to meet them and then I left early because I was tired. I was waiting outside for my roomie to pick me up. Um just like on my phone probably, from here to the door [indicates a distance of about ten feet] from the bouncer . . . not like you know, well . . . And this older drunk guy comes out of the bar, he is like yelling at everyone, belligerent, never seen him before in my life, and he walks past me and I just look up from my phone and he looked at me and I just look like down and he turns around. Never seen him before and he starts coming at me, and I'm like what is this guy doing and he shoves me . . .

Victoria: Oh, my goodness.

Savannah: And literally [I've] never spoken a word to the dude. Still the weirdest experience of my life. I land in this like bush, kind of, like big bush, so I kind of like bounce out of it. And so, I shoved him back and he's got me on the ground onto the concrete.

Victoria: Jesus.

Savannah: And then it didn't hurt, but he was like hitting me so that I just come up and threw a left hook and hitting him in the face.

Victoria: Oh, wow good for you.

Savannah: Then this like cop rolls up, and he's like are you okay and the guy takes off running and I was like yeah I'm fine, I don't know that guy, like I don't know what just happened. And like the bouncer came over and was like, what happened? I seriously was like, I don't know. But, at that moment like I was happy I knew how to throw a punch. (Savannah, Personal Communication, April 4, 2017)

Savannah felt empowered by this experience and credited her fast action to her boxing skills and, whether rightly or wrongly, further conflated boxing with self-defense. There is, of course, no way to determine whether it was truly her boxing skills that saved her from further harm as I readily admit that there were other factors that may have influenced the outcome (i.e., her attacker's size, stature, speed, intoxication, etc.) and some might argue that the outcome could well have been different resulting in more harm to Savannah. But speculative questioning of the outcome supports larger structures of gender socialization that defines femininity in terms of rape culture where femininity means violability and weakness. Heterosexual gender roles are not only played out, but they are institutionally enforced, and through enforcement they are embodied (MacKinnon 1987). In questioning Savannah's recollection of the events that transpired, including her attributing her defense to "her left hook", I am undermining her physicality and her ability to fight because, as McCaughey (1997) argues, this would require an unlearning of the broadly understood gender socialization. To acknowledge Savannah's successful self-defense means subscribing to a femininity that is not socially endorsed, one that accepts aggressiveness, overcomes proclivities to be submissive, nice, passive, and any physical hesitancy. I am, therefore, reluctant to engage in any questioning of Savannah's account as I too, would be subscribing to heteronormative culture understandings of femininity that undermines women's physicality.

Although Savannah's was one of only two stories that emerged where women had utilized their boxing skills as a form of defense, her experience was not typical. The more typical scenario was that of gym participants who had fortunately not had their boxing skills tested in a real-life attack. Therefore, the pragmatic limitations of equating cardio-boxing to self-defense cannot be ignored. The idea that cardio-boxing taught basic defensive skills was prominent in this research. It is understandable that in acquiring skills that are not only empowering and instilling of confidence but also reward physically aggressive behaviors that have previously been attributed solely to men, women felt more confident and able to defend themselves. Women were able to reclaim their power through their embodiment of behaviors that challenge the existing gender order. However, having discussed the transition from cardio-boxing to adversarial boxing in chapter 6, the reality of being hit or hitting someone is more complex than simply relying on muscle memory, especially as not everyone reacts the same when confronted with real violence.

BOXING, SELF-DEFENSE, AND VIOLENCE

There have been a number of scholarly articles that have criticized the sport of boxing as being "organized brutality" (Lundbery 1986). Boxing, specifically, has received criticism for its viciousness, with some arguing that this disqualifies is from even being considered a sport (Cynarski and Litwiniuk 2006). In 2019 alone, three professional boxers died as a result of blows to the head during boxing matches; Maxim Dadashev aged 28, Hugo Santillan aged 23, and Patrick Day aged 27 (Graham 2019). The response to such claims have long focused on the defensive merits of engaging the sport where "Boxing also makes a man self-reliant and resourceful when assaulted by sudden or unexpected dangers or difficulties" (Edwards 1888, 33). The acceptance of women in the fighting sports has been slow (see chapter 2 for a more detailed overview), with women only officially being accepted in the Golden Gloves in 1995, meaning that the inclusion of women in recreational boxing is a relatively recent development. Couple this with the purposeful marketing of cardio-boxing to women consumers (see chapters 3 and 4), it is not unexpected that issues that impact women more broadly would also emerge in these gym spaces. The overt or more subtle offering of self-defense as a justification for engaging the sport brings the issue of violence to the fore, specifically the threat of violence to women and their ability to defend themselves. This capitalizes on discourses that differentiate between harmful violence and defensive violence, the latter framed as being more defendable or justifiable.

The subject of violence more broadly often emerged as it related to understandings of cardio-boxing and boxing can be utilized for self-defense. As argued by Hollander (2009) in relation to self-defense, there is a general belief that violence should not be the solution to violence. This philosophical underpinning leads to the rejection of women engaging in behaviors that are perceived as being violence as "Women need to be safe from violence without having to learn self-defense, and we must develop better means of conflict resolution than physical violence" (Russell et al. 2007, 5). This is compounded by beliefs that women who were exposed to violent behaviors through self-defense courses would cause them to enjoy using these newly acquired skills a little too much (Russell et al. 2007), and then utilize them in situations where they were not needed. Interestingly, this assertion came from a focus group study of women who avoided self-defense courses exploring their reasons for making that decision. Extrapolating on this justification, Russell et al. (2007, 4) argue this implies "that women who are not vulnerable are dangerous to themselves and others." While acknowledging the already mentioned differences between self-defense and boxing, I agree with Hollander (2009) when she questions the merits of this claim. Like Hollander (2009), I have yet to encounter a woman who has purposely exposed herself to an unsafe situation due to their engagement with the sport. In my experience, the greater my engagement with the sport, the more I recognized its inherent limitations as a self-defense technique.

Interestingly, my perspective was not unique. This inverse relationship developed with many participants indicating that the greater the exposure to boxing, the more caution and acknowledgement there was that street fighting or being attacked outside of the gym space brought in other unknowns that increased risk and danger. In talking about the difference between boxing and being attacked, Anna said "But boxing you're like, oh shoot they have a weapon…Yeah that's when the running comes in" (Anna, Personal Communication, January 27, 2017). Elizabeth also said, "you, might have a false sense of security, so at the same time you might think you're a bad ass, right, then you get yourself in trouble and you really don't know what you're doing. It's more of the exercise at the cardio-boxing gym" (Elizabeth, Personal Communication, April 21, 2017).

Furthermore, some of the women interviewed commented that there were certain people or groups in the gym spaces that had a different perception of their own abilities as compared to how they were perceived by others. It was expressed that these gym-goers had a confidence that was not reflected by their skill set, a "false perception of what you're capable of" (Elizabeth, Personal Communication, April 21, 2017). To be clear, I am not suggesting that this false sense of security or self, results from women's inability to defend themselves. Nor am I agreeing with the oft-touted view that it is too dangerous for women to attempt to defend themselves; a criticism that has gained both social and cultural traction by feminist researchers that oppose self-defense as a tactic more broadly (Hollander 2009; McCaughey 2000). Rather, I am drawing attention to what could be described as an aggrandized perception of self that is related to the mislabeling of cardio-boxing as self-defense and/or the consumer belief that they have acquired fighting skills. Furthermore, the philosophical position that argues "violence begets violence" (Rosenblum 2007) makes no differentiation between the violence of an attack and defensive violence. They are simply lumped together, ignoring the contextual and motivational factors, as well as the impacts of the violence, most importantly that defensive violence is *responsive*. I agree with Hollander (2009) when she argues that responsive violence can be qualitatively differentiated from assaultive violence perpetrated by an attacker. However, if boxing should not be considered self-defense, then it is important to consider how participants here conceptualize it as it relates to violence.

Sports violence is difficult to define (Young 2019). In the sociology of sports literature there is an abundance of terms that are used, often interchangeably, to convey violence and behaviors/actions that are violent (Cashmore 2000; Coakley and Donnelly 2009). Likewise there are numerous theoretical approaches advanced to explain violence and aggression, too many to adequately review here (Atkinson and Young 2008; Berkowitz 1978; Bushman and Anderson 2001; Deutschmann 2007; Eller 2006; Kerr 2004;

Muir and Seitz 2004; Priks 2010). While the focus here is not to review the complexities and arguments offered by this literature, it must be noted that boxing has been subject to considerable scholarly criticism from varying fields for its brutality as well as the harm it causes to the body, particularly the brain. Therefore, boxing would meet sports sociologists Jay Coakley and Peter Donnelly's (2009, 187–188) definition of sports violence, "the use of excessive physical force, which causes or has the potential to cause harm or destruction." Despite public opinions, scholarly criticism, and the advancement of medical concerns, those engaged in the sport often adopt "interpretive frames" (Hughes and Coakley 1991) that socialize them to the norms within their sport. This dictates behaviors that are both acceptable and unacceptable within the sport.

The focus here is not to examine or diminish the legitimacy of concerns expressed over the violent nature of the sport of boxing, rather it is to examine how it is perceived by the participants in this study. For women who are socialized to suppress their own aggression, anger and violence (Allen 1986; McCaughey 1997), it is important to understand how they view their participation in the sport, especially as for women boxing is "characterized as disreputable and dangerous" (Hargreaves 1994, 183). This wider public perception of the incompatibility of women with the sport is further compounded by the aforementioned belief that women's utilization of violence is dangerous, ineffective against men's violence, and could lead to further harm and therefore it is never appropriate as a solution (Hollander 2009). This is especially important to examine when boxing has been found to be a useful vehicle for the legitimation of women's anger and aggression (Van Ingen 2011), a finding supported by this very study.

The dominant understanding of boxing by the participants included here largely rejected dominant social and cultural understandings of the sport as violence. By labeling boxing as sport allowed participants to separate it from violence. This view was often coupled with a caveat that provided qualifiers for if, and when, it could be considered violence. The most common qualifier for its preclusion from violence was likening the risk of harm to those experienced in other sports. For example, when asked whether boxing is violence, Angelina argued "Um, I guess no because I consider it, to me, it's not that different from soccer. I haven't ever gotten more hurt from boxing than soccer. Um, and soccer isn't violent to me so I would have to say no" (Angelina, Personal Communication, February 16, 2017). In addition to soccer, basketball, American football, target shooting, MMA, hockey, and horseback riding were also brought up as comparatives that led to equal if not more harm. Julie's comments were similar, yet she explored the topic further in her qualification of what does and does not constitute violence,

I think that there's a violent side to it. Um, so for me it's kind of the same as with shooting. Um, so I think that on it's own, and you know, and you're target shooting it is not necessarily inherently violent, but it can cross into violence, and um so for me, with boxing and MMA and all of that, I think that there is strategy involved. I think it is absolutely a sport, there's very much logic and skill and practice that goes into it. Um but I think especially when it gets into the ring, and you get kind of down to the self-protective core that we all have when we have to have it, um it can turn violent. And I think that, you know, there's a reason we have referees in sports like this, and you know, because I think someone has to be there to say, this is the line between sport and violence, and I'm going to stop you before you get to that purely violent part. Um, you know, and some people are probably more prone than others to crossing that line um but I think part of what comes with it, you know, you see this a lot with professional fighters, is they have to just have this desire to destroy their opponent. (Julie, Personal Communication, February 5, 2017)

The physical regimes associated with developing the skill and expertise of becoming a boxer distanced it from violence for Julie, but she still suggested that there is an underlying violence that is only contained through regulations and referees. This suggests the distinction is not clear cut, something that was supported by Emelia's comment in response to the question whether she thought boxing was violence, "I think a lot of people do unfortunately. Like, I definitely think, it's really hard to justify people hitting each other and then being like oh it's okay…it's dangerous…he can get hit incorrectly and you can be brain-dead the rest of your life" (Emelia, Personal Communication, July 17, 2017).

In a similar manner, by distinguishing it as sport the women often spoke of the motivations and situational context of those participating as opposed to the goals of those engaging in behaviors they clearly saw as violence. For example, Hannah argued that real violence is "If you just like were out and pick a fight, I don't know, [and] punch somebody upside the head that you know if you punch you're going to hurt him because you're doing it. I guess that's violence" (Hannah, Personal Communication, June 20, 2017). Faye also emphasized the intent as being what differentiates violence from sport, saying,

I think, what I consider violence I think of you trying to hurt someone else. And I think [boxing] you're not ever trying to hurt anyone. Even though it's, it's considered a little bit more of a violent sport. I don't think your goal is to hurt somebody. (Faye, Personal Communication, December 15, 2016)

The intent to cause meaningful harm was a common characteristic for defining violence. Angelina agreed with Faye when she suggested that the goals in boxing were not the same as for those who want to commit violence. She argued,

> Yeah, well I mean, I guess trying to hurt someone for the express purpose of hurting them. At least with boxing you're trying to hurt them to win the fight, but the purpose is to win the fight. Not to pummel them. And there's usually respect for your opponent, you don't actually want to like harm them . . . in a meaningful way. (Angelina, Personal Communication, February 16, 2017)

Caroline took this further, arguing that,

> I would consider verbal aggression like cussing or you know like pointing a gun at someone . . . I would consider that violence. You know . . . Or you know like even fighting in an uncontrolled setting that would be violence . . . but like a lot of like martial arts sports they're in controlled settings and there are certain moves that you cannot do to your opponent and if you actually think about it, I guess like I am, there are like less deaths. (Caroline, Personal Communication, February 13, 2017)

Other participants focused on consent being key to demarcating the boundaries of violence. When both parties consent to spar/fight in a bout then the general perception was that this negated any classification of violence. In discussing the difference between the two, Savannah argued,

> If you and I were like about to box, or about to spar, that's nonviolence because we know we are both doing it. But if I go up to a guy on the street and I'm like "hey we're sparring" and punch him, like that's violence. So, I would say if both people were like willing then it's not, but if it's a [situation] where one person is not, you know, aware of the situation or doesn't want to participate I will feel like that's violence. (Savannah, Personal Communication, April 4, 2017)

In her book *Consensual Violence: Sex, sports, and the Politics of Injury*, Jill Weinberg (2016) discusses the importance of consent and regulations in the process of social decriminalization of behaviors that are otherwise considered taboo. Weinberg draws attention to the construction of these behaviors in the broader social climate, something that she argues is largely shaped by media framing that can garner the support and trust of the public. The creation of rules, therefore, has legitimated previously private actions between two people into semi-public commercialized spaces. These acts of violence have been made palatable through state sanctioning. Boxing has been "civilized" (Elias 1994) where otherwise violent acts have been transformed into consensual acts. Further legitimating the narrative of consent as a characteristic that delineates sport from violence are the heroic narratives that dominate popular constructions of the sport.

Boxing has long been associated with honor where displays on masculine athleticism are grounded in a genealogy that has been shaped by militarism, courage, and honorable masculinities (Woodward 2007). This construction persists, painting boxers as gladiatorial-like opponents that are engaged in a heroic endeavor. Their athleticism is celebrated by the masses who watch them overcome not only their opponent but the struggles they have brought to the sport that they then embody in their face-off in the ring. This is not new symbolism as boxing more broadly is associated with transcending class and race barriers and as a vehicle for escaping tragedy through disciplinary reform of the physical body. This often includes histories that have to be overcome such as Mike Tyson being involved in thefts and robberies as he grew up in an impoverished neighborhood in Brownsville (Cynarski and Litwiniuk 2006). Other examples include Joe Louis joining the army, cementing the American dream by conforming to the militarism that has been instilled in boxing narratives (Woodward 2007). George Foreman followed a similar trajectory, and infamously Muhamad Ali used boxing as a platform for resistance and was stripped of his Championship title, rejected for being unpatriotic when he refused to conscript as an act of political resistance, before reconfiguring his image through the platform of boxing as someone who "stood tall as a man who stood by and literally fought for his principles" (Sugden 1996, 46).

For women, although these narratives exist, they are less about escaping a life of crime or making political statements, rather the focus is on personalized stories such as overcoming past childhood abuses and sexual assault. Consider Quanitta Underwood, an American boxer fighting in the 2012 London Olympics, who received considerable media attention including detailed coverage in the *New York Times*. Instead of focusing on her athletic accomplishments and her boxing career the majority of the coverage is about her father's sexual abuse and her efforts through boxing to overcome it (Bearak 2012). Therefore, in popular cultural constructions of boxing, the focus is less on the act of consenting to be punched or punching someone, and instead on the reclamation of power and courageous heroism in overcoming history and controlling your own destiny. Boxing becomes a transformative vehicle for salvation, providing refuge and a means for empowerment. It is unsurprising that even at the most amateur level, the same narratives are upheld and are reproduced in the gym spaces that are selling the idea of boxing.

Despite the subjective nature of violence, motivations, consent, and regulations were key factors that led participants to differentiate boxing from violence. This distinction, however, ignores the violence that is inherent to sports (Smith 1983), something that Young (2019, 2) argues is rarely "taken seriously." Every sport is based on competition where rivalries play out through acts of aggression to lesser or greater degrees. These acts of aggression are more overt in sports such as boxing where the competition is based on face to face confrontation. A few participants argued that the violence in boxing is reflective of the violent nature of the society we live in. Hannah argued "I just feel like our world today is so violent, everything is so violent" (Hannah, Personal Communication, June 20, 2017). In her mind, a violent society led to the normalization of behaviors that otherwise would have been rejected.

Antonio agreed with Hannah but also argued that the violence inherent in boxing was not only a reflection of society but was innate to all humans.

> Yeah it is violence. I mean football is violence. I mean everything can be violent. Basketball, if you hit someone in the air and fall and break their leg that's violent. You know what I mean, but that's what America was made on like, that's in our blood. I just feel like, that it's natural. Like even animals you know were made to combat and reproduce and just we all have different defense mechanisms. Like fighting is just natural you know. It's just . . . it's just in us. (Antonio, Personal Communication, July 9, 2017)

This view is not new, with the nature versus nurture debate influencing many different fields of academic inquiry. Although I am in no way advancing Antonio's position that violence is inherent to human nature, it has been noted that "Fight and violence are as old as the history of mankind and under certain conditions – socially acceptable and justified" (Cynarski and Litwiniuk 2006, 3).

CONCLUSION

This chapter has examined the narratives of self-defense and how they have emerged in the cardio gym spaces. Although none of the cardio gyms officially offered self-defense, the narratives emerged as it related to broader understandings of violence against women. This is not surprising considering that boxing gyms are a microcosm of society. Given that we live in a time where the potential for violence against women is high, the self-defense narrative as a marketing tool offers a pragmatic and accessible (not for all) means for women to claw back some of their control and power. A cursory online search for women's self-defense brings up thousands of classes ranging from "self-defense-survival-boot-camp" to "female awareness" Krav Maga, and even "Mommy and Me" self-defense classes. In addition, there is a large market of products that are sold for the purposes of assisting in self-protection or self-defense, many of them marketed based on gender. It is not surprising then that cardio-boxing gyms also want to capitalize on this market. Therefore, although they are not selling self-defense, they are capitalizing on these narratives.

Many of the women felt empowered by these narratives and the reclamation of power that accompanied the learning and embracing of boxing skills. This is not necessarily a bad thing, yet there were concerns that the conflation of boxing and self-defense led to a false sense of security, one that led women to believe they were better able to defend themselves if they were attacked even if they had never hit someone or been hit. More experienced pugilists saw the potential for danger and cautioned that this was creating a mirage of power that can only be shattered if their learned skills are put to the test—something they themselves would have to seek out at full-contact gyms or test in a real-life situation. Despite this potential for a false sense of security there were a few women who had successfully defended themselves when they were attacked. They credited this to their boxing skills. The chapter ended with a further examination of the complexities of defining violence in society as it relates to participants' perceptions of boxing and how this relates to larger understandings of sport and violence.

Chapter 8

The Female Fight

Sport and the Spectacle

INTRODUCTION

During the course of this project, I was able to attend multiple fights that ranged from professional fights to white-collar events that did not permit registered fighters to compete. These events were boxing and MMA, amateur and professional, and included both men and women. Focusing in on amateur fights, there was a wide spectrum of events ranging from a Greek life sponsored charity boxing tournament, to *Rough N' Rowdy*, to an amateur boxing match where a woman boxer was the headliner on the fight card. *The Boxing Event,* renamed for anonymity, was a charity endeavor where Greek organizations at one of the local universities pit members against each other in an annual boxing competition. The touring event *Rough N' Rowdy* was also held locally, an event that encourages people with no fighting experience to test their skills in the ring. Unlike the impromptu, clandestine, and unsanctioned fights of the "all women's fight club" discussed in chapter 5, these events were organized, promoted, and well attended. Focusing on women participants, this chapter examines the spectacle of the fight, with particular attention to the days leading up to the fight, advertising, and promotion as well as the atmosphere of the fight spaces that prioritize the anticipation, tension and overall entertainment experience for the fans in attendance. This chapter unpacks these women's experiences as they relate to not only the competition itself but also the preparation and training they endured in relation to gender.

PREPARING FOR THE FIGHT

Women fighters communicated that there were regimens and/or training schedules they followed to both mentally and physically prepare for a boxing match. Anna, an experienced amateur boxer who throughout her boxing career competed at the national level, said the following of her typical training regimen.

> Let's see um my typical day um my training. I'll do strength and conditioning which will vary each day but that ranges from a hour to two hours um, I . . . I would say probably everyday average an hour and a half of strength and conditioning and that'll be you know light weight, high rep, um a lot a lot of running um, I don't, because of my stress fracture, I haven't been able to run, but elliptical, doing something where you keep your heart rate in that fat burning range, um and then that'll, you'll do that for like 45 to 60 minutes, then you'll do like some general strength, where it's like body weight exercises, pushups, pull ups, stuff like that. (Anna, Personal Communication, March 11, 2017)

As expected, this was not that different from what male fighters said, or the widely documented regimens analyzed by Loïc Wacquant (2004), Kath Woodward (2007), Benita Heiskanen (2012), Lucia Trimbur (2013), to mention but a few. As noted by Heiskanen (2012, 35), "the pugilistic workout regimen itself is remarkably resistant to change." What was interesting however, was at the last minute the fight that Anna was preparing for was canceled. This was somewhat of a relief for her as she felt that her coach had been somewhat distracted by a more imminent fight scheduled for another boxer—a male professional fighter. Of the cancellation Anna said,

> This has nothing to do with my coaches' ability to coach, but there were a lot of distractions going on. And, I told you last week that I didn't feel like fully prepared. Not in my ability, I know I'm confident if I even went tomorrow, I could win the tournament. There is a difference between being skill wise prepared and mentally prepared . . . I want to go there and perform the way I can, and not be like 70 percent. (Anna, Personal Communication, March 11, 2017)

Further probing also revealed that from Anna's perspective, USA Boxing's organization of the tournament was poor, "I didn't even know until like a month, maybe even less, before where the hotels were even at, or like they didn't even put the fact sheet out for the tournament until a month before which normally you need to plan two months in advance for a tournament" (Anna, Personal Communication, March 11, 2017). She describes it as a "weight being lifted" (Anna, Personal Communication, March 11, 2017), but there was some carefully portrayed resentment that she did not get to spar enough in preparation for the tournament; something she reluctantly attributed to her coach's focus on his male professional fighter.

The prioritizing of male over female fighters is not a unique happening. It has been widely documented in the sports literature that there is still some resistance to women's acceptance in boxing, especially from coaches and trainers that occupy the lower levels of the boxing hierarchy where there is little fiscal gain to be had by including women (Heiskenan 2012). This resistance to women is compounded by the historically engrained gendered prowess of combative sports. As argued by feminist scholar Jane Gallop (1988, 18), those hesitant to the inclusion of women are not disturbed by "physical violence but the physical as it violated the rational categories that would contain and dominate it." Coaches of this "old school" mentality have been found to prioritize prizefighters over those engaging the sport at the lower levels or for recreation (Heiskanen 2012). This meant that for the less formal competitions, those more easily classified as white-collar boxing events, such as the Greek sponsored *The Boxing Event,* the fighters experienced what I can only characterize as a crash course in training.

The Boxing Event is a USA Boxing sanctioned event sponsored by a fraternity and a local fight gym. The event provides a night of amateur boxing matches between fraternity men, as well as sorority women. The requirements for participation included agreeing to, and completing, a program of training at the sponsoring fight gym. The coaches at the fighting gym can then assess and match fighters based on weight and skill. The fighters are then subjected to a weigh-in (emulating a real fight) in the days leading up to the event (Fieldnote, November 7, 2017). Penelope, a nineteen-year-old college student, signed up to participate in *The Boxing Event.* At the time of the competition, Penelope had been attending one of the cardio-boxing gyms for approximately three years and was a member of a sorority at one of the local universities. In talking about the event, she said "it's not too legit . . . But it's just, it's a boxing match, there's like three rounds, a minute and a half each I think with like a minute break in between" (Penelope, Personal Communication, November 1, 2016). In explaining the amount of time she had to prepare for the fight, Penelope said,

> Yea, so it's not too long, but they don't, they don't even start promoting it until like September . . . and then they pick sign-ups like September 15th, and then I was like I'm going to do it, you know. A lot, a lot of girls doing it haven't boxed before. So, it makes me even more confident that I can do it (laughs) if I am fighting someone who hasn't boxed, so I don't know. (Penelope, Personal Communication, November 1, 2016)

The fighters participating in the event, that was held every year in November, had less than eight weeks to prepare. Penelope felt that her experience with cardio-boxing gave her a significant advantage over other competitors who had little or no boxing experience. Although she communicated this advantage, she still participated in the training program associated with the fight event. Penelope's experience at the fight gym was different from what she was used to at the cardio-gym,

Penelope: I don't know, for training they haven't taught us how to do much, the people in the rings are always guys that already know what they're doing just kind of doing it for fun. Whereas I feel like they should be teaching the girls and the people that haven't sparred before how to spar.
Victoria: So, what do you do there then?
Penelope: Ummm you just kind of fend for yourself. You, they have some heavy bags and you can share those with people, because they only have three, but there's like 50 people there so, it's . . . yea, and a lot of people jump rope and do abs and stuff, coz they always have the timer going for rounds, coz someone's always in the ring sparring, but then, I don't know . . . coz there's two hours and a lot of people come later, coz there's less people there later, I don't know. It hasn't been super helpful for me. (Penelope, Personal Communication, November 1, 2016)

The lack of direction and instruction that Penelope was used to having at the cardio-gym was notably absent from the fight gym. Those at the fight gym were left to engage in the necessary roadwork for their own conditioning and skill development, which is a normative practice in fight gyms and requires the fighter to demonstrate the bodily labor necessary to become a boxer (Heiskenan 2012) outside of instruction and coaching. It communicates to those in the space, fellow fighters, coaches, and spectators that they are indeed serious about their pursuit of a fight career. They were also adhering to Hoffman's (2006) three stages of boxing: the air, leather, and adversarial phases.

Furthermore, it is possible that the lack of structured instruction provided to the *The Boxing Event* fighters was reflective of the event being a white-collar boxing event. As found by Trimbur (2011, 189), "Trainers know that the practices that boxing client perform are different from those that are competitive fighters, and it is imputed, not legitimate." By providing a watered-down, or lesser workout, the white-collar or recreational boxer leaves feeling like they have completed an authentic and rigorous boxing workout despite it being a carefully crafted illusion. Yet, for Penelope, a stranger to the cultural norms and etiquettes of a more traditional fight gym but someone who had been involved in cardio-boxing with some knowledge of boxing regimens, the lack of one-on-one instruction seemed odd. Given, the short time frame to train for her fight, coupled with having no fight experience, she felt that a more comprehensive and interactive level of instruction should have been provided. She worried more specifically about the lack of instructional sparring that was offered, "There's been one day that they've let everyone spar, and I think one spar before you're actually going out fighting . . . isn't good enough (laughs) . . . not for me to feel safe at least" (Penelope, Personal Communication, November 1, 2016).

As was the case with other women mentioned in this book (see chapters 4 and 5), instead of engaging the space of the traditional fight gym, one that Penelope found unhelpful to her goals, she sought out private instruction from a boxing trainer she knew. This trainer provided the instructional sparring experience Penelope felt she needed to feel comfortable getting into the ring. This instruction took place outside of the gym setting in the trainer's back garden, where he not only introduced Penelope to sparring but also brought in another more experienced female fighter to increase her skill. Penelope recounted the event with excitement,

> He got a girl named Louise, who did *The Boxing Event* last year, she knocked her girl out second round, and so I was scared, but she has like a brown belt in Ju Jitsu, a black belt in Karate and six years of martial arts, and I was like, I do not want to fight her. And then he had me do it, coz he's like I want to see where you stand and I was like, oh my god, and then we did four rounds, and she hurt me a few times, but it wasn't anything bad and that made me feel even more confident because I know how good she is and I could keep up with it. So, it was cool. (Penelope, Personal Communication, November 1, 2016)

Here, Penelope modified her approach to the sport of boxing when she felt the resources available to her were not inclusive—the instruction at the fight gym did not meet her wants or needs, nor was it welcoming. And, while the fighting gym and *The Boxing Event* were happy to capitalize on the spectacle of the white-collar boxing tournament, the reality was that the training provided was limited, especially for women participants. Penelope, as did other women who participated in this event, sought out women-friendly resources that she felt were more appropriate for her fight preparation, emphasizing again that when it comes to adversarial boxing the deeply rooted maleness of the sport still acts to limit access to women. Beyond the training regimens, it is also useful to examine the motivations the women had in pursuing fights whether for recreation or as part of a larger career.

Motivated to Fight

Motivations for getting in the ring for a fight differed considerably and largely depended on the event, the fighter, and the level of engagement they had with the sport. Noticeably, of all the women fighters included in this study those that had fight experience were all white, in their early 20s, and from middle-class backgrounds. Some of this is likely reflective of the demographical geography of the area, but it must be noted that this region can be described as being majority white, with one in every 5.5 people in the state living in poverty (WelfareInfo 2019). However, it is also reflective of more generalized patterns in boxing that show that women that pursue the sport often come from more varied backgrounds than male fighters. In her study of Gleason's Gym, Trimbur (2013) found that of the more than 300 women fighters who frequented the gym, the majority were middle class and came from educated backgrounds. They "worked as teachers, writers, artists, public relations specialists, nurses, administrative assistants, firefighters, and police officers or are college students" (Trimbur 2013, 94). This observation was reflected here as many of the women were highly educated or from seemingly middle-class backgrounds. Of those who were engaged in adversarial boxing, they were fitness instructors, college students, beauty pageant contestants, and administrative assistants. Others I came into contact with either through sparring or in gym spaces were sales managers, pursuing medical careers—one of my regular sparring partners left the area to pursue a surgical residency, or other similarly classified white-collar professions. This was contrasted heavily with the backgrounds of the male fighters who are the subject of other ethnographic studies (Heiskanen 2012; Jump 2020; Trimbur 2013; Wacquant 2004), as well as many of the male sparring partners or fighters I encountered here. For example, Antonio had a more traditional background that would more readily fit within the stereotypical narrative of a person who turns to fighting as a career. When asked to describe why he first started fighting, he said,

Antonio: When I was in . . . I guess it was maybe my senior year of high school, I don't know, we would just have some little A team, at a club, we was just dancing and long story short these guys came over and just, they just jumped us. Like it was seven of us and we probably got jumped by like, no exaggeration, probably like 30 people.

Victoria: That's horrible. I'm sorry that happened.

Antonio: And then after they jumped us, one of em had our phones I guess and they called us, and were like, "we're sorry we thought you was someone else we was beefing with um". . . . We looked like this other people they was beefing with. It was like "apology not accepted sir." But um and then in [name of a town] I'm pretty sure I got jumped cause I was black. I mean that's the only thing I can think of, cause I was just standing on the porch and I just see a bottle like pass my face. Like I felt the wind and it was a beer bottle. So, I looked around and only one guy is staring at me. And so, I looked at him and like, we're probably you know six feet away or so, and uh and I said, "did you throw that?" And he said "yeah." I said "why?" He said "I don't give a . . . I don't give a F," you know. So I had no shoes on, so I was like okay. I went to get my shoes on. I come back outside. There was like seven guys around, you know. I'm just tryna deal with him. So, uh so as I come outside I kinda pause, I see the seven guys and then they just rush me, start beating my ass. I don't know. It's really how it went, like I'm so confused like there was no like confrontation before. Just he threw a beer bottle, I asked him why, you know I thought I was gonna beat him up, one on one. Let's go. I was doing some young stupid stuff. But yeah, I ended up getting jumped. I always thought I could whoop three people, but it was pretty hard. They have to be really shitty fighters to beat up three people. Like cause you know, it's just, it's just hard, the third one is always gonna get you. It's a lot harder than it looks. Like I see some guys before I got jumped, like man I coulda done this and that. It's a lot harder than you think but um. So, I had um I had experiences. So after football was over I was like I gotta compete. I still love playing sports. I play basketball in high school and um . . . I did it and I was like well you know I always like to be in shape anyways. I was like this is cool. I can get in shape. I can learn how to fight. Why not? You know like . . . you never know, you know, I've been jumped a few times. I'm not a confrontational person but I will defend myself but um I'm like why not. So I started doing it for about six months maybe and I was like oh I'm kinda good at it. (Antonio, Personal Communication, July 9, 2017)

Pride featured heavily as a motivation for Antonio, but as an African American man living in a predominantly rural white region of the United States, this pride was situated in the structural and institutionalized racism he had experienced throughout his life. Although he had opportunities to pursue a football career beyond high school, he felt he was subject to increased surveillance because of his race. This increased scrutiny led to an arrest in college that ended his college career. It also was the catalyst for violence that foraged his path into pursuing fighting as a career option.

Similarly, I also briefly engaged in sparring drills with a very promising fighter, an eighteen-year-old Cuban man named Matteo. When I encountered Matteo he was saving all his paychecks to get boxing lessons from my coach, and we were sometimes paired up for drills. Matteo was quick, athletic, and worked hard. However, when I entered the gym for training one day he was notably absent. When I inquired as to his whereabouts, I was informed he had been arrested for drug possession and distribution. The story told was that he crashed his car and lost consciousness. When he woke up he found himself handcuffed and his vehicle being subject to a police search which resulted in them discovering not only drugs, but a scale in the trunk of his car (Fieldnote, August 12, 2018). Matteo's legal troubles created a significant barrier to his pursuing boxing as a career, but his story fits more with the dominant narrative of boxing being a vehicle for social and economic security (Heiskanen 2012; Wacquant 2004; Woodward 2007). It was a means to escape structural inequality, such as racism and financial hardship, in an effort at social mobility. Despite the dominance and popularity of this narrative more broadly, this did not emerge as a narrative for women fighters in this study.

Women's motivations were not about escaping structural oppression or increased state surveillance, nor were they about class mobility or economic security. Anna, for example, saw boxing as a calling,

> Like yes training stinks and it's, like you go through hell for lack of a better word, but like getting your hand raised and like winning that belt or the gold medal. I mean it's obviously not the end goal as far as life goes but that feeling is just euphoric like it's amazing and then I think really just me personally like, just having Jesus in my life obviously it's to glorify Him and I think that this is the road that He has me on and if I felt otherwise . . . it I would go a different avenue, but I will always love boxing. Like no matter where the Lord has me it's just putting all of the time and the effort into something and then you know reaching that goal and getting that gratification is just awesome. (Anna, Personal Communication, January 23, 2017)

Anna's faith played a strong roll in her boxing career and her life more broadly, she expressed an almost fatalistic view of her path in the sport crediting her wins to her devotion, and her losses to spiritual tests and further directions from God. This was unique to Anna and represented the intersection of two aspects of her life that were instrumental to the formation of her identity.

The sport of boxing provides a means for transformation whether it is through the physical rigor of the training, the bodily labor of competition, or the empowerment of reclaiming their sense of self and physicality. Wacquant (1995, 501) has argued that boxing is "the vehicle for the project of *ontological transcendence* whereby those who embrace it seek to literally fashion themselves into a new being." It is through the physical routine and regimen of the sport that the athletes build their sense of self. Heiskenan (2012, 37) argues that this transcendence should not be seen as finite, rather it is ongoing and therefore should be viewed as a "continual ontological contestation," which better represents the fluctuating nature of identity formation as it relates to the forever changing outside world, as well as how the individual fits within this world. It is, therefore, not surprising that Anna views her faith as being integral to her boxing career. As she herself stated,

> I was in a place like emotionally and just in life where I didn't have Jesus, I didn't know what I was doing, I was really struggling um in a lot of areas and so then February 8th of 2015, whenever I accepted Jesus and really had a purpose

for my life I knew He had given me boxing for a reason. (Anna, Personal Communication, January 23, 2017)

Identity can be conceptualized as the "interface between the personal and the social and the 'inside' and the 'outside'" (Woodward 2007, 15). For Anna, a devout believer in the Christian Faith, her physical and bodily labor—the sacrifice she makes for her sport, is an important part of her spiritual journey. This definition allows for the investment of the mental and physical through the commitment to the bodily regimes and practices of the sport as they manifest through individual agency and structural subjectification. Important to her conceptualization, is Anna's agentic expression of gender as it relates to her individual decision-making and performance, as well as the more traditional positioning of the boxer and the sport of boxing within the economic, gender, racial, and political structures it has more historically been associated with. Through this lens, the underrepresentation of women in the sport compounds the importance of Anna's participation. She not only represents herself but also other women who want to excel in a male-dominated sport, and despite the hostility she meets, Anna is made more resolute in her positioning due to her strong faith. Identity through this lens has political ramifications and offers the potential for resistance to the very structural barriers that impose its meaning *on* and *to* the larger society.

Penelope and Savannah, who both took part in *The Boxing Event,* expressed fewer complex motivations for their choice to train and fight; however, unlike Anna, they did not view boxing as a career option. Savannah said she was initially influenced or pressured by others into entering the fight,

> I kind of got talked into that. I mean like I said I've been thinking about it, I wanted to do a fight. Um, one of my friends was the head of the event, and asked me if we can find another girl, [and asked] would you do this? It was the first women's fighting event at the University, and I was like sure. I'm not one to like turn down an opportunity. So, I like to be out of my comfort zone so that's definitely out of my comfort zone. So, I was like I've been doing this for a while and I think it would be a good experience. And you know the other girl . . . had experience, she was bigger than me. So, I just decided to go for it and I was like you know why, why come to the classes if you're going to turn down an opportunity to use the skills I've learned. But, uh it was fun. (Savannah, Personal Communication, April 4, 2017)

Penelope also liked the challenge of pushing herself outside of her comfort zone. In explaining her motivations for fighting, she said,

> I like working towards goals. Like I do pageants too, when I think half of the reason I do those is just coz it's something to work towards, and it's something

that like, it's out, its completely out of my comfort, it's nothing like this. (Penelope, Personal Communication, November 1, 2016)

The importance of testing the limits of the body and pushing themselves into behaviors they, and the larger society, viewed as being inappropriate for women was important to both Penelope and Savannah. My own motivations are grounded in pushing myself, pursuing a goal, and resisting deeply engrained gender expectations. Beyond the self-satisfaction of meeting certain fitness goals, boxing became, and arguably still is, a defining component of my identity. This manifested in different ways ranging from the acquisition of friends who share a passion for the sport, to changes in presentations of self (i.e., how I hold myself physically), to coming to realize that I was in fact in pretty good shape (yes, even fighting shape!) In addition, the more I engaged the sport, the greater pleasure I garnered from upending people's assumptions about me as a middle-class white woman with a white-collar occupation by informing them about my quite serious hobby. Boxing for many women, myself included, becomes a reflection of our everyday existence within a larger gender structure that limits women's embracement of their bodily and physical capital but also was a means to demonstrate their athletic achievements.

Important to the women here was the elevation of other women fighters in the public eye. As already discussed in chapter 3, women in the sports of boxing and MMA who garner celebrity status for their athleticism and success in the sport provided visual influence and confirmation that women not only belong in the sport but they can have a successful career. Anna spoke very highly of Claressa Shields, who at the time of our conversation was only just beginning to garner public recognition. Anna said,

Seeing, you know, Claressa come up, and this terminology is used a lot, it's just paving the way you know, for us. Really that's what she's doing, and Heather Hardy, who's in a lower weight class, she's featherweight, I think that's around 120, 125, she's a dominant force. But Claressa coming so prominently from the amateurs having that much of a prestigious career in the amateurs and then you know, doing what she's doing in the pros, I know she's only had two fights, but I mean being on the undercard of Ward vs Kovalev, which was the biggest fight of the year, one of the biggest fights of the decade, and then right after that coming and fighting as the boxing event . . . but that's never been done, it was huge. And for it to be in women's history month, and on the week of international women's day. It was just a huge week for women in general and it's definitely going to open huge opportunities for women to have the boxing event on a card, whether it's a historical event, whether it's a small card or a big card it doesn't matter. And for it to be on *Showtime* that's huge. (Anna, Personal Communication, March 11, 2017)

The visibility and achievements of other women boxers had a strong impact on women choosing to fight at the amateur level. In seeing their success, they too were inspired to persevere in the sport independent of the barriers to their success.

WEIGHT AND DIET

Instrumental to fight preparation is weight loss and maintenance. This has already been briefly touched upon as a factor that impacts women entering boxing as a weight-loss or exercise regimen in chapter 3, but here the focus is the practice of "making weight" before a tournament or fight. It has been argued that the number of weight categories in boxing makes it, at least in principle, an "egalitarian sport" (Heiskanen 2012, 37) due to the acceptance and inclusion of different body types. For most boxers, however, their everyday weight can and does differ significantly from their competition weight sometimes by as much as 20 lbs. For women boxers competing at the professional level, there is no unified agreement as to the number of weight categories, but for men since 2015 there have been 17 recognized weight divisions, an expansion on the previously recognized eight categories. At the amateur level, there are ten weight divisions for women, yet at the Olympics there are still only three divisions as compared to the ten for men (Hauser and Sammons 2020). The ability to make weight and the diet regimes that accompany this feat have been analyzed in the literature (Davis 2017; Jennings and Velázquez 2015; Pettersson et al. 2012) with particular attention being paid to the detrimental health effects these practices have on the body (Daniele et al. 2016; Degoutte et al. 2006; Fogelholm 1994; Steen and Brownell 1990). It is unsurprising that weight dominated some of the concern women boxers had about competing in the ring.

Anna was especially vocal about her struggle with making weight before a competition. Of preparing for a national competition, Anna said the following about finding herself considerably above her required fight weight,

> My coach always said like don't get above four to six pounds, seven at the most above your weight. And I've definitely dealt with that and struggled just dropping the two weight classes, it's hard to stay and I, I've not been perfect, I've gone up and down and that's hard on your body and I don't think people really understand like the toll that your body takes going up and down and up, even boxers they don't understand it fully. (Anna Personal Communication, January 23, 2017)

Some of the documented health risks for dropping weight include severe dehydration (Daniele et al. 2016), increased heart rate, muscle glycogen depletion, hydroelectrolytic disturbances, impaired thermoregulation (Fogelholm 1994), growth and development issues if done during adolescence (Artioli et al. 2010), psychological effects such as short-term memory loss, inability to concentrate, increased confusion, rage, fatigue, and depression (Steen and Brownell 1990; Horswill et al. 1990; Filaire et al. 2001; Degoutte et al. 2006). It has also been established in the literature that the constant attention and pressure to maintain weight, or the focus on weight cycling, makes pugilists more susceptible to long-term eating disorders such as bulimia, anorexia, and binge eating, with vulnerability being greater for female that for male athletes (Fogelholm 1994).

The lesser weight divisions for women's competitions mean that boxers are forced to either drop a considerable amount of weight or add weight. Again, the difficulty associated with attaining the correct weight was talked about as it related to the Olympics. The toll this had on women boxers both mentally and physically was emphasized.

> Going towards 2016 is when I had to make that choice do I go up in weight or do I go down because that was my dream in 2012 when I won the Junior Olympics cause I was like okay this is awesome this is my first national championship um, this is actually something that's attainable. And so, I know [I] had a couple of years to think about it. I thought they were gonna add more weight classes in 2013, they announced they weren't and then um coming up on like 2014, 2015 is when they pick the team, so you really, that's the year that you have to, are you gonna do it or not, all in or not . . . I ended up losing 24 pounds in three months. You know I'm this elite athlete thinking I'm already on weight, it was tough to get to 152 at times because you know you walk around at 158 just cause your body settles in different weight ranges. (Anna, Personal Communication, January 23, 2017)

Having fewer weight categories for women means the weight cycling can be more dramatic. Ultimate Fighting Championship fighter Valerie Latourneau has been vocal about the gender-based differences in weight cutting for athletes in her campaign for the addition of a flyweight division (Carroll 2017). Latourneau explained that the practice of losing water weight by spending time in a sauna is not as effective for women as it is for men. She argued,

> I can remember one time I got some help from my friend David Loiseau during a weight cut and he was so desperate. He couldn't believe how much time I had to spend in the sauna to get on weight. I was in there for hours and hours and I was barely sweating. All of the guys had come and gone and got themselves on weight. I had started my cut before them and I was still there after, it was taking forever. Weight cutting for women is a different game and you've got to work

with somebody who knows about that to make sure you can do it the healthiest way possible. (Latourneau as cited in Carroll 2017)

Given the difficulties and associated health risks that are associated with making weight that differentially impact women, it is not surprising that nutrition and diet featured highly in women boxers' training regimen. This does not mean that this was not a problem for male boxers, rather that diet and nutrition were more dominant concerns for women in conversations about fight preparedness. As argued by Ariel,

> I try to keep a regimented plan and I'm on one right now. You have to watch your salt because you retain water and it's certain things that people don't, other athletes even, don't even have to worry about, like the salt intake or how much fat you get, because with boxers you want more carb then fat. You don't want to retain any fluids, um, we do some laxative teas, might help with digestion. (Ariel, Personal Communication, January 25, 2017)

Conversations about nutrition were a reoccurring happening with my own coach. Having some medical issues such as hashimotos thyroiditis, as well as being in my mid-30s, I struggled, and still do, with losing weight. His concern was always coached in the uncertainty of if/when I secured a fight that I would have to lose 8–10 pounds. Even at my lightest (149 pounds), training six days a week, sometimes twice a day, eating 1200 calories a day, I found myself starving for both energy and nutrients. However, unlike some of the other women featured here, I was not pursuing boxing as a career and as a result I could always opt out of fighting or refuse to engage in weight-loss practices that I felt were detrimental to my health (i.e., laxative teas). Yet, at times, I felt pressured to justify why I was not yet in "fight shape" (Fieldnote, January 14, 2018). This is something I often deflected with humor and self-deprecation, responding "this is my shape," referencing my own body (Fieldnote, January 14, 2018).

THE SPECTACLE OF THE FIGHT

The lights are low as I enter the large, cavernous space of what seems to be a basement room under a larger auditorium. There is loud rap music thudding through the space that centers on a long runway leading up to a boxing ring illuminated by bright lights that swirl and dance across the space. There are folding chairs surrounding the ring on all four sides, and gaggles of sorority and fraternity members crowd the space, most wearing their colors or letters in coordinated outfits or matching attire. Sponsors and local businesses sit in booths on the outsides of the room, and a weird mix of parents, locals, and university students fill the seats. Feeling a little out of my element, I look for the bar thinking a drink would help, however, a security officer is quick to inform me that "no alcohol is being served at this event." The event starts with the singing of the national anthem, a common occurrence at fights, and I look to the audience who all quickly get to their feet as a young woman enters the ring, microphone in hand, ready with her rendition. (Fieldnote, November 3, 2017)

There was a stark difference in events that hosted serious amateur boxers and those who would more readily be classified as white-collar events. The more serious amateur fights I attended were held in gym spaces that had been adapted to host the event (i.e., cleared of exercise machines, chairs laid out, and floors stripped of matting). They were attended by locals, family members, and those who frequented the gyms—that is, those involved in the local fight scene/community. They were not heavily advertised or attended by members of the public (I often found out about the event only because I knew one of the boxers personally). Although there was music playing, you could still hear yourself talk, and it tended to be a mix of music genres. There were of course all the markers of boxing such as a ring, judges, a referee, cornermen, and, in some instances, ring girls. However, the overall feeling of these events were calmer and more family orientated than the large white-collar tournaments, especially because they began in the early evening. Furthermore, the amateur events did not always relegate women's fights to appearing before the men's, as, in some instances, they were the main card because the boxers were more advanced in their career than the men. There were less of the elements of spectacle (beyond the matches themselves) that are associated with televised professional boxing. This contrasted with the gregarious spectacle of the white-collar events like *Rough N' Rowdy and The Boxing Event.*

The Boxing Event capitalized on the notable markers of a fight, those familiar to the audience and any public audience who watches mediatized boxing. There was a ring, loud music, referees, judges, and scantily clad ring girls. However, there was also the flashing and roaming lights building an atmosphere, large, televised viewing screens in the space, loud thudding music, and an overall atmosphere of excitement and danger. These events were held in large buildings such as sports venues and coliseums. Large concession stands were set up for snacks (some had alcohol, others did not). As argued by sports sociologist Jay Coakley (1994, 303), "throughout history sport has always been used as a form of entertainment. However, sports have never been so heavily packaged, promoted and presented, and played as commercial products as they are today." Here, the white-collar boxing events have been thoroughly packaged and commodified into an evening of entertainment. Interestingly, along with the prioritizing of consumerism, those attending the events also fully embraced dominant narratives that have been heavily proliferated by the media some of which were rooted in race and class stereotypes.

At *The Boxing Event,* I found myself struck by the capitalization of stereotypes, albeit implicit, that understands boxing to be the sport of the dangerous underclass as summarized in this fieldnote.

> There is obvious excitement in the air as young people flit around me, giggling, and shouting out greetings to their friends. I am however, struck by the number of white sorority women wearing their hair in boxer or cornrow braids. Having noticed it, I can't seem to shake the obvious cultural appropriation that seems to be now very obvious to me. These women are not fighting, so they are not needing to tie back their hair in order to keep it out of their faces and/or contain it under the protection of head gear. Rather, they are emulating what they think it means to be a boxer or at least attend a boxing match. The noticeable absence of any nonwhite people and the dominance of rap music blaring from the speakers, makes me question the racial undertones of such decisions, ones that may well be subconscious but seem quite overt. (Fieldnote, November 3, 2017)

Here, gendered and racialized themes that revolve around black masculinity become integral to those attending the event. The construction of white-collar boxing is grounded in assumptions about "the proximity to the masculinity of the racial Other" (Trimbur 2011, 199) that do not only help construct the identity of those doing the boxing (i.e., the white collar boxers) but also those attending the event. It is this narrative, one that equates boxing with blackness, that is capitalized on, commodified, and consumed by the audience at *The Boxing Event.*

Similarly, *Rough N' Rowdy* capitalizes on the gendered, classed, and raced understandings of poor white men. These events are hosted in various cities across the United States but predominantly in regions characterized as being demographically rural and white. Consider, for example, that the event has been hosted in West Virginia, Kentucky, Ohio, and North Carolina to audiences that exceed 2,000 people. The events social media account promotes the tournament by having their prospective fighters "call out" their opponents. These men engage in performative displays of hegemonic masculinity. They are often featured shirtless, peacocking on the screen, hurling insults about the other man's masculinity—or lack thereof—and challenging them to prove their toughness in the ring. For example, in a video posted to Instagram that is typical of this promotional approach, there are two men who have been filmed separately but then the videos have been cut, stitched, and manipulated to indicate they are engaging each other in a conversation—a verbal exchange. After introducing himself, the first man says "You probably know me better as 'Lights Out Lang', and I'm sure your saw the fucking clinic I put on last Rough N' Rowdy I put on in Providence Rhodes Island." To which the other man then replies "You're fast but you ain't got any fucking power. You fought a girl last time for three fucking rounds and you couldn't even knock her out. I'd of killed that son of a bitch in ten seconds if I'd of fought that bastard, you ain't shit." To which the video is cut to show the other man's response, "Nothing personal man, but if you think I'm going to fight you in fucking Levis, I'm going to knock you the fuck out" (Rough N' Rowdy 2020). This male posturing is accompanied by gimmicks, nicknames, framing their opponent as feminine with the intention to deride, and using props (crowns, guns, knives, smashing property, etc.) that emphasize a certain form of masculinity; one that is not only toxic but rooted in limited understandings of lower-class, rural white masculinity in the United States.

Rough N' Rowdy capitalizes on the historically embedded understandings of white masculinity in the United States. With the advancement of civil rights, deindustrialization, and the rise of the feminist movement in the second half of the twentieth century, the perception that white masculinity being in crises has been circulated (Cooley 2010). While nonwhite fighters do participate, the fight card is dominated by white men from rural communities. Through the focus on physical toughness in the prelude video clips, self-claimed fight names, and the spectacle in the ring, these men can demonstrate their superiority to not only women but to the modern construction of man—one that is viewed as effete. Sociologist Michael Messner (1992) argues that violence is no longer a part of most men's lives, so these events provide a vehicle for a reclamation of the power and dominance that has been since lost. For example, in 2017, *Rough N' Rowdy* was hosted in McDowell County, West Virginia, in the small community of Welch. In the 1950s, McDowell County boosted a population of 100,000 due to the then booming coal industry. There was a bustling downtown that supported smaller villages and communities in the surrounding area. The closing of the coal mines, however, lead to economic devastation and considerable flight from the region with as many as four in every five people leaving the county. The once-thriving downtown has been reduced to shuttered businesses, and McDowell County now is West Virginia's poorest county with one of the country's lowest life expectancies. There is little to do in town, but every year during the month of March, *Rough N' Rowdy* comes to town (Lowery 2017). These events, therefore, provide a means to reclaim this ideal of hegemonic masculinity in a region of the United States where traditional avenues for achieving it are stunted. Once a year, men can demonstrate their physical toughness to prove themselves and to show others they are indeed "a badass" (Morgan as cited in Lowery 2017). For women, however, the narrative is different.

Rough N' Rowdy features women's fights, but they are far fewer in number. Also, from these communities, the majority of these women do not fit dominant understandings of femininity or middle-class white beauty. With a few exceptions[1], the descriptions of these fighting women fixate on some identifying quality—usually unflattering—that differentiates her from her opponent. Some are described as "toothless hillbillies" (Rough N' Rowdy 2019), others "jacked country girls" (Rough N' Rowdy 2019), referring to her muscular form, and others "overweight" or "fat" (Rough N' Rowdy 2018). Further contrast is made between the women fighters and the ring girls who enter the ring wearing very few clothes to compete for the title of best ring girl. The ring girls are objectified and sexualized with the commentators openly discussing their body parts under the guise of "judging" a winner. This contrasts heavily with the commentary on women fighters where their fighting is called "sloppy." In one such fight, the commentator joked about the woman's size, speculating out loud on the size of the woman's waist guard concluding with ridicule that "it must be huge" (Rough N' Rowdy 2018). This is part of a pattern whereby women who participate as fighters have their bodies generally mocked. Male fighters are also subject to mocking, yet this tends to be limited to their fighting prowess and not involve the subjection of their bodies to a sexualized male gaze. The spectacle of *Rough N' Rowdy* is in the lack of experience the fighters have in the ring coupled with the entertainment that this event brings to economically struggling towns.

As argued by theorist Guy Debord (1995, 12) in discussing the spectacle, "All that once was directly lived has become mere representation." The world has become spectacular, a society of the spectacle whereby,

The spectacle is both the outcome and the goal of the dominant mode of production. It is nothing added to the real world—not a decorative element, so to speak. On the contrary, it is the very heart of society's real unreality. In all its specific manifestations—news or propaganda, advertising or the actual consumption of entertainment—the spectacle epitomizes the prevailing model of social life. (Debord 1995, 13)

In the case of the boxing fan, the spectator is alienated from their own lives watching their actions as if removed. At *Rough N' Rowdy*, the audience, both on social media and at the event itself, watch the performative tension scripted between the two would-be novice boxers from the safety of the stands or in their own living room. Debord (1995) suggests the more the spectator observes the less actual engagement they have, losing understanding of their own wants, wishes, and sense of self. They are manipulated and through this lens deprived of their own judgment. As argued by scholars of sports science, Verner Møller and Jakob Østergaard Genz (2014), through this lens, the spectator or consumer can be viewed as a victim, where something has been done to him/her. I agree with their assertion that "the spectator does make a choice . . . [yet it is] unfair to underestimate spectators by describing them as uncritical sleepers" (Møller and Genz 2014, 262). In the case of sporting events, the consumer makes a choice to attend, watch, and to ignore, whether purposefully or through a disavowal, the harms and costs to others that has allowed for their consumption. They are not victims to the spectacle, rather they are accomplices in the carnivals of violence and harm that pervade them. They are contributing to the classicist, sexist, and racist exploitation that these large events capitalize on.

PROTECT YOURSELF AT ALL TIMES: FACING YOUR OPPONENT IN THE RING

As noted by Trimbur (2011), the illusion of control that white-collar/novice boxers feel they have is not only uninformed but quickly exposed when they enter a real bout. White-collar events are more bloody and brutal than experienced amateur and professional tournaments. This was quickly evident when events were compared. The more serious amateur boxers working toward careers in the sport had considerable experience sparring and, although nervous, entered the ring with a plan. As indicated by Anna,

> You're on deck and then you're kinda going through some things in your mind of like okay this is what we wanna start off with. Your coach is telling you, start off with this, like most of the time he gives me a combination to start off with and he's like the first round is yours, I'm not gonna tell you anything else. Um and then you know he'll like help me throughout the fight and we'll adjust but you're just kinda thinking like okay I've trained super hard for this and nobody's gonna take this away. (Anna, Personal Communication, January 23, 2017)

For the white-collar or novice boxer, the lack of experience with fighting created self-doubt and fear of the ring. Penelope found herself questioning why she even agreed to fight in the days leading up to her fight. She said,

> I can't do this, I was freaking out and my roommate was trying to give me like a pep talk and I was just like, I don't want to do it, coz there's so many people there first of all and it's just like, um . . . I had no idea what to expect because I, it was Thursday and Friday, and I fought on Friday, Thursday night I saw the girls like, the girls that went on Thursday night they were fighting and

they were all way better than they were at training, so I was like should I, am I underestimating the girl that I am fighting. (Penelope, Personal Communication, November 10, 2016)

In addition, the lack of the control they have in the ring means the matches are more likely to devolve into brutal and bloody displays of offensive punches. For example, Penelope did not realize she had an injury until the fight was stopped. She said,

> I didn't know it was bleeding because I had a cold, so I thought it was just snot, which is really gross (laughs) but I had no idea, yea, it's like I can't touch it, after they were like your nose is bleeding and I was like ahhh, okay, but she, I watched the video back, and I don't even think she even hit me in the face. (Penelope, Personal Communication, November 10, 2016)

The lack of defensive knowledge coupled with the spectacle of the event itself means these events capitalize on the gruesomeness and violence of the sport (Trimbur 2011).

The Politics of Injury

Getting seriously hurt did not seem to be a priority concern for many of the women athletes. Savannah's response to questioning how she felt about the risk of harm was typical. She said, "I really don't worry. I mean I don't want to get knocked out or go to the hospital, but you wear so much headgear it's not really [a] concern" (Savannah, Personal Communication, April 4, 2017). Women often emphasized their lack of concern by listing injuries they received by participating in other sports or activities. They did recognize that there was a risk of injury, although they saw it as a reasonable expectation of engaging the sport. This reflects the self-regulation and routinization of injury that Woodward (2007) notes is common to boxing training. Men too held similar views, yet they did report a greater number of injuries than the women boxers and therefore an increased concern for long-term effects. Matt, an amateur MMA fighter, having suffered a concussion from a sparring session said the following,

> Yeah it kinda opened my eyes to realize, okay being tough does not mean you're good. Being tough means you can take a beating and I don't wanna take beatings, I want to not get hit. So, um the concussion kinda opened my eyes to, I have to be more careful. I can't be as you know headstrong, aggressive as I might want to be um and then of course you're always, you're always, that's always in the back of your mind. But when it becomes a passion and you're

driven for it, it's like the risk of this is worth the reward of this. So that's kinda where I'm at with it. (Matt, Personal Communication, July 25, 2017)

When injuries were reported by women, the overall approach was less about risk versus reward and more about learning from their mistakes. They would analyze how and why the harm occurred opposed to emphasizing that the harm would pay dividends in the future. Consider that Evangeline very pragmatically analyzed the cause of what she deemed was her worse injury in the following way,

Evangeline: My only real significant injury was actually when I was fighting with some boys. It was a boy sparring division and I was fighting for first place. I got kicked in the ribs, and I cracked about three of them . . . and, it was my own fault. Looking back, it was my own fault because I dropped my hands . . .
Victoria: Yeah?
Evangeline: I was wide open and, you know. Here I am attacking him like crazy . . . he had every right to kick me, you know, that was, I wouldn't expect him to go any easier on me. (Evangeline, Personal Communication, July 17, 2017)

For those women more involved in combat sports there was a general acceptance that injuries were going to happen. To mitigate harm they would only engage adversarial boxing with the support and presence of their coach, in controlled environments, and sometimes even switched to "point sparring" (Evangeline, Personal Communication, July 17, 2017). While I personally did not brush off or minimize injuries, I too fell into this category of accepting that boxing increases your susceptibility to injuries and over a three-year period, I received a few bloody lips, a black eye, and the odd scrape and/or bruise. Ironically, one of the worst injuries I sustained was a sprained ankle that resulted from being pushed by a 220 lbs man in sparring. During the course of the round, I was in close to his body, hitting him repeatedly in the body, instead of moving away from me, he shoved me hard with his hip and shoulder yelling "get off me!" (Fieldnote, September 24, 2019). This caused me to fall and twist in such a way that I sprained my ankle. Instead of immediately bowing out of the session, and with encouragement from my coach, I finished the round. The adrenaline and my own stubbornness muting the pain. This exacerbated the injury, as three hours later, my ankle had swollen to the size of a tennis ball. I would not attribute the latter to engaging adversarial boxing per se, but rather to a misjudgment on the part of my sparring partner which resulted in an accidental injury.

Interestingly, others reported injuries that were due to more general mishaps in the gym spaces opposed to adversarial sparring. Caroline for example, spoke about a hand injury, saying,

I hurt um my left hand . . . like I hurt my first two knuckles pretty bad and they were bruised for two months and I couldn't punch or hit anything with them. So, I had to like punch with my right hand and um and during kickboxing I kind of got like a hairline [fracture], I kicked the heavy bag with my toe . . . yeah and that was bruised for about three months. (Caroline, Personal Communication, February 13, 2017)

I too experienced a range of injuries in addition to the above-mentioned sprained ankle, which include an acromioclavicular joint separation, from training outside of the ring some of which caused considerably more pain, medical treatment and recovery time than anything caused by adversarial boxing. I attribute many of these injuries to mishaps and/or clumsiness when navigating the gym equipment and machines, so much so my coach took to calling me "awkward Ninja" (Fieldnote, May 17, 2017). It was meant in jest, but it betrayed an inherent worry that led to his increased surveillance when I was navigating new exercises.

Novice boxers with lesser experience however expressed increased anxiety over the potential for harm as compared to those with more experience. For example, Penelope expressed increased anxiety in the days leading up to her fight, and she confessed being concerned about being hurt related to an under-lying medical condition that meant she was at high risk for blood clots. She said,

I have, just coz a lot of the reason I didn't think I would do, and the reason I didn't do it last year is because I'm on blood thinners, which if I get hit in the nose, my nose will bleed for so long . . . and even if I get just like a random nosebleed I'll cover like a whole handtowel with blood . . . and so, if it's an injury hit, I don't, I think that would be worse. But I hope my defense is good enough. (Penelope, Personal Communication, November 1, 2016)

This anxiety is reasonable considering the newness of the ring for white-collar boxers and the brutality of novice boxing events; however, contrary to other research that found that visible injuries are symbolic of risk taking (Satterlund 2012), women tended to mitigate or downplay the injuries they had sustained. This makes sense when situated with the larger gender struc-ture as women do not have the same need to embody manhood by displaying visible symbols (blood and injury) of their masculinity.

The most pronounced reaction to women boxing was not made by those already traversing the gym spaces but rather emerged in interac-tions in the women's everyday lives. Many of the women spoke about their loved ones expressing concern for serious injury. Caroline said, her mom often,

Worries about the head injuries that it could cause and um the permanent damage to my body . . . and my brain. So like a lot of my friends don't understand
why I want to do it but they asked me, if how I'm going to like if my face gets
messed up or you know like after so many fights will have you have the looks
you know . . . or will you need to have like plastic surgery. (Caroline, Personal
Communication, February 13, 2017)

Caroline, however, asserted that these were not concerns that ever entered
her mind. Others reported similar responses from friends and families, but
also several unsolicited comments and interactions from others who found
out they boxed.

Many women, as was I, were subject to jokes about being tough, fierce,
and/or scary due to our engagement with the sport. I cannot count the number
of times that someone I am acquainted with or had been recently introduced
to say something to the effect of "So you can beat me up?" or lift their fists
when I come in the room. Some of this is meant to humor but other comments are just odd. For example, I am not sure what men who ask me about
my ability to beat them up are expecting me to say. If I were to answer
"yes," then what would happen next? Is he going to try and hit me? Not to
mention that these interactions always occur outside of a boxing facility in
social, professional, and semi-professional settings. These types of questions
appear mocking, patronizing (implying "how cute" she thinks she can beat
me up) and threatening all at the same time. It is a reflection of skepticism
that women can successfully express their physicality, as well as a representation of the discomfort with the gender transgression (i.e., women engaging
in activities reserved for men) that boxing provides. Other women reported
similar experience and found it frustrating and sometimes tiresome that their
engagement with the sport became a central focus of others despite their
varied interests in life.

CONCLUSION

This chapter provides an overview of the women's experiences with the spectacle of the fight as it relates to two very different types of events: the white-
collar versus the more serious amateur boxing event. Drawing on fieldnotes
and conversations with fighters entering the ring, the experiences of women
were examined as they are related to motivations to fight, training regimens,
weight cycling, and cutting, weight divisions before the spectacle of the
boxing competitions were analyzed as it related to the spectacle and commodification of sport more broadly. The career boxers and those more serious
were involved in events that focused on the competition with less pomp and

circumstance surrounding the event itself. These fights were promoted and attended by those in the fight community and though they were open to the public, the focus was about the boxers' advancement in the sport itself. Both events, however, had far fewer women fighters than men, leading them to sometimes be overlooked as serious pugilists.

Furthermore, motivations for novice women's engagement with the sport at this level were different from the motivations of men. Men's motivation was heavily influenced by masculinity and pride as well as the more traditional explanations discussed in other ethnographic works. Women instead had a variety of reasons for competing, the most prominent being pushing themselves to experience things they would not otherwise be comfortable doing. In preparing for the events when women found the resources provided were not to their liking, they deviated calling on their own networks to find training that fit their needs.

Unlike the regimens of the women working toward a career in the sport, technique, skill, and the importance of months of bodily labor that the boxer undertakes in preparation for a fight is largely absent from white-collar boxing. For both men and women, these carnival events neglect the disciplining aspects of combat sports and promote the most exciting and prominent aspects of boxing as being enough—such as pad work and sparring. Roadwork, shadow boxing, strength training, and defensive drills are largely absent from the short preparatory period the novice boxers undertake. I would argue that in the face of events such as *Rough N' Rowdy*, this is purposeful, as this tournament is not about boxing per se but about the commodification of the sport for the purposes of entertainment and consumerism.

All of the women here, whether novice or career boxers, were still an anomaly as they were one of few to make it to fight cards in a sea of male competitors. Although I have been critical of the training—or lack thereof—for large white-collar events, I want to recognize the courage that each of these women demonstrated in pursuing their goals of taking on a boxing match. This does not mean however that the large spectacle events such as *Rough N' Rowdy* and *The Boxing Event* are beyond reproach, as these events are less about boxing as a sport and more about the commodification of it as a means to reassert masculinity and dominance, and for capital acquisition.

NOTE

1. There was one former homecoming queen who received considerable attention for getting in the ring.

Conclusion

There are a number of noteworthy scholarly studies on the sport of boxing where the boxing gym has provided a rich site for sociological inquiry. Unlike these studies, however, the purpose here was to center women in the analysis and to widen the focus beyond professional pugilists to include amateur, novice, and recreational boxers. This has allowed for a widening of inquiry beyond traditional fight gyms (those stereotypically associated with boxing) to include the much more commercial spaces of cardio-boxing gyms where many women are first introduced to the sport, or work, and teach others as boxing instructors and trainers. The goal was to explore and examine amateur, novice, and recreational engagements in the sport as it has been increasingly commodified and coopted into workout regimes for those wanting to improve their fitness. By adopting Edward Wright's (2019) definition of white-collar boxer as one that conveys a novice status instead of being reflective of occupational or socio-economic class, this allowed for the exploration of the marketing of the sport as a commodity. The commodification and consumerism surrounding the sport have increased access to women of varying ages and provided cardio-gym spaces that are less overtly masculine and hostile to women, leading to tremendous benefits for those that consume what is offered.

An important finding, and one that is consistent with similar research (Jennings 2015; McCaughey 1997; Nash 2017; Trimbur 2013, Van Ingen 2011), is the transformational effects the bodily labor of boxing has on women, both physically and psychologically. Women engaging the sport at all levels reported feeling empowered, stronger, and more confident, as well as feeling healthier. Importantly, it was found that boxing also provided an outlet for the expression of anger and aggression. Culturally, women are socialized to suppress feelings of anger and aggression and the bodily, physical, and spatial assumptions that accompany them. In a patriarchal society where women are rewarded for exhibiting characteristics that promote their subordination to men, it is not surprising that many of the participants here reported a resulting increase in confidence and a feeling of empowerment when given permission and space to undermine such behaviors. Boxing provided a vehicle for such expression as women directly embodied (Wacquant 2004) the reimagining of the relationship of their bodies to anger, aggression, and violence. They engaged in new social scripts.

I have also highlighted that beyond the benefits of attracting women to the sport, the commodification of consumerism of the sport is not without criticism. As argued by Zygmunt Bauman (1987), "Men and women are integrated into society as, above all, consumers" (Bauman 1987, 166). This extends beyond market logics to aspects of everyday life and was evidenced in the appropriation and incorporation of boxing in songs, advertisements, fitness apparel, and even lingerie. As a consequence, "every item of culture becomes a commodity [and] . . . all perceptions and expectations . . . are trained and moulded inside the new 'foundational' institution – that of the market" (Bauman 1987, 166). Boxing, as well its high-profile athletes, are commodified to capitalize on the female-dominated fitness market. To attract women consumers, sales techniques revolve around feminizing products. It was not uncommon to find products touting slogans such as "hit like a girl," or bedazzled boxing gloves, or fitness and boxing gear in overtly feminine colors. These products covertly reify existing gender roles and norms as products are designed to reflect ideals of masculinity and femininity— that is, pink for a girl and blue for a boy. However, their broader meaning is rarely noted. They become banal (Goold et al. 2013), fading out to the periphery (Miller 2010). But their very presence acts to reinforce the existing patriarchal structure.

In addition, many participants reflected on the objectification and sexualization of women's bodies as they engaged the sport, both at the professional level where traditional ideals of white, middle-class, feminine beauty, and sex appeal are capitalized on to sell the sport, and at the novice level as women traversed the spaces of the boxing gyms. Women were quickly classified by both men and women gym-goers as either conforming to emphasized femininity or violating it, something that was most overtly illustrated in media coverage of professional fighters such as Cris Cyborg Justino, who frequently is subjected to negative commentary on her physique and questions about her sexuality due to her appearance (Jennings 2015). It was noted that purposely highlighting feminine characteristic was a tactic utilized to make women's participation in combat sports more palatable/less threatening to men. The consequences of this played out at the interactional level, where women felt they had to/were told to appear feminine to fit within a gendered image that was created by not only USA Boxing but also when they interacted with others in gyms.

Furthermore, the historical construction of the sport was upset by women who not only engaged the sport but did so with greater skill than the men occupying the same spaces. This often led to men exiting spaces where their masculinity was challenged or complaining about their experiences. Women had to engage in considerable emotional work to navigate not only the gym spaces but men's preconceived gender assumptions. This was most pronounced at fight gyms where there was greater hostility toward women in the sport. This manifested in different ways ranging from the lack of changing rooms to the atmosphere and behaviors of the gym-goers in these spaces. These hostile behaviors acted as a barrier for women accessing these spaces as many women chose to avoid or not return to these gyms. Coaches, in particular, acted as gatekeepers who either allowed or denied access to these spaces. This meant that women who wanted to go beyond exercise to fight and/or compete had to not only navigate their own femininity in accessing these spaces but also the perceived threats they pose to masculinity especially when participating in inter-gendered sparring.

In addition, in *Fighting Sports, Gender and the Commodification of Violence: Heavy Bag Heroines*, I have acknowledged the importance of boxing as a cultural, political, and economic landscape for social relations. This landscape includes the space as well as the spatiotemporal processes of the body as it engages the physicality of the sport and sites necessary for that engagement. In an attempt to circumvent the gendered nature of these social relations, some women carved out their own spaces outside of traditional gyms to engage in adversarial boxing. These spaces included a boxing instructors' back garden as well as an unsanctioned women's fight club. Women's fight club was explored as it related to women's resistance to traditional gendered scripts that felt suffocating to some of their members. Women embraced their anger, aggression, and bodily labor to express frustration at the heteronormative gender order and the Fight Nights were perceived as liberating women from the tethers of femininity that controlled their everyday lives. Contrary to the women who sought out contact boxing in more traditional fight gyms, the fight club purposely excluded men. The emotional work of gender maneuvering was not required of them as being a woman was not something they had to navigate. Instead, they embraced deep emotional bonding and post-fight discussions that promoted greater connectivity.

In an examination of the relationship between boxing, violence, and self-defense, I have drawn on the work of Bauman (1987). He notes that consumerism extends beyond the material to include the symbolic, something that constructs self, identity, and relationships with others. Relationships with others as a theme emerged in the constant societal presence of the very real threats of men's violence toward women. The narrative of self-defense capitalizes on common understandings of masculinity and femininity where women are automatically socially constructed as being weaker than men. This manifested in marketing and sales techniques in cardio-boxing spaces and was brought into the gym spaces by women who had personal experiences with violence and emerged in narratives about future safety in the face of potential violence. Although this was very often empowering to women to feel better equipped to defend themselves, there were an abundance of unofficial scripts drawn on to sell memberships, teach classes and "ring-ready" programs for the purposes of capitalist profit-making.

Without dismissing or undermining the very real feelings of empowerment that many women reported as a result of engaging the sport, the majority of white-collar/novice boxers reported feeling better able to defend themselves having never entered the ring, thrown a punch at a person, or having been hit. This is in line with Lori Holyfield's (1999) commentary on consumer adventure where she argued that many people want the appearance of risk and the emotional dividends that result without the real danger. For many, the limited classes of the boxercise gym were enough, as were the fight programs claiming to get people ready to fight. But for those looking to try adversarial boxing, these programs fell short, lacked authenticity, and were further undermined by experiences in gyms that allowed full-contact sparring. In cardio-boxing gyms, these programs reinforced individualized scripts of self-defense and protection from future violence but very often neglected what some have argued is a core component of self-defense—the practicing of the moves on another person.

But as boxing gyms are a microcosm of the society in which we live, it is not surprising that women, independent of their level of engagement, consumed and reproduced the narratives of self-defense. Given that we live in a time where the United Nations has ranked the United States as one of the top ten worse countries for women's safety in the world and we had a sitting President that is a repeat offender when it comes to sexually assaulting women, the self-defense narrative as a marketing tool offers a pragmatic means for women to claw back some of their control and power, even if it is only symbolic or merely an appearance of power. The danger resides in it being merely a mirage of power that can easily be destroyed if women's learned skills are put to the test—something they themselves would have to seek out at full-contact gyms or test in real-life situation.

The last substantive chapter focused on women's experiences as novice and amateur boxers who entered the ring. By comparing the spectacle of local white-collar events, those that purposely attracted and promoted novice boxers, with the more traditional amateur fights of those pursuing the sport as more than recreation, I was able to highlight the ever-present spectacle of consumerism, as well as some of the exploitative practices of large tourna-ments such as *Rough N' Rowdy*. As women's participation was rare, they were often ridiculed as spectacle or novelty with the focus being their bodies or physique opposed to their boxing skills. Women who participated in these events felt the resources provided to prepare were not welcoming to women and chose to capitalize on their own connections to ready themselves for their match. Although women have made tremendous gains, a deep-rooted inequality still exists as it relates to endorsements, coaching support, weight classes (or lack thereof), and public acceptance that women want to and do fight.

MOVING FORWARD: SO, WHAT NOW?

Some may argue that the happenings in a boxing gym have little bearing on the larger society, and any findings from this study are with little conse-quence. As others have before me (Jump 2020; Nash 2017; Trimbur 2013; Wacquant 2004), I would vehemently argue against such a critique as gym spaces, including boxing gyms, are reflective of the society in which we live. They act as microcosms of the larger gender issues, both interactional and structural, that are constantly navigated in everyday life. This study has dem-onstrated that despite the considerable advances of the feminist movement, institutionalized inequalities persist both in the sport of boxing as well as in the spaces that shape it. Women are still having to unlearn a socialization that dictates appropriate female behavior as being one that rejects the expression of aggression and anger in physical ways and embraces passivity and weak-ness. Boxing undermines this, as women are quick to learn techniques and skills that embrace these culturally tabooed characteristics in reclamation of their own bodies.

Expression through the physical and the notion that women own their bodies is not a new idea; however, even in this day and age, this ownership has parameters. These parameters need to be challenged, questioned, and critiqued in a way that is open to furthering women's embracing of the physi-cal as empowering. This means challenging the narratives and discourses that designate women as predominantly nonviolent both in gyms spaces and beyond. While I am not arguing that women should be violent, or that boxing is violence, but I am suggesting that there needs to be a strengthening of the willingness to acknowledge, as well as increased attention paid to, how the embracing of the physical body that has a capacity for violence can challenge assumptions about systemic power relations. Not only do women experience transformation, empowerment, and pleasure from engaging the sport of box-ing, but their presence also confuses and unsettles men. The body can be used as an effective tool to disrupt and confront gender hierarchies at the individual, institutional, and structural levels. As argued by Martha McCaughey (1997, 200), "Keeping women away from violence, or denying the aggressive potential in them, preserves the association of violence and masculinity and upholds a false similarity within the category 'women'." It is important not only to acknowledge this, but to carve our spaces where such embedded assumptions can be contested. This should not be limited to cardio-boxing spaces but should include the more traditional fight gyms as well as novice and white-collar events that marginalize the participation of women.

If women are ready to contest gender scripts and engage in exhaustive emotional work of gender maneuvering as they fight for their place in the sport at the interactional level, there also needs to be more work at the institutional and structural level. Calls to challenge the maleness of the institution of sport is not new, and I recognize that this study is one of many to point to the continued gender inequality that women have to contend with. Key to change is continued pressure to address wage disparities, endorsement deals, and the lack of media coverage of women's sports more generally (Groombridge 2017; Hargreaves and Anderson 2014b). This would include recognizing the role of capitalist consumerism as not only a gateway to women's access to the sport but also as an exploitative mechanism that reduces women pugilists to overly sexualized body objects, relegating their athleticism to being secondary to their attractiveness to men. There also needs to be an increased awareness as to the role of commodity marketing as it reifies patriarchal bifurcated gender roles of heterosexual gender as they seek to capitalize on feminizing products, so much so it leads to a "magical thinking" (Baudrillard 1998, 31) divorcing the products from their utility and their broader social meaning (i.e., glitter- or rhinestone-covered boxing gloves).

Although the focus here has been on women, specifically white-collar and/ novice women boxers in the analysis, my adherence to the dualistic categories of heteronormative gender could not only been critiqued as reinforcing dualistic and dated gender categories, but it has left a gap in the literature for further exploration. This study was limited to its participants and I acknowledge that there needs to be increased attention on novice and white-collar boxing especially as it relates to nonbinary gender as it intersects with age, race, class, and ableism. Although I was able to touch on some of these issues in brief, the geographical situating of this project in the rural United States meant that the majority of participants were white, able-bodied, and under 30. What is more, the women involved were overwhelmingly middle class, something that is again reflective of not only the region but larger patterns that have been revealed about women boxers (Trimbur 2013). This is further compounded by the inclusion of my own experiences as a white, middle-class woman engaging the sport. As with all ethnographic research, my social positioning influences relationships, views, and understanding of the world around me. Although I have strived to accurately reflect the positions of those included in the study, there remains a degree of subjectivity in the shared understandings and experiences between the researcher and the research participants (Ferrell and Hamm 2016). This does not, however, invalidate the findings I have presented, rather they should be situated in the parameters of the study—a small but in-depth study of women's boxing in rural America.

Future research should attempt to expand on this study in other geographic locations and delve deeper into the spectacle of white-collar boxing events, especially ones such as *Rough N' Rowdy* that purposely capitalize on what can be termed a crisis in masculinity (Friday 2003). These spectacle events attract considerable participation and public support despite their overt and troublesome treatment of not only their women fighters, but the men as well. Yet, they have provided outlets for novice women boxers who might not otherwise get a chance to engage the sport. This needs further unpacking considering that accessibility to the sport for many women might not afford them the best experiences. It is with all this in mind that I turn to some concluding thoughts.

CONCLUDING REMARKS

With the introduction of the commodification of the sport for white-collar and novice boxers, as well as an increased mediated presence of extremely talented women boxers in the public eye, such as Claressa Shields, it becomes apparent that there has been considerable advancement for women's boxing. Joyce Carol Oates (1987, 72) statement that "boxing is for men and is about men, and is men" no longer stands. Independent of the level of engagement, women report a myriad of beneficial experiences including physical, cognitive, psychological, and emotional that result from trying boxing. I too experienced these things and would advocate strongly on the benefits of boxing. Having experienced my own body transformation, tested myself both physically and mentally in the ring, and embraced the title "amateur boxer" as an instrumental part of my identity, I am convinced that boxing *is* for women. For many women, the unsettling of the gender hierarchy that boxing provides and the potential uncomfortableness this can cause, is not enough to dissuade them from pursuing a sport that allows for full-body engagement and expression.

Yet, there were some concerns that emerged revolving around consumerist exploitation, false marketing (i.e., identifying as boxer yet never participating in adversarial boxing), the spatial infringement of male spaces, and lingering hostilities toward women in more traditional fight gyms. Sadly, these hostilities are characteristic of women laying claim to any space that has historically been exclusively male. From male-dominated careers, to physical labor, women are resilient in their battles for inclusion. Fighting sports are no different, but they do deliver personal transformations for those who dare traverse these spaces. Independent of whether the participants think of their behavior as "real" boxing or not, does not diminish the important unlearning of feminine scripts that limit women's body ownership and physical expression. From the amateur and professional fighters that jumped in the ring, to the women who solely hit the heavy bag—the heavy bag heroines—the benefits of boxing reflect resistance to larger gender hierarchies and scripts that socialize women to ignore or suppress aggression and anger. This powerful emotion influenced many women's cathartic experiences with the sport of boxing as they fought for their voices, space, and place in the boxing gym.

Bibliography

Adams, Terry and C.A. Tuggle. 2004. "ESPN's SportsCenter and Coverage of Women's Athletics: "It's a Boys' Club."" *Mass Communication and Society,* 7, no. 2: 237–248. doi:10.1207/s15327825mcs0702_6

Allen, Jeffner. 1986. *Lesbian Philosophy: Explorations.* Palo Alto, CA: Institute of Lesbian Studies.

Anderson, Eric and Ann Travers, eds. 2017. *Transgender Athletes in Competitive Sports.* New York: Routledge.

Anderson, Linda A. and Susan C. Whiston. 2005. "Sexual Assault Education Programs: A Meta-analytic Examination of their Effectiveness." *Psychology of Women Quarterly,* 29, no. 4: 374–388. doi:10.1111/j.1471-6402.2005.00237.x

Angleman, Amy J., Shinzato, Yoshihiko, Van Hasselt, Vincent B. and Stephen A. Russo. 2009. "Traditional Martial Arts Versus Modern Self-Defense Training for Women: Some Comments." *Aggression and Violent Behavior,* 14, no. 2: 89–93. doi:10.1016/j.avb.2008.12.001

Antico, Pete [Producer] and Gary Stretch [Director]. 2019. *Through My Father's Eyes: The Ronda Rousey Story.* Wrekin Hill Entertainment.

Artioli Guilherme G., Gualano Bruno, Franchini Emerson, Scagliusi Fernanda B., Takesian Mariane, Fuchs Marina and Antonio H. Lancha. 2010. "Prevalence, Magnitude, and Methods of Rapid Weight Loss among Judo Competitors." *Medicine and Science in Sports and Exercise*, 42, no. 3: 436–442. doi:10.1249/MSS.0b013e3181ba8055

Atkinson, Michael and Kevin Young. 2008. *Deviance and Social Control in Sport.* Champaign, IL: Human Kinetics.

Austin, D. Mark, Gagné, Patricia and Angela Orend. 2010. "Commodification and Popular Imagery of the Biker in American Culture." *Journal of Popular Culture,* 43, no. 5: 942–963.

Bart, Pauline B., and Patricia H. O'Brien. 1985. *Stopping Rape.* New York: Pergamon.

Bartky, Sandra L. 1988. "Foucault, Femininity, and the Modernization of Patriarchal Power." In *Feminism and Foucault: Reflections of Resistance*, edited by Irene Diamond and Lee Quinby, pp. 129–154. Boston, MA: Northern University Press.

Baudrillard, Jean. 1981. *For a Critique of the Political Economy of the Sign.* St. Louis, MO: Telos Press Ltd.

Baudrillard, Jean. 1998. *The Consumer Society: Myths and structures.* London: Sage.

Baugh, Christine M., Robbins Clifford A., Stern, Robert A., Ann C. McKee. 2014. "Current Understanding of Chronic Traumatic Encephalopathy." *Current Treatment Options in Neurology,* 16, no. 9: 306. doi:10.1007/s11940-014-0306-5

Bauman, Zygmunt. 1987. *Legislators and Interpreters: On Modernity, Post-Modernity and Intellectuals.* Cambridge, UK: Polity Press.

Bearak, Barry. 2012. "The Living Nightmare." *The New York Time,* February 11, 2012. https://www.nytimes.com/2012/02/12/sports/quanitta-underwood-a-contender-for-olympic-gold-and-a-survivor.html?pagewanted=all&_r=0

Beauchez, Jérôme. 2017. *Boxing, the Gym, and Men: The Mark of the Fist,* Translated by Michael C. Behrent. Switzerland: Palgrave Macmillon.

Becker, Howard S. 1963. *Outsiders: Studies in the Sociology of Deviance.* New York: Free Press.

Becker, Howard S. 1967. "Whose Side Are We On?" *Social Problems,* 14, no. 3(Winter): 239–247.

Bederman, Gail. 1995. *Manliness and Civilization: A Cultural History of Gender and Race in the United States, 1880-1917.* Chicago, IL: University of Chicago Press.

Bem, Sandra, L. 1993. *The Lenses of Gender.* New Haven, CT: Yale University Press.

Berkowitz, L. 1978. "Whatever Happened to the Frustration-Aggression Hypothesis?" *The American Behavioral Scientist,* 21, no. 5: 691–709. doi:10.1177/000276427802100505

Bernstein, Alina. 2002. "Is it Time for a Victory Lap? Changes in the Media Coverage of Women in Sport." *International Review for the Sociology of Sport*, 37, no. 3–4: 415–428. doi:10.1177/101269020203700301

Billings, Andrew C. and Brittany D. Young. 2015. "Comparing Flagship News Programs: Women's Sports Coverage in ESPN's SportsCenter and FOX Sports 1's Sports Live." *Electronic News*, 9, no. 1: 3–16. doi:10.1177/1931243115572824

Biscomb Kay and Gerald Griggs. 2012. "'A Splendid Effort!': Print Media Reporting of England's Women's Performance in the 2009 Cricket World Cup." *International Review for the Sociology of Sport*, 48, no. 1: 99–111. doi:10.1177/1012690211432061

Blackshaw, T. 2016. "Bauman on Consumerism – Living the Market-Mediated Life." In *The Sociology of Zygmunt Bauman: Challenges and Critique,* edited by M. H. Jacobson and P. Poder, pp. 115–136. Abingdon, UK: Routledge.

Boddy, Kasia. 2014. "Watching Women Box." In *Routledge Handbook of Sport, Gender and Sexuality,* edited by Jennifer Hargreaves and Eric Anderson, pp. 254–262. New York: Routledge.

Bodner, Allen. 1997. *When Boxing Was a Jewish Sport.* Westport, Ct: Praeger Publishers.

Bordo, Susan. 1993. *Unbearable Weight: Feminism, Western Culture and the Body.* Berkeley, CA: University of California Press.

Bourdieu, Pierre. 1984. *Distinction: A Social Critique of the Judgment of Taste.* Translated by Richard Nice. Cambridge, MA: Harvard University Press.

Bourdieu, Pierre. 1990. *The Logic of Practice.* Translated by Richard Nice. Stanford, CT: Stanford University Press.

Bourdieu, Pierre. 2010. *Distinction.* Abingdon, UK: Routledge (Original work published 1979).

Brecklin, Leanne R. 2008. "Evaluation Outcomes of Self-Defense Training for Women: A Review." *Aggression and Violent Behavior*, 13, no. 1: 60–76. doi:10.1016/j.avb.2007.10.001

Briggs, Daniel. 2013. *Deviance and Risk on Holiday: An Ethnography of British Tourists in Ibiza.* Basingstoke, UK: Palgrave Macmillan.

Bruce, Toni. 2013. "Reflections on Communication and Sport: On Women and Femininities." 1, no. 1–2: 125–137. doi:10.1177/2167479512472883

Bryson, I. 1990. "Challenges to the Male Hegemony in Sport." In *Sport, Men, and Gender Order: Critical Feminist Perspectives,* edited by Michael A. Messner and Don F. Sabo, pp. 173–184. Champaign, IL: Human Kinetics.

Bunsell, Tanya. 2013. *Strong and Hard Women: An Ethnography of Female Bodybuilding.* New York: Routledge.

Bushman, Brad J. and Craig A. Anderson. 2001. "It is Time to Pull the Plug on Hostile versus Instrumental Aggression Dichotomy?" *Psychological Review*, 108, no. 1: 273–279. doi: 10.1037/0033-295X.108.1.273

Buszek, Maria Elena. 2006. *Pin-Up Grrrls: Feminism, Sexuality, Popular Culture.* Durham, NC: Duke University Press.

Butler, Judith. 1990. *Gender Trouble: Feminism and the Subversion of Identity.* New York: Routledge.

Butler, Judith. 1993. *Bodies that Matter.* New York: Routledge.

Butler, Judith. 1998. "Athletic Genders: Hyperbolic Instance and /or the Overcoming of Sexual Binarism." *Stanford Humanities Review*, 6, no. 2: 102–129.

Butler, Judith. 1999. "Performativity's Social Magic." In *Bourdieu: A Critical Reader,* edited by Richard Shusterman, pp. 113–128. New York: Routledge.

Cahill, A. J. 2001. *Overcoming Objectification: A Carnal Ethics.* New York: Routledge.

Cahn, Susan K. 1994. *Coming on Strong: Gender and Sexuality in Twentieth Century Women's Sport.* New York: New York Free Press.

Caple, Helen, Greenwood, Kate and Catharine Lumby. 2011. "What League?: The Representation of Female Athletes in Australian Sports Coverage." *Media International Australia*, 140: 137–146. doi:10.1177/1329878X1114000117

Carroll, Helen J. 2014. "Joining the Team: The Inclusion of Transgender Students in United States School-Based Athletics." In *Routledge Handbook of Sport, Gender and Sexuality,* edited by Jennifer Hargreaves and Eric Anderson, pp. 367–375. New York: Routledge.

Carroll, Peter. 2017. "Valerie Letourneau: Weight-cutting for women is a Different Game." *MMA Fighting,* December 14, 2017. https://www.mmafighting.com/20 17/12/14/16761128/valerie-letourneau-weight-cutting-for-women-is-a-different -game

Cashmore, Ellis. 2000. *Sports Culture: An A-Z Guide.* New York: Routledge.

Cermele, Jill. 2010. "Telling Our Stories: The Importance of Women's Narratives of Resistance." *Violence Against Women,* 16, no. 10: 1162–1172. doi:10.1177/1077801210382873

Chan, Wendy and George S. Rigakos. 2002. "Risk, Crime and Gender." *The British Journal of Criminology,* 42, no. 4: 743–761. https://www.jstor.org/stable/23638964

Chang, Heewon. 2008. *Autoethnography as Method.* New York: Taylor & Francis.

Channon, Alex, and George Jennings. 2014. "Exploring Embodiment through Martial Arts and Combat Sports: A Review of Empirical Research." *Sport in Society,* 17, no. 6: 773–789. doi:10.1080/17430437.2014.882906

Channon, Alex and Christopher R. Matthews, eds. 2015. *Global Perspectives on Women in Combat Sports: Women Warriors around the World.* New York: Palgrave Macmillon.

Chen, Jieru, Walters, Mikel L., Gilbert, Leah K., and Nimesh Patel. 2020. "Sexual Violence, Stalking, and Intimate Partner Violence by Sexual Orientation, United States." *Psychology of Violence*, 10, no. 1: 110–119. doi:10.1037/vio0000252

CNN. 2017. "Women Who Fight." *YouTube,* January 20, 2017. https://www.youtube.com/watch?v=aJBtGzM5W9o

Coakley, Jay J. 1994. *Sport in Society: Issues and Controversies.* New York: McGraw-Hill Education.

Coakley, Jay J. and Peter Donnelly. 2009. *Sports in Society: Issues and Controversies,* 2nd edition. Toronto, ON: McGraw-Hill Ryerson.

Coen, Stephanie E., Rosenberg, Mark W. and Joyce Davidson. 2018. ""It's Gym, like G-y-m not J-i-m": Exploring the Role of Place in the Gendering of Physical Activity." *Social Science & Medicine,* 196: 29–36. doi: 10.1016/j.socscimed.2017.10.036

Collins, Victoria E. 2015. *State Crime, Women and Gender.* Oxon, UK: Routledge (Taylor Francis).

Collins, Victoria E. and Dawn L. Rothe. 2017. "The Consumption of Patriarchy: Commodification to Facilitation and Reification." *Contemporary Justice Review,* 20, no. 2: 161–174. doi: 10.1080/10282580.2017.1307110

Collins, Victoria E. and Dawn L. Rothe. 2019. *The Violence of Neoliberalism: Crime, Harm and Inequality.* London, UK: Taylor & Francis Group.

Connell, Raewyn. 1987. *Gender and Power, Society, the Person and Sexual Politics.* Cambridge: Polity Press.

Connell, Raewyn W. 1995. *Masculinities.* Cambridge: Polity Press.

Connell, Raewyn W. and Messerschmidt, James W. 2005. "Hegemonic Masculinity: Rethinking the Concept." *Gender and Society,* 19, no. 6: 828–859.

Cooky, Cheryl and Michael A. Messner. 2018. *No Slam Dunk: Gender, Sport and the Unevenness of Social Change.* New Brunswick, NJ: Rutgers.

Cooky, Cheryl and Nicole M. Lavoi. 2012. "Playing but Losing: Women's Sports after Title IX." *Contexts,* 11, no. 1: 42–46.

Cooky, Cheryl, Messner, Michael. A, and Robin H. Hextrum. 2013. "Women Play Sports, but Not on TV: A Longitudinal Study of Televised News Media." *Communication & Sport,* 1, no. 3: 203–230. doi:10.1177/2167479513476947

Cooky, Cheryl, Messner, Michael A. and Michela Musto. 2015. "It's Dude Time!" A Quarter Century of Excluding Women's Sports in Televised News and Highlight Shows."*Communication & Sport,* 3, no. 3: 261–287. doi:10.1177/2167479515588761

Cooky, Cheryl, Wachs, Faye L., Messner, Michael A. and Shari L. Dworkin. 2010. "It's Not About the Game: Don Imus, Race, Class, Gender and Sexuality in Contemporary Media." *Sociology of Sport Journal,* 27, no. 2: 139–159. doi:10.1123/ssj.27.2.139

Cooley, Will. 2010. ""Vanilla Thrillas": Modern Boxing and White-Ethnic Masculinity." *Journal of Sport and Social Issues,* 34, no. 4: 418–437. doi:10.1177/0193723510379992

Cooper, Drea and Zackary Canepari. 2016. "T Rex: Her Fight for Gold." *Independent Lens,* August 2, 2016. https://www.pbs.org/independentlens/films/t-rex-her-fight -for-gold/

Cover, R. 2015. "Sexual Ethics, Masculinity and Mutual Vulnerability: Judith Butler's Contribution to an Ethics of Non-Violence." *Australian Feminist Studies,* 29, no. 82: 435–451. doi:10.1080/08164649.2014.967741

Crawford, June, Kippax, Susan, Onyx, Jenny, Gault, Una and Pam Benton. 1992. *Emotion and Gender: Constructing Meaning from Memory.* London: Sage.

Crocket, H. 2012. "This is Men's Ultimate: (Re)creating Multiple Masculinities in Elite Open Ultimate Frisbee." *International Review for the Sociology of Sport,* 48, no. 3: 318–333.

Crouse, Karen. 2013. "Why Female Athletes Remain on Sport's Periphery." *Communications & Sport,* 1, no. 3, 237–240. doi:10.1177/2167479513487722

Cummings, Nina. 1992. "Self-Defense Training for College Women." *Journal of American College Health,* 40, no. 4: 183–138. doi:10.1080/07448481.1992 .9936280

Cunningham, George B., Fink, Janet S. and Linda Jean Kenix. 2008. "Choosing an Endorser for a Women's Sporting Event: The Interaction of Attractiveness and Expertise." *Sex Roles,* 58, no. 5–6: 371–378. doi:10.1007/s11199-007-9340-z

Cynarski, Wojciech and Artur Litwiniuk. 2006. "The Violence in Boxing." *Archives of Budo,* 2: 1–10.

Daniele, Gianlorenzo, Weinstein, Richard N., Wallace, Paul W., Palmieri, Vincenzo and Massimiliano Bianco. 2016. "Rapid Weight Gain in Professional Boxing and Correlation with Fight Decisions: Analysis from 71 Title Fights." *The Physician and Sports Medicine,* 44, no. 4: 349–354. doi:10.1080/0091384 7.2016.1228421

Dardenne, Benoit, Dumont, Muriel and Thierry Bollier. 2007. "Insidious Dangers of Benevolent Sexism: Consequences of Women's Performance. *Journal of Personality and Social Psychology,* 9, no. 5:764–779. doi:10.1037/0022-3514.93.5.764

Davidson, Joyce, Bondi, Liz and Mick Smith, eds. 2005. *Emotional Geographies.* Burlington: Ashgate Publishing.

Davis, Philip. 2017. "Comment On: "It is Time to Ban Rapid Weight Loss from Combat Sports". *Sports Medicine,* 47, no. 8: 1673–1675. doi:10.1007/ s40279-017-0713-3

Davis-Delano, Laurel R., Pollack, April and Jennifer Ellsworth Vose. 2009. "Apologetic Behavior Among Female Athletes: A New Questionnaire and Initial

Results." *International Review for the Sociology of Sport,* 44, no. 2–3: 131–150. doi:10.1177/1012690209335524

Dawson Hoff, Victoria. 2015. "The Fat-Burning Boxing Workout that Keeps Victoria's Secret Models in Top Form." *Elle,* May 19, 2015. http://www.elle.com/beauty/health-fitness/how-to/a28441/kelly-gale-pop-up-workout-boxing/

Debord, Guy. 1995 [1967]. *The Society of the Spectacle.* New York: Zone Books.

Deffenbacher, Jerry L., Oetting, Eugene R., Lynch, Rebekah S. and Chad D. Morris. 1996. "The Expression of Anger and its Consequences." *Behavior Research and Therapy,* 34, no. 7: 575–590. doi:10.1016/0005-7967(96)00018-6

Degoutte Fabrice, Jouanel P., Begue R.J., Colombier M., Lac G., Pequignot J.M. and Edith Filaire. 2006. "Food Restriction, Performance, Biochemical, Psychological, and Endocrine Changes in Judo Athletes." *International Journal of Sports Medicine,* 27, no. 1: 9–18. doi:10.1055/s-2005-837505

DeKeseredy, Walter, Dragiewicz, Molly and Martin D. Schwartz. 2017. *Abusive Endings: Separation and Divorce Violence Against Women.* Oakland, CA: University of California Press.

Delorme, Nicolas. 2014. "Were Women Really Underrepresented in Media Coverage of Summer Olympic Games (1984-2008)?: An Invitation to Open a Methodological Discussion Regarding Sex Equity in Sports Media." *Mass Communication and Society,* 17, no. 1: 121–147. doi:10.1080/15205436.2013.8 16740

Deming, Richard. 1977. *Women: The New Criminals.* New York: Thomas Nelson Inc.

Denzin, Norman K. 2009. *On Understanding Emotion,* 2nd edition. New Brunswick, NJ: Transaction Publishing.

Deutschmann, Linda. 2007. *Deviance and Social Control,* 4th edition. Toronto, ON: Nelson.

Donnelly, Peter. 2004. "Sport and Risk Culture." In *Sporting Bodies, Damaged Selves: Sociological Studies of Sports-Related Injuries,* edited by Kevin Young, pp. 29–57. Oxford: Elsevier.

Douglas, Kitrina. 2009. ""Storying Myself": Negotiating a Relational Identity in Professional Sport." *Qualitative Research in Sport and Exercise,* 1, no. 2: 176–190.

Duffy, M. (2007). Doing the Dirty Work: Gender, race, and Reproductive Labor in Historical Perspective. *Gender & Society,* 21, no. 3: 313–336.

Duncan, Margaret Carlisle. 1986. "Gender Warriors in Sport: Women and the Media." In *Handbook of Sports and Media,* edited by Arthur A. Raney and Jennings Bryant, pp. 247–269. New York: Routledge.

Duncan, Margaret Carlisle and Cynthia A. Hasbrook. 1988. "Denial of Power in Televised Women's Sports." *Sociology of Sport Journal,* 5, no. 1: 1–21. doi:10.1123/ssj.5.1.1

Dunn, Katherine. 2000. "Lucia Rijker—War with Christy Martin—War with Christy Martin—War Rumors and More Rumors." *Cyber Boxing Zone,* March 3, 2000. http://www.cyberboxingzone.com/boxing/kd3300.htm

Dunn, Katherine. 2009. *One Ring Circus: Dispatches from the World of Boxing.* Tuscon, AZ: Schaffner Press.

Dworkin, Shari L. 2004. "A Women's Place is in the Cardiovascular Room?? Gender Relations, the Body, and the Gym." In *Athletic Intruders: Ethnographic Research on Women, Culture and Exercise,* edited by A. Bolin and J. Granskog, pp. 131–158. Albany, NY: State University of New York Press.

Dworkin, Shari L., and Faye Linda Wachs. 2009. *Body Panic: Gender, Health, and the Selling of Fitness.* New York: New York University Press.

Dyksta, Steph. 2019. "The Transformative Power of Boxing for Women." *GirlsGoneStrong.com.* https://www.girlsgonestrong.com/blog/confidence/em powerment/transformative-power-boxing-women/?utm_source=facebook&utm_m edium=ggs-page&utm_campaign=facebook-blog-posts&utm_content=transforma tive-power-boxing-women&fbclid=IwAR1vCwJvL6qVuUBZCsj4yo9nv-InaEGX L_2u0tvkxZmpAlK_9NabgfTob44

Eastwood, Clint, Ruddy, Albert. S., Rosenburg, Tom., Haggis Paul. (Producers) and Clint Eastwood (Director). 2004. *Million Dollar Baby* [Motion picture]. United States: Warner Brothers Picture.

Edwards, William. 1888. *Art of Boxing and Science of Self Defense, Together with a Manual of Training.* New York: Excelsior Publishing House. http://www.nycs teampunk.com/bartitsu/manuals/TheArtOfBoxingAndManualOfTraining1888.pdf

Elias, Norbert. 1994. *The Civilizing Process.* Oxford, UK: Basil Blackwell.

Eller, Jack David. 2006. *Violence and Culture: A Cross Cultural and Interdisciplinary Perspective.* Toronto, ON: Wadsworth Publishing.

Elling, Agnes and Annelies Knoppers. 2005. "Sport, Gender and Ethnicity: Practises of Symbolic Inclusion/Exclusion." *Journal of Youth and Adolescence,* 34, no. 3: 257–268. doi:10.1007/s10964-005-4311-6

Faber, S.D. and J.W. Burns. 1996. "Anger Management Style, Degree of Expressed Anger, and Gender Influence Cardiovascular Recovery from Interpersonal Harassment." *Journal of Behavioral Medicine,* 19, no. 1: 31–53. doi:10.1007/ BF01858173

Faludi, Susan. 1999. *Stiffed: The Betrayal of the American Man.* New York: Harper Perennial.

Ferrell, Jeff and Mark S. Hamm, eds. 2016. *Ethnography on the Edge: Crime, Deviance, and Field Research.* Boston, MA: North Eastern University Press.

Filaire Edith, Maso F., Degoutte Fabrice, Jouanel P. and Lac G. 2001. "Food Restriction, Performance, Psychological State and Lipid Values in Judo Athletes." *International Journal of Sports Medicine,* 22, no. 6: 454–459. doi:10.1055/s-2001-16244

Finley, Nancy J. 2010. "Skating Femininity: Gender Maneuvering in Women's Roller Derby." *Journal of Contemporary Ethnography,* 39, no. 4: 359–387. doi:10.1177/0891241610364230

Fisher, Bonnie, Francis Cullen, and Michael Turner. 2000. *The Sexual Victimization of College Women.* Washington, DC: U.S. Department of Justice.

Fisher, Mark. 2009. *Capitalist Realism: Is There No Alternative?* Winchester, UK: Zero Books.

Fiske, John, 1992. "Cultural Studies and the Culture of Everyday Life." In *Cultural Studies,* edited by Lawrence Grossberg, Cary Nelson and Paula A. Triechler, pp. 154–173. New York: Routledge.

Fogelholm Mikael. 1994. "Effects of Bodyweight Reduction on Sports Performance." *Sports Medicine*, 18: 249–267. doi:10.2165/00007256-199418040-00004.

Follansbee, Patti A. 1982. *Effects of a Self-Defense Program on Women's Psychological Health and Well-being. Dissertation Abstract International*, 43: 2388.

Follo, Giovanna. 2012. "A Literature Review of Women and the Martial Arts: Where are we Right Now?" *Sociology Compass,* 6, no. 9: 707–717. doi:10.1111/j.1751-9020.2012.00487.x

Forell Caroline Anne. 2005. "The Meaning of Equality: Sexual Harassment, Stalking, and Provocation in Canada, Australia, and the United States." *Thomas Jefferson Law Review,* 28, Summer: 151–166.

Foucault, Michel. 1979. *Discipline and Punish.* New York: Vintage.

Fox, Jesse and Bridget Potocki. 2016. "Lifetime Video Game Consumption, Interpersonal Aggression, Hostile Sexism, and Rape Myth Acceptance: A Cultivation Perspective." *Journal of Interpersonal Violence,* 31, no. 10: 1912–1931.

Friday, Krister. 2003. "A Generation of Men Without History: Fight Club, Masculinity, and the Historical Symptom." *Postmodern Culture*, 13, no. 3: 1–34. doi:10.1353/pmc.2003.0016.

Friday, Nancy. 1977. *My Mother/My Self: The Daughter's Search for Identity.* New York: Delacorte.

Friedland, Roger and Robert R. Alford. 1991. "Bringing Society Back In: Symbols, Practices, and Institutional Contradictions." In *The New Institutionalism in Organizational Analysis,* edited by Walter W. Powell and Paul J. DiMaggio, pp. 232–263. Chicago, IL: University of Chicago Press.

Gallop, Jane. 1988. *Thinking Through the Body.* New York: Columbia University Press.

Garfinkel, Harold. 1967. *Studies in Ethnomethodology.* Englewood Cliffs, NJ: Prentice-Hall.

Garis, Laurence de. 2000. "'Be a Buddy to your Buddy': Male Identity, Aggression, and Intimacy in a Boxing Gym." In *Masculinities, Gender Relations, and Sport,* edited by Jim McKay, Michael A. Messner, and Don Sabo, pp. 87–107. Thousand Oaks, CA: Sage.

Gelsthorpe, Loraine. 1990. "Feminist Methodologies in Criminology." In *Feminist Perspectives in Criminology,* edited by Loraine Gelsthorpe and Allison Morris, pp. 89–106. Milton Keynes, UK: Open University Press.

Gems, Gerald. R. 2014. *Boxing: A Concise History of the Sweet Science.* Lanham, MD: Rowman & Littlefield.

Gill, Rosalind. (2007). *Gender and the Media.* Cambridge: Polity Press.

Glick, Peter and Susan T. Fiske. 1996. "The Ambivalent Sexism Inventory: Differentiating Hostile and Benevolent Sexism." *Journal of Personality and Social Psychology,* 70, no. 3: 491–512.

Goday-Pressland, Amy. 2014. "The Weekend as a Male Entity: How Sunday Newspaper Sports Reporting Centres around Male Activities, Interests and Languages (2008-2009)." *Leisure Studies,* 33, no. 2: 148–163. doi:10.1080/02614367.2013.833286

Goldberg, Emma. 2019. "Selling Self Defense." *The Baffler,* April 26, 2019. https://thebaffler.com/latest/selling-self-defense-goldberg

Goold, Benjamin, Loader, Ian and Angélica Thumala. 2013. "The Banality of Security: The Curious Case of Surveillance Cameras. *British Journal of Criminology,* 53, no. 6: 977–996.

Gorn, Elliott. 1986. *The Manly Art: Bare-Knuckle Prize Fighting in America.* Ithaca, NY: Cornell University Press.

Graham, Robert M. 2019. "Knockout: In Boxing, Brain Damage Is the Goal-Why do we Applaud a Sport Dedicated to Hurting People?" *MedPage Today,* November 14 2019. https://www.medpagetoday.com/neurology/headtrauma/83336

Gramsci, Antonio. 1971. *Selections from the Prison Notebooks.* New York: International Publishers.

Grau, S.L., Roselli, G., and C. R. Taylor. 2007. "Where's Tamika Catchings? A Content Analysis of Female Athlete Endorsers in Magazine Advertisements." *Journal of Current Issues & Research in Advertising,* 29, no. 1: 55–65. doi:10.1080/10641734.2007.10505208

Green, Sarah, Griffin Martha, Renzi Maggie [Producers] and Karyn Kusama [Director]. 2000. "Girl Fight." *Sony Pictures Releasing Screen Gems.* Culver City, CA: Sony Pictures Entertainment.

Greenwell, T. Christopher, Simmons, Jason M., Hancock, Meg., Shreffler, Megan and Dustin Thorn. 2017. "The Effects of Sexualized and Violent Presentations of Women in Combat Sport." *Journal of Sport Management,* 31, no. 6: 533–545. doi:10.1123/jsm.2016-0333

Griffin, Pat. 2014. "Overcoming Sexism and Homophobia in Women's Sports: Two Steps Forward and One Step Back." In *Routledge Handbook of Sport, Gender and Sexuality,* edited by Jennifer Hargreaves and Eric Anderson, pp. 265–274. New York: Routledge.

Griggers, Cathy. 1992. Lesbian Bodies in the Age of (Post)mechanical Reproduction. *Postmodern Culture,* 2, no. 3. doi:10.1353/pmc.1992.0020

Groombridge, Nic. 2017. *Sports Criminology: A Critical Criminology of Sport and Games.* Chicago, IL: Polity Press.

Halberstam, Jack. 1998. *Female Masculinity.* Durham, NC: Duke University Press.

Halbert, Christy. 1997. "Tough Enough and Woman Enough: Stereotypes, Discrimination, and Impression Management among Women Professional Boxers." *Journal of Sport and Social Issues,* 21, no. 1: 7–36.

Hall, Stuart. 1997. "The Work Representation." In *Representation: Cultural Representations of Signifying Practices,* edited by Stuart Hall, pp. 13–74. London: Sage.

Hamm, Mark. 2005. "Doing Terrorism Research in the Dark Ages: Confessions of a Bottom Dog." In *Edgework: The Sociology of Risk-Taking,* edited by Stephen Lyng, pp. 273–291. New York: Routledge.

Hardin, Marie, Chance, Jean, Dodd, Julie E. and Brent Hardin. 2002. "Olympic Photo Coverage Fair to Female Athletes." *Newspaper Research Journal,* 2, no. 2–3: 64–78. doi:10.1177/073953290202300206

Harding, Sandra. 2004. "Can Men be Subjects of Feminist Thought?" In *Feminist Perspectives on Social Research*, edited by Sharlene Nagy Hesse-Biber and Michelle L. Yaiser, pp. 177–197. New York: Oxford University Press.

Hargreaves, Jennifer. 1994. *Sporting Females: Critical Issues in the History and Sociology of Women's Sports.* New York: Routledge.

Hargreaves, Jennifer. 1996. "Bruising Peg to Boxerobics: Gendered Boxing – Images and Meaning." In *Boxer: An Anthology of Writings on Boxing and Visual Culture,* edited by David Chandler, John Gill, Tania Guha and Gilane Tawadros, pp. 120–131. London: Institute of International Visual Arts.

Hargreaves, Jennifer. 1997. "Women's Boxing and Related Activities: Introducing Images and Meanings." *Body and Society,* 3, no. 4: 33–49.

Hargreaves, Jennifer and Eric Anderson, eds. 2014a. *Routledge Handbook of Sport, Gender and Sexuality.* Abingdon: Routledge.

Hargreaves, Jennifer and Eric Anderson 2014b. "Sport, Gender and Sexuality: Surveying the Field. In *Routledge Handbook of Sport, Gender and Sexuality,* edited by Jennifer Hargreaves and Eric Anderson, pp. 3–18. New York: Routledge.

Hartt, Brian. 2014. "Is this What a Man Looks Like? Nihilistic Tautologies and the Splitting of Self Chuck Palahniuk's *Fight Club.*" *The College of New Jersey,* xvi: 1–9. https://joss.tcnj.edu/wp-content/uploads/sites/176//2014/04/2014-Hartt-Submission.pdf

Harvey, Geraint, Vachhani, Sheena J. and Karen Williams. 2014. "Working Out: Aesthetic Labour, Affect and the Fitness Industry Personal Trainer." *Leisure Studies,* 33, no. 5: 454–470. doi:10.1080/02614367.2013.770548

Hass, N. 2000. When Women Step into the Ring. *New York Times,* October 1, 7. https://www.nytimes.com/2000/10/01/style/when-women-step-into-the-ring.html

Hauser, Thomas and Jeffrey T. Sammons. 2020. "Rules, Organizations, Techniques, and Styles: Weight Divisions." *Encyclopedia Britannica,* May 14, 2020. https://www.britannica.com/sports/boxing/Women-in-boxing#ref29790

Havan, J. 2004. "The Week." *BusinessWorld,* June 21, 2004. 1.

Hearn, Jeff. 1998. *The Violence of Men: How Men Talk About and How Agencies Respond to Men's Violence to Women.* Thousand Oaks, CA: Sage Publications Inc.

Heiser, Christina. 2019. "This is Why Boxing is Becoming such a Popular Workout Choice." *aSweatLife,* January 23, 2019. https://asweatlife.com/2019/01/this-is-why-boxing-is-becoming-such-a-popular-workout-choice/

Heiskanen, Benita. 2012. *The Urban Geography of Boxing: Race, Class, and Gender in the Ring.* New York: Routledge.

Henley, Nancy M. 1977. *Body Politics: Power, Sex, and Nonverbal Communication.* Englewood Cliffs, NJ: Prentice-Hall.

Heywood, Leslie and Shari L. Dworkin. 2003. *Built to Win: The Female Athlete as Cultural Icon.* London: University of Minnesota Press.

Hickey, William. 1913. *Memoirs,* vol 1. London: Hurts and Blacken.

Hoagland, Sarah. 1988. *Lesbian Ethics: Towards New Value.* Palo Alto, CA: Institute of Lesbian Studies.

Hoffer, Richard. 1996. "Gritty Woman." *Sports Illustrated,* April 15, 1996. https://vault.si.com/vault/1996/04/15/gritty-woman-christy-martin-is-knocking-down-stereotypes-even-as-she-refuses-to-champion-the-cause-of-women-in-the-ring

Hoffman, Steve G. 2006. "How to Punch Someone and Stay Friends: An Inductive Theory of Simulation." *Sociological Theory,* 24, no. 2: 170–193. doi:10.1111/j.0735-2751.2006.00287.x

Holland, Jesse. 2014. "Sponsor Blasts UFC for Conduct Double Standard. *MMA Mania,* April 21, 2014. https://www.mmamania.com/2014/4/21/5636616/sponsor-blasts-ufc-conduct-double-standard-offers-5k-reward-ronda-rousey-ko-mma

Holland, Samantha. 2004. *Alternative Femininities: Body, Age and Identity.* Oxford, UK: Berg.

Hollander, Joyce A. 2009. "The Roots of Resistance to Women's Self-Defense." *Violence Against Women,* 15, no. 5: 574–594. doi:10.1177/1077801209331407

Holyfield, Lori. 1999. "Manufacturing Adventure: The Buying and Selling of Emotions." *Journal of Contemporary Ethnography,* 28, no.1: 3–32.

Holyfield, Lori and Gary Alan Fine. 1997. "Adventure and Character Work: The Collective Taming of Fear." *Symbolic Interaction,* 20, no. 4: 343–363. doi:10.1525/si.1997.20.4.343

Hong, E. 2012. "Women's Football in the Two Koreas: A Comparative Sociological Analysis." *Journal of Sport and Social Issues,* 32, no. 1: 115–134. doi:10.1177/0193723511434328

Horswill Craig A., Park Sung Han and James N. Roemmich. 1990. "Changes in the Protein Nutritional Status of Adolescent Wrestlers.' *Medicine & Science in Sports Exercise*, 22, October: 599–604. doi:10.1249/00005768-199010000-00010

Hughes, Robert and Jay Coakley. 1991. "Positive Deviance among Athletes: The Implications of Overconformity to the Sport Ethic." *Sociology of Sport Journal,* 8, no. 4: 307–325. doi:10.1123/ssj.8.4.307

Ivanov, Dimitar. 2020. "Is Boxing Considered a Martial Art? Why Yes and Why No." *ShortBoxing.* https://shortboxing.com/is-boxing-a-martial-art/

Jackman, Mary R. 1994. *The Velvet Glove: Paternalism and Conflict in Gender, Class, and Race Relations.* Berkeley, CA: University of California Press

Jarvis, Brian. 2007. "Monsters Inc.: Serial Killers and Consumer Culture." *Crime, Media, Culture,* 3, no. 3: 326–344. doi:10.1177/1741659007082469

Jennings, L.A. 2015. *She's a Knockout!: A History of Women in Fighting Sports.* London: Rowman & Littlefield.

Jennings, George and Beatriz Cabrera Velázquez. 2015. "Gender Inequality in Olympic Boxing: Exploring Structuration through Online Resistance against Weight Category Restrictions." In *Global Perspectives on Women in Combat Sports: Women Warriors around the World,* edited by Alex Channon and Christopher R. Matthews, pp. 89–103. New York: Palgrave Macmillan

Johansson, Thomas. 1996. "Gendered Spaces: The Gym Culture and the Construction of Gender." *YOUNG,* 4, no. 3: 32–47. doi:10.1177/110330889600400303

Jump, Deborah. 2020. *The Criminology of Boxing, Violence and Desistance.* Bristol, UK: Bristol University Press.

Kane, Mary Jo and Jo Anne Buysse. 2005. "Intercollegiate Guides as Contested Terrain: A Longitudinal Analysis." *Sociology of Sport Journal*, 22, no. 2: 214–238. doi:10.1123/ssj.22.2.214

Kane, Mary Jo, LaVoi, Nicole. M. and Janet S. Fink. 2013. "Exploring Elite Female Athletes' Interpretations of Sport Media Images: A Window into the Construction of Social Identity and "Selling Sex" in Women's Sports." *Communication & Sport*, 1, no. 3: 1–31. doi:10.1177/2167479512473585

Kelly, Liz. 1988. *Surviving Sexual Violence.* Minneapolis, MN: University of Minnesota Press.

Kerr, J, H. 2004. *Rethinking Violence and Aggression in Sport.* London, UK: Routledge.

Kilbourne, Jean. 2010. *Killing Us Softly 4: Advertising's Image of Women.* Media Education Foundation Online Store.

Kimmel, Michael S. 1994a. *The Gender of Desire: Essays on Male Sexuality.* New York: State University of New York Press.

Kimmel, Michael S. 1994b. "Masculinity as Homophobia: Fear, Shame, and Silence in the Construction of Gender Identity." In *Theorizing Masculinity,* edited by Harry Brod and Michael Kaufman, pp. 142–164. Thousand Oaks, CA: Sage Publications.

Kissling, Elizabeth Arveda. 1991. "Street Harassment: The Language of Sexual Terrorism." *Discourse & Society,* 2, no. 4: 451–460. https://www.jstor.org/stable/42888749

Kleck, Gary, and Susan Sayles. 1990. "Rape and Resistance." *Social Problems*, 37, no. 2: 149–62. doi:10.2307/800645

Klein, Melissa. 1997. "Duality and Redefinition: Young Feminism and the Alternative Music Community." In *Third Wave Agenda: Being Feminist, Doing Feminism*, edited by Leslie Heywood and Jennifer Drake, pp. 207–225. Minneapolis, MN: University of Minnesota Press.

Koss, Mary P., Dinero, Thomas E., Seibel, Cynthia and Susan L. Cox. 1988. "Stranger and Acquaintance Rape: Are There Differences in the Victim's Experience?" *Psychology of Women Quarterly,* 12, no. 1: 1–24. doi:10.1111/j.1471-6402.1988.tb00924.x

Krane, Vikki and Shannon M. Baird. 2005. "Using Ethnography in Applied Psychology." *Journal of Applied Sport Sociology,* 17, no. 2: 87–107.

Kring, Ann M. 2000. "Gender and Anger." In *Gender and Emotion: Social Psychological Perspectives,* edited by Agneta H. Fischer, pp. 211–231. Cambridge: Cambridge University Press. doi:10.1017/CBO9780511628191.011

Kruger, Barbara. 1982. *No Progress in Pleasure.* Buffalo, NY: Cepa.

Lafferty, Yvonne and Jim McKay. 2004. "'Suffragettes in Satin Shorts'? Gender and Competitive Boxing." *Journal of Qualitative Sociology,* 27, no. 3: 249–276. doi:10.1023/B:QUAS.0000037618.57141.53

Lather, Patti. 1991. *Getting Smart: Feminist Research and Pedagogy within the Post-Modern.* New York: Routledge.

Laurendeau, Jason. 2006. "'He Didn't Go in Doing a Skydive': Sustaining the 'Illusion' of Control in an Edgework Activity." *Sociological Perspectives,* 49, no. 4: 583–605. doi:10.1525/sop.2006.49.4.583

Laurendeau, Jason. 2008. "'Gendered Risk Regimes': A Theoretical Consideration of Edgework and Gender." *Sociology of Sport Journal*, 25, no. 3: 293–309. doi:10.1123/ssj.25.3.293

Laurendeau, Jason and E. Gibbs Van Brunschot. 2006. "Policing the Edge: Risk and Social Control in Skydiving." *Deviant Behavior*, 27, no. 2: 173–201. doi:10.1080/01639620500468535

Lefebvre, Henri. 1991. *The Productions of Space*. Translated by Donald Nicholson-Smith. Oxford, UK: Blackwell.

Lerner, Harriet E. 1977. "The Taboos Against Female Anger." *Menninger Perspective*, 8, no. 4: 4–11.

Linson, Art, Chaffin, Cean, Grayson Bell, Ross [Producers] and David Fincher [Director]. 1999. *Fight Club*. Fox 2000 Pictures: 20th Century Fox.

Logan, T.K. and Kellie R. Lynch. 2018. "Dangerous Liaisons: Examining the Connection of Stalking and Gun Threats Among Partner Abuse Victims." *Violence and Victims*, 33, no. 3: 399–416. doi:10.1891/0886-6708.v33.i3.399

Logan, T. K. and Robert Walker. 2017. "Stalking: A Multidimensional Framework for Assessment and Safety Planning." *Trauma, Violence, & Abuse*, 18, no. 2: 200–222. doi:10.1177/1524838015603210

Lois, Jennifer. 2001. "Peaks and Valleys: The Gendered Emotional Culture of Edgework. *Gender & Society*, 15, no. 3: 381–406. www.jstor.org/stable/3081890

Lois, Jennifer. 2005. "Gender and Emotion Management in the Stages of Edgework." In *Edgework: The Sociology of Risk-taking*, edited by Stephen Lyng, pp. 117–152. New York: Routledge.

Lorde, Audre. 1984. *Sister Outsider*. Trumansburg, NY: The Crossing Press.

Love, Adam. 2014. "Transgender Exclusion and Inclusion in Sport." In *Routledge Handbook of Sport, Gender and Sexuality*, edited by Jennifer Hargreaves and Eric Anderson, pp. 376–383. New York: Routledge.

Lowery, Wesley. 2017. "This is Rough N Rowdy, Where a Forgotten Town Dukes it Out Once a Year." *The Washington Post*, March 21 2017. https://www.washingt onpost.com/national/this-is-the-rough-n-rowdy-where-a-forgotten-town-dukes-it -out-once-a-year/2017/03/21/a8f14ffa-034d-11e7-b1e9-a05d3c21f7cf_story.html

Lundberg George D. 1986. "Boxing Should Be Banned in Civilized Countries—Round 3." *JAMA*, 255, no. 18: 2483–2485. doi:10.1001/jama.1986.03370180109044\

Lyng, Stephen. 1990. "Edgework: A Social Psychological Analysis of Voluntary Risk-taking." *American Journal of Sociology*, 95, no. 4: 851–886. www.jstor.org/stable/2780644

Lyng, Stephen. 2005. *Edgework: The Sociology of Risk-taking*. New York: Routledge.

MacKinnon, Catherine A. 1987. *Feminism Unmodified: Discourses on Life and Law*. Cambridge: Harvard University Press.

Madden, Margaret E. and Thomas J. Sokol. 1997. "Teaching Women Self-Defense: Pedagogical Issues." *Feminist Teacher*, 11, no. 2: 133–151. https://www.jstor.org /stable/40545790

Mandel, Hadas and Moshe Semyonov. 2006. "A Welfare State Paradox: State Interventions and Women's Employment Opportunities in 22 Countries." *American Journal of Sociology*, 111, no. 6: 1910–1949. doi:10.1086/499912

Marcus, Sharon. 1992. "Fighting Bodies, Fighting Words: A Theory and Politics of Rape Prevention." In *Feminists Theorize the Political,* edited by Judith Butler and Joan W. Scott, pp. 385–403. New York: Routledge.

Markula, Pirkko. 2001. "Beyond the Perfect Body: Women's Body Image Distortion in Fitness Magazine Discourse." *Journal of Sport and Social Issues,* 25, no. 2: 158–179. doi:10.1177/0193723501252004

Masser, Barbara and Dominic Abrams. 2004. "Reinforcing the Glass Ceiling: The Consequences of Hostile Sexism for Female Managerial Candidates." *Sex Roles,* 51: 9–10. doi:10.1007/s11199-004-5470-8

McCaughey, Martha. 1997. *Real Knockouts: The Physical Feminism of Women's Self-defense.* New York: New York University Press.

McCaughey, Martha. 2000. "Kicking into Consciousness through Self-Defense Training: Getting Physical in Both Theory and Practice." In *Just Sex: Students Rewrite the Rules on Sex, Violence, Activism, and Equality,* edited by Jodi Gold and Susan Villari, pp. 157–166. Lanham, MD: Rowman & Littlefield.

McDonald, Paula and Sara Charlesworth. 2016. "Workplace Sexual Harassment at the Margins." *Work, Employment & Society,* 30, no. 1: 118–134. https://www.jstor.org/stable/10.2307/26655451

McKay, Jim. 1997. *Managing Gender: Affirmative Action and Organizational Power in Australian, Canadian, and New Zealand Sport.* New York: State University of New York Press.

McKay, Steph and Christine Dalliere. 2009. "Campus Newspaper Coverage of Varsity Sports: Getting Closer to Equitable and Sports-Related Representations of Female Athletes?" *International Review of the Sociology of Sport,* 44, no. 1: 25–40. doi:10.1177/1012690208101484

McNaughton, Melanie Joy. 2012. "Insurrectionary Womanliness: Gender and the (Boxing) Ring." *The Qualitative Report,* 17, no. 33: 1–13.

Mead, George Herbert. 1934, 1950. "Mind, Self, and Society" edited by Charles W. Morris. Chicago, IL: University of Chicago Press.

Mennesson, Christine. 2000. ""Hard" Women and "Soft" Women: The Social Construction of Identities Among Female Boxers." *International Review for the Sociology of Sport,* 35, no. 1: 21–33. doi:10.1177/101269000035001002

Merz, Mischa. 2000. *Bruising: A Journey through Gender.* Sydney: Picador.

Messerschmidt, James. 2002. "On Gang Girls, Gender and a Structured Action Theory: A Reply to Miller." *Theoretical Criminology,* 6, no. 4: 461–475. doi:10.1177/136248060200600404

Messner, Michael. 1988. "Sports and Male Domination: The Female Athlete as Contested Ideological Terrain." *Sociology of Sport Journal,* 5, no. 3, 197–211. doi:10.1123/ssj.5.3.197

Messner, Michael A. 1992. *Power at Play: Sports and the Problem of Masculinity.* Boston, MA: Beacon Press.

Messner, Michael A. 2000. "When Bodies are Weapons." In *Gender through the Prism of Difference,* edited by Maxine Baca Zinn et al. Boston: MA: Allyn and Bacon.

Messner, Michael A. 2002. *Taking the Field: Women, Men and Sports.* Minneapolis, MN: University of Minnesota Press.

Messner, Michael A, Duncan, Margaret Carlisle and Cheryl Cooky. 2003. "Silence, Sports Bras, and Wrestling Porn: The Treatment of Women in Televised Sports News and Highlights." *Journal of Sport and Social Issues*, 27, no. 1: 38–51. doi:10.1177/0193732502239583

Messner, Michael and Donald Sabo, eds. 1990. *Sport, Men, and the Gender Order: Critical Feminist Perspectives*. Champaign, IL: Human Kinestics Books.

Miller, Daniel. 2010. *Stuff*. Cambridge, UK: Polity Press.

Miller, Eleanor M. and Stephen Lyng. 1991. "Assessing the Risk of Inattention to Class, Race/Ethnicity, and Gender: Comment on Lyng." *American Journal of Sociology*, 96, no. 6: 1530–1534. https://www.jstor.org/stable/2781910

Miller, William J. and James H. Frey. 1996. "Skydivers as Risk Takers: An Examination." *Humanity & Society*, 20, no. 4: 3–15. doi:10.1177/016059769602000402

Møller, Verner and Jakob Østergaard Genz. 2014. "Commercial Sport—Debordian Spectacle or Barthesian Mythology?" *Catalan Journal of Communication & Cultural Studies*, 6, no. 2: 257–271. doi:10.1386/cjcs.6.2.257_1

Morgan, Rachel E. and Grace Kenna. 2018. "Criminal Victimization, 2016: Revised." *United States Department of Justice Bureau of Justice Statistics*. October 2018. NCJ 25212

Morley, Jill, Georgiev, Tchavdar [Producers] and Jill Morley [Director]. 2013. *Fight Like a Girl*. Vision Films.

Muir, Kenneth B. and Trina Seitz. 2004. "Machismo, Misogyny and Homophobia in a Male Athletics Subculture: A Participant-Observation Study of Deviant Rituals in Collegiate Rugby." *Deviant Behavior*, 25, no. 4: 303–327. doi:10.1080/01639620490267294

Mullaney, Jamie. 2007. ""Unity Admirable but Not Necessarily Heeded": Going Rates and Gender Boundaries in the Straight Edge Hardcore Music Scene." *Gender & Society*, 21: 384–408. doi:10.1177/0891243207299615

Nash, Meredith. 2017. "Gender on the Ropes: An Autoethnographic Account of Boxing in Tasmania, Australia." *International Review for the Sociology*, 52, no. 5: 734–750. doi:10.1177/1012690215615198

National Association of Anorexia Nervosa and Associated Disorders. 2020. "Eating Disorder Statistics." *ANAD*. https://anad.org/education-and-awareness/about-eating-disorders/eating-disorders-statistics/

National Organization for Women. 2020. "Violence Against Women in the United States: Statistics." *Now.org*. https://now.org/resource/violence-against-women-in-the-united-states-statistic/

Oates, Joyce Carol. 1987. *On Boxing*. London, UK: Bloomsbury.

O'Connell, Liam. 2019. "Total Revenue of the Global Sports Apparel Market from 2012 to 2025 (in Billion U.S. Dollars)*." *Statista*, November 29, 2019. https://www.statista.com/statistics/254489/total-revenue-of-the-global-sports-apparel-market/#:~:text=The%20global%20sports%20apparel%20market%20generated%20around%20181%20billion%20U.S.,billion%20U.S.%20dollars%20in%202025

O'Malley, Pat and Steve Mugford. 1994. "Crime, Excitement, and Modernity." In *Varieties of Criminology: Readings from a Dynamic Discipline*, edited by Gregg Barak, pp. 189–212. Westport, CT: Praeger.

Ovid. 1990. "Letter XVI: Paris to Helen." In *Heroides.* Translated by H. Isbell. Harmondsworth: Penguin Books.

Owton, Helen. 2015 "(Re)inventing the Body-Self: Intense, Gendered, and Heightened Sensorial Experiences of Women's Boxing Embodiment." In *Global Perspectives on Women in Combat Sport: Women Warriors around the World,* edited by Alex Channon and Christopher R. Matthews, pp. 221–236. Basingstoke: Palgrave Macmillan.

Padavic, Irene and Babara Reskin. 2002. *Women and Men at Work,* 2nd edition. Thousand Oaks, CA: Sage.

Palahniuk, Chuck. 1996. *Fight Club: A Novel.* New York: W. W. Norton.

Paradis, Elise. 2012. "Boxers, Briefs or Bras? Bodies, Gender and Change in the Boxing Gym." *Body & Society,* 18, no. 2: 82–109. doi:10.1177/1357034X12440829

Perasso, Valeria. 2017. "100 Women: Is the Gender Pay Gap in Sport Really Closing?" *BBC News,* October 23, 2017. https://www.bbc.com/news/world-41685042

Peterson, Richard A. 2005. "Problems in Comparative Research: The Example of Omnivorousness." *Poetics*, 33, no. 5–6: 257–282. doi:10.1016/j.poetic.2005.10.002

Pettersson, Stefan, Ekström, Marianne P. and Christina M. Berg. 2012. "The Food and Weight Combat: A Problematic Fight for the Elite Combat Sports Athlete." *Appetite,* 59, no. 2: 234–242. doi:10.1016/j.appet.2012.05.007

Place, Janey. 1998. "Women in Film Noir." In *Women in Film Noir,* edited by E. Ann Kaplan, pp. 47–68. New York: Palgrave Macmillan

Priks, Mikael. 2010. "Does Frustration Lead to Violence? Evidence from the Swedish Hooligan Scene."*Kyklos,* 63, no. 4: 450–460. doi:10.1111/j.1467-6435.2010.00482.x

Propertius. 1994. "The Advantage of Spartan Athletics." In *The Poems.* Translated by G. Lee. Oxford: Oxford University Press.

Quinsey, Vernon L. and Douglas Upfold. 1985. "Rape Completion and Victim Injury as a Function of Female Resistance Strategy." *Canadian Journal of Behavioral Science,* 17, no.1: 40–50. doi:10.1037/h0080128

Renzetti, Claire M. 2013. *Feminist Criminology.* New York: Routledge.

Renzetti, Claire, Follingstad, Diane and Ann Coker, editors. 2017. *Preventing Intimate Partner Violence: Interdisciplinary Perspectives.* Chicago, IL: Policy Press.

Rezzadeh, Kevin. 2019. "Is Traumatic Brain Injury Preventable in Amateur Boxing Competition? *Clinical Correlations,* January 18, 2019. https://www.clinicalcorre lations.org/2019/01/18/is-traumatic-brain-injury-preventable-in-amateur-boxing-c ompetition/

Rightler-McDaniels, Jodi L. 2014. "Changes Through the Lens?: US Photographic Newspaper Coverage of Female Athletes." *Sport in Society,* 17, no. 8: 1076–1094. doi:10.1080/17430437.2013.838354

Robson, Colin. 2000. *Small-Scale Evaluation: Principles and Practice.* London, UK: Sage.

Rosenblum, Gianine D. 2007. "Self Defense as Clinical Intervention." *Association of Women in Psychology Annual Meeting,* March 2007. San Francisco, CA.

Ross Karen and Cynthia Carter. 2011. "Women and News: A Long and Winding Road." *Media, Culture and Society,* 33, no. 8: 1148–1165. doi:10.1177 /0163443711418272

Ross, Sally R., Ridinger, Lynn L. and Jacquelyn Cuneen. 2009. "Drivers to Divas: Advertising Images of Women in Motorsport." *International Journal of Sports Marketing and Sponsorship*, 10, no. 3: 7–17. doi:10.1108/IJSMS-10-03-2009-B003

Roth Amanda and Susan A. Basow. 2004. "Femininity, Sports, and Feminism: Developing a Theory of Physical Liberation." *Journal of Sport and Social Issues*, 28, no. 2: 245–265. doi:10.1177/0193723504266990

Rough N' Rowdy. 2018. "Girl Fight Gets Sloppy -RNR 3." *YouTube*, July 31 2018. https://www.youtube.com/watch?v=YyoiMuG2gjU

Rough N' Rowdy. 2019. "Jacked Country Girl Fights Small Girl." *YouTube*, October 23 2019. https://www.youtube.com/watch?v=rSs4Pdu5Akg

Rough N' Rowdy. 2019. "Toothless Hillbilly Fights Young Wrestling Champ– RNR 8." *YouTube*, May 15 2019. https://www.youtube.com/watch?v=gO2z69SqHB8

Rough N' Rowdy. 2020. "My Fame Ain't From Wearing Jeans in the Ring…It's from Knocking Motherfuckers Out for the Past 10 Years." *Instagram roughnrowdy*. January 21, 2020. @roughnrowdy.

Russell, Glenda M., McCarroll, M. C. and J.S. Bohan, J. S. 2007. "When Feminists Resist Self-Defense: Traditional Gender Roles or Feminist Ideology?" Paper presented at the Annual Meeting of the Association for Women in Psychology, March 2007. San Francisco, CA.

Satterlund, Travis D. 2012. "Real, but Not Too Real: A Hierarchy of Reality for Recreational Middle-Class Boxers." *Sociological Perspectives*, 55, no. 3: 529–551.

Scheper-Hughes, Nancy. 1994. "Embodied Knowledge: Thinking with the Body in Critical Medical Anthropology." In *Assessing Cultural Anthropology*, edited by Robert Borofsky, pp. 229–242. New York: McGrawhill.

Schippers, Mimi. 2002. *Rockin' Out of the Box: Gender Maneuvering in Alternative Hard Rock*. New Brunswick, NJ: Rutgers University Press.

Schippers, Mimi. 2007. "Recovering the Feminine Other: Masculinity, Femininity, and Gender Hegemony." *Theory and Society*, 36, no. 1: 85–102.

Schirmer, Eleni. 2017. "Fighting for the Lights: Claressa Shields' Big Night for Women Fighters." *ESPN*, March, 10, 2017. http://www.espn.com/espnw/voices/article/18872047/fighting-lights-claressa-shields-big-night-women-fighters

Schwalbe, Michael L. 1996. *Unlocking the Iron Cage: The Men's Movement, Gender Politics, and American Culture*. New York: Oxford University Press.

Schwalbe, Michael L. 2005. "Identity Stakes, Manhood Acts, and the Dynamics of Accountability." *Studies in Symbolic Interaction*, 28: 65–81. doi:10.1016/S0163-2396(04)28010-3

Searles, Patricia and Ronald J. Berger. 1987. "The Feminist Self-Defense Movement: A Case Study." *Gender and Society*, 1, no. 1: 61–84. doi:10.1177/089124387001001004

Searles, Patricia and Patti Follansbee. 1984. "Self-Defense for Women: Translating Theory into Practice." *Frontiers: A Journal of Women Studies*, 8, no. 1: 65–70. https://www.jstor.org/stable/3346096

Sheeran, Ed, Mac, Steve, McDaid, Johnny, Burruss, Kandi, Cottle, Tameka and Kevin Briggs. 2016. Shape of You [Recorded by Ed Sheeran]. On *Divide* [CD]. United States: Asylum/Atlantic Records.

Sheffer, Mary Lou and Brad Schultz. 2007. "Double Standard: Why Women have Trouble getting Jobs in Local Television Sports." *Journal of Sports Media*, 2, no. 1: 77–101. doi:10.1353/jsm.0.0005

Shilling, Chris. 1993. *The Body and Social Theory.* London, UK: Sage.

Smith, Michael D. 1983. *Violence and Sport.* Toronto, ON: Butterworths.

Smith, Sharon G., Chen, Jieru, Basile, Kathleen C., Gilbert, Leah K., Merrick, Melissa T., Patel, Nimesh, Walling, Margie and Anurag Jain. 2017. *The National Intimate Partner and Sexual Violence Survey (NISVS): 2010 –2012 State Report.* Atlanta, GA: National Center for Injury Prevention and Control, Centers for Disease Control and Prevention.

Sparkes, Andrew C., Brighton, James and Kay Inckle. 2014. "Disabled Sporting Bodies as Sexual Beings: Reflections and Challenges." In *Routledge Handbook of Sport, Gender and Sexuality,* edited by Jennifer Hargreaves and Eric Anderson, pp. 179–188. New York: Routledge.

Sparkes, Andrew. 2000. Autoethnography and Narratives of Self: Reflections on Criteria in Action. *Sociology of Sport Journal,* 17: 21–43.

Spezia, M. 2017. "Claressa Shields Ready to Headline Unprecedented Boxing Main Event." *Detroit Free Press,* March 9, 2017. http://www.freep.com/story/sports /2017/03/09/claressa-shields-ready-headline-unprecedented-boxing-main-event/9 8921148/

Spitzberg, B. H., and W.R. Cupach. 2014. *The Dark Side of Pursuit: From Attraction to Obsession and Stalking,* Second edition. New York: Routledge.

Spohn, Ryan, Bjornsen, Abby and Emily M. Wright. 2017. "Factors Associated with Reporting of Sexual Assault among College and Non-College Women." *Journal of Aggression, Conflict & Peace Research*, 9, no. 4: 279–289. doi:10.1108/ JACPR-05-2017-0298

Stone, Jacqui and John Horne. 2008. "The Print Media Coverage of Skiing and Snowboarding in Britain: Does it Have to be Downhill all the Way?" *Journal of Sport and Social Issues,* 32, no. 1: 94–112. doi:10.1177/0193723507311673

Strauss, Anslem L. 1978. *Negotiations: Varieties, Contexts, Processes, and Social Order.* San Francisco, CA: Jossey-Bass.

Steen, Stephen N., and Kelly D. Brownell. 1990. "Patterns of Weight Loss and Regain in Wrestlers: Has the Tradition Changed?" *Medicine and Science in Sports and Exercise*, 22, no.6: 762–768. doi:10.1249/00005768-199012000-00005

Sugden, John. 1996. *Boxing and Society: An International Study.* Manchester, UK: Manchester University Press.

Sullivan, Deborah. 2004. *Cosmetic Surgery: The Cutting Edge of Commercial Medicine in America,* 2nd edition. News Brunswick, NJ: Rutgers University Press.

Swasey, Elizabeth J. 1993. "NRA Woman's Voice." *American Rifleman,* February, 18.

Tasker, Yvonne and Diane Negra. 2007. "Introduction: Feminist Politics and Postfeminist Culture." In *Interrogating Postfeminism,* edited by Yvonne Tasker and Diane Negra, pp. 1–25. Durham, NC: Duke University Press.

Theberge, Nancy. 1993. "The Construction of Gender in Sport: Women, Coaching, and the Naturalization of Difference." *Social Problems,* 40, no. 3: 301–313. doi:10.2307/3096881

Theberge, Nancy. 1994. "Toward a Feminist Alternative to Sport as a Male Preserve." In *Women, Sport, and Culture,* edited by Susan Birrell and Cheryl L. Cole, pp. 181–192. Champaign, IL: Human Kinetics Books.

Thomas Reuters Foundation. 2018. "The World's Most Dangerous Countries for Women." *Thomas Reuters Foundation Annual Poll.* https://poll2018.trust.org/

Thomas, Sandra P., ed. 1993. *Women and Anger.* New York: Springer Publishing Company.

Thomas, Sandra P. and R. L. Williams. 1991. Perceived Stress, Trait Anger, Modes of Anger Expression, and Health Status of College Men and Women. *Nursing Research,* 40, no. 5: 303–307.

Toulmin, Vanessa. 1999. *A Fair Fight: An Illustrated Review of Boxing on British Fairgrounds.* Oldham: World's Fair Publications.

Trail, Gailen T. and Jeffrey D. James. 2001. "The Motivation Scale for Sport Consumption: Assessment of the Scale's Psychometric Properties." *Journal of Sport Behavior,* 24, no. 1: 108–127.

Trimbur, Lucia. 2011. "Buying and Selling Blackness: White-Collar Boxing and Racialized Consumerism." In *Reconsidering Social Identification: Race, Gender, Class and Caste,* edited by Abdul R. Janmohamed, pp. 177–206. Oxfordshire: Routledge.

Trimbur, Lucia. 2013. *Come Out Swinging: The Changing World of Boxing in Gleason's Gym.* Princeton, NY: Princeton University Press.

Trujillo, Nick. 2000. "Hegemonic Masculinity on the Mound: Media Representations of Nolan Ryan and American Sports Culture." In *Reading Sport: Critical Essays on Power and Representation,* edited by Susan Birrell and Mary G. McDonald, pp. 14–39. Boston, MA: Northeastern University Press.

Turner, Jacob S. 2014. "A Longitudinal Content Analysis of Gender and Ethnicity Portrayals on ESPN's SportsCenter from 1999-2009." *Communication & Sport,* 4, no. 4: 303–327. doi:10.1177/2167479513496222

Turner, Ralph H. 1976. "The Real Self: From Institution to Impulse." *American Journal of Sociology,* 81, no. 5 :989–1016.

Ullman, Sarah E. 1997. "Review and Critique of Empirical Studies of Rape Avoidance." *Criminal Justice and Behavior,* 24, no. 2: 177–204. doi:10.1177/0093854897024002003

Ullman, Sarah E. 2007. "A 10 Year Update of "Review and Critique of Empirical Studies of Rape Avoidance." *Criminal Justice and Behavior,* 34, no. 2: 411–429. doi:10.1177/0093854897024002003

Ullman, Sarah E. and Raymond A. Knight. 1992. "Fighting Back: Women's Resistance to Rape." *Journal of Interpersonal Violence,* 7, no. 1: 31–43. doi:10.1177/088626092007001003

Ullman, Sarah E. and Raymond A. Knight. 1993. "The Efficacy of Women's Resistance Strategies in Rape Situations." *Psychology of Women Quarterly,* 17, no. 1: 23–38. doi:10.1111/j.1471-6402.1993.tb00674.x

United Nations Population Fund. 2014. "Gender Equality: Ending Widespread Violence Against Women." *United Nations Population Fund.* www.unfpa.org/gender/violence.htm.

University of Western Ontario. 2017. "Study explores how gender defines the gym." *Phys.org,* December 1, 2017. https://phys.org/news/2017-12-explores-gender -gym.html

Vaccaro, Christain A. and Melissa L. Swauger. 2016. *Unleashing Manhood in the Cage: Masculinity and Mixed Martial Arts.* Lanham, MD: Lexington Books.

Van Ingen, Cathy. (2011). Spatialities of Anger: Emotional Geographies in a Boxing Program for Survivors of Violence. *Sociology of Sport Journal,* 28, no. 2: 171–188. doi:10.1123/ssj.28.2.171

Wacquant, Loïc J.D. 1992. "The Social Logic of Boxing in Black Chicago: Toward a Sociology of Pugilism." *Sociology of Sport Journal,* 9, no. 3: 221–254. doi:10.1123/ssj.9.3.221

Wacquant, Loïc J.D. 1995a. "Pugs at Work: Bodily Capital and Bodily Labour Among Professional Boxers." *Body and Society,* 1, no. 1: 65–93. doi:10.1177/135 7034X95001001005

Wacquant, Loïc J.D. 1995b. "The Pugilistic Point of View: How Boxers Think and Feel About their Trade." *Theory and Society,* 24, no. 4: 489–535. https://www.jstor .org/stable/657882

Wacquant, Loïc J.D. 1998a. "The Prizefighter's Three Bodies." *Ethnos: Journal of Anthropology* 63, no. 3–4: 325–352. doi:10.1080/00141844.1998.9981579

Wacquant, Loïc J.D. 1998b. "A Fleshpeddler at Work: Power, Pain, and Profit in the Prizefighting Economy." *Theory and Society,* 27, no.1: 1–42. doi:10.1023/A:1006817716428

Wacquant, Loïc J.D. 2001. "Whores, Slaves, and Stallions: Languages of Exploitation and Accommodation Among Professional Fighters." *Body and Society,* 7, no. 2–3: 181–194.

Wacquant, Loïc J.D. 2004. *Body & Soul: Notebooks of An Apprentice Boxer.* New York: Oxford University Press.

Walklate, Sandra. 1997. "Risk and Criminal Victimization—a Modernist Dilemma?" *The British Journal of Criminology,* 37, no. 1: 35–45. https://www.jstor.org/stable /23637919

Wang, Stephanie. 2017. "Some Say Indiana School's Dress Code Blames Girls For Boys' Bad Behavior." *USA Today,* November 27, 2017. https://www.usatoday .com/story/news/nation-now/2017/11/27/indiana-school-dress-code/897288001/

Warshaw, Robin. 2019. *I Never Called It Rape,* reprint. New York: Harper Perennial.

Webber, Jonetta D. and Roberta M. Carni. 2013. "Where are the Female Athletes in Sports Illustrated?: A Content Analysis of Covers (2000-2011)." *International Review for the Sociology of Sports,* 48, no. 2: 196–203. doi:10.1177/1012690211434230

Wedgwood, Nicole. 2004. "Kicking Like a Boy: Schoolgirl Australian Rule Football and Bi-gendered Female Embodiment." *Sociology of Sport Journal,* 21, no. 2: 140–162. doi:10.1123/ssj.21.2.140

Weinberg, Jill D. 2016. *Consensual Violence: Sex, Sports and the Politics of Injury.* Oakland, VA: University of California Press.

WelfareInfo. 2019. "Poverty in Kentucky." *WelfareInfo.* https://www.welfareinfo.o rg/poverty-rate/kentucky/

West, Candace and Sarah Fenstermaker. 1995. Doing Difference. *Gender & Society,* 9, no. 1: 8–37. doi:10.1177/089124395009001002

West, Candace, and Don H. Zimmerman. 1987. "Doing Gender." *Gender & Society,* 1, no. 2:125–151.

Whiteside, Erin and Marie Hardin. 2012. "On Being a "Good Sport" in the Workplace: Women, the Glass Ceiling, and Negotiated Resignation in Sports Information." *International Journal of Sport Communication,* 5, no. 1: 51–68. doi:10.1123/ijsc.5.1.51

Wilkins, Amy C. 2004. ""So Full of Myself as a Chick": Goth Women, Sexual Independence and Gender Egalitarianism." *Gender & Society,* 18, no. 3: 328–349. https://www.jstor.org/stable/4149405

Winkler Irwin, Chartoff, Robert, Winkler, Charles, Chartoff, William, Winkler, David, King-Templeton, Kevin, Stallone, Sylvester [Producers] and Ryan Coogler. 2015. "Creed." CA: Warner Bros. Pictures.

Winkler Irwin, Chartoff, Robert, Winkler, Charles, Chartoff, William, Winkler, David, King-Templeton, Kevin, Stallone, Sylvester [Producers] and Steven Caple Jnr [Director]. 2018. "Creed II." CA: Warner Bros. Pictures.

Woodward, Kath. 2007. *Boxing, Masculinity and Identity: The 'I" of the Tiger.* New York: Routledge.

Woodward, Kath. 2014. "Legacies of 2012: Putting Woman's Boxing into Discourse." *Contemporary Social Science,* 9, no. 2: 242–252. doi:10.1080/21582041.2013.83 8295

Wright, Edward J. 2019. "On White-Collar Boxing and Social Class." *The Sociological Review,* 67, no. 6: 1400–1416. doi:10.1177/0038026119829762

Yang, Melissah. 2015. "The Money Rhonda Rousey Makes Falls Short Compared to Men's Earnings, & that's a Problem UFC Needs to Address." *Bustle,* August 3, 2015. https://www.bustle.com/articles/101567-the-money-ronda-rousey-makes-fa lls-short-compared-to-mens-earnings-thats-a-problem-ufc

Young, Iris Marion. 1990. *Throwing Like a Girl and Other Essays in Feminist Philosophy and Social Theory.* Bloomington, IN: Indiana University Press.

Young, Kevin. 2019. *Sport, Violence and Society,* 2nd edition. New York: Routledge.

Yu. Fay [Producer]. 2012. "Hidden in America: Underground Fight Clubs." Season 1, Episode 4 [46 minutes].

Zoucha-Jensen, Janice M. and Ann Coyne. 1993. "The Effects of Resistance Strategies on Rape." *American Journal of Public Health*, 83, no. 11: 1633–1634. doi:10.2105/ajph.83.11.1633

Index

About the Author

Victoria E. Collins is an associate professor and graduate program coordinator in the School of Justice Studies at Eastern Kentucky University. Victoria's research and teaching interests include state crime/crimes of the powerful, victimology, violence against women, and the sociology of sport. Victoria has published three books *State Crime, Women and Gender* (Routledge, Taylor & Francis), *The Violence of Neoliberalism: Crime, Harm and Inequality* co-authored with Dawn Rothe, and *Explorations in Critical Criminology: Essays in Honor of William Chambliss* co-edited with Dawn Rothe. Some of Victoria's recent publications have appeared in journals such as *Crime, Media, Culture, Social Justice, Critical Criminology, Contemporary Justice Review*, and *Critical Sociology*.

9 781793 600639